Falling Off the Edge of the World

Two Years in Saudi Arabia

By Shelly Anderson

ISBN: 978-1-304-05983-3

Printed in the United States of America

Desert Wind Books

This book is dedicated to Pop Norris, whose wandering spirit was never to wander

This adventure is for you Pop

And to my dear friends, Bonnie and Chris, you left too soon

Always remembered with love

Acknowledgements

The writing of "Falling Off the Edge of the World" has been quite a journey. I have never worked harder on anything in my entire life, nor cried so many tears, nor felt such joy in what I was creating. I discovered that actually writing the story was easy compared to what seemed like endless re-writes and editing. If I'd known all this at the beginning I doubt I'd have had the courage to continue, nor even start. And I worked a full-time job through it all.

To our cherished friend Lynn Olson who made the all-important phone call to friend Barry Dunleavey, the gentleman who would become my mentor and editor. Barry held that Creative Writing class, my first step forward with the book project. Lynn also proofread the final manuscript in a most professional way.

My heartfelt thanks to Barry Dunleavey, who told me early on that the real writing was in the re-write. Oh how right you were Barry! If not for your patience, wisdom, and knowledge to guide me I don't believe I could have completed this project. Thanks for picking me up when I fell, and motivating me when I was ready to quit, all with a quiet, gentle spirit that kept me going.

To Bob Rockwell who professionally formatted my book, put it all together, and sent it off to the printer. Awesome job Bob, many thanks.

To my Mom and Dad, and many friends in Canada and Texas, who believed in me and encouraged me to keep going.

To my BFF Kim who kept all my Saudi letters, notes and cassette tapes because she knew that one day I'd need that material to help write my book. Your encouragement and love never faltered.

To my dear friend Carol who lived it with me. No other friend can ever know what Saudi Arabia was really like. Thanks for all your valuable input and clever help with details.

To Wilf and Bev, you loved my Saudi letters and shared them with friends. You too encouraged me to write the book. Thanks for the wonderful "Shelly of Arabia" CD that I shall treasure always.

To Pat Eisler and the lab staff at the former Grace Hospital in Calgary, Canada who saw me off on my adventure in Saudi. Years later I still cherish wonderful memories of the Grace Hospital and the family we all found there.

To Ernest Koury and his exceptionally talented staff at Eureka! Media Group in El Paso, Texas, who designed and produced the fantastic cover for my book. Special thanks to Omar, Ana and Enrique who remained patient and gracious through all my requests for changes. And thanks to Joe Campbell who recommended Eureka! Media.

And, most importantly, to my Ghanem, the most patient of husbands. So many weekends spent at home because I needed to work on my book, and you never once complained. You encouraged me at every step and shared my journey.

Creed of the Peaceful Traveler

Grateful for the opportunity to travel and to experience this world, and because peace begins with the individual, I affirm my personal responsibility and commitment to:

Journey with an open mind and gentle heart.

Accept with grace and gratitude the diversity I encounter.

Revere and protect the natural environment which sustains all life.

Appreciate all cultures I discover.

Respect and thank my hosts for their welcome.

Offer my hand in friendship to everyone I meet.

Support travel services that share these views and act upon them.

By my spirit, words, and actions encourage others to travel the world in peace.

Author unknown

The Desert Has Many Teachings

In the desert,
Turn toward emptiness,
Fleeing the self.
Stand alone,
Ask no one's help,
And your being will quiet,
Free from the bondage of things.

Those who cling to the world,
Endeavor to free them;
Those who are free, praise.
Care for the sick,
But live alone,
Happy to drink from the waters of sorrow,
To kindle Love's fire
With the twigs of a simple life.
Thus you will live in the desert

Mechthild of Magdeburg

Falling Off the Edge of the World

Two Years in Saudi Arabia

Shelly Anderson

Chapters

Preface

"Travel is fatal to prejudice, bigotry and narrow-mindedness."
Mark Twain

At the age of thirty-three I left my familiar world behind and took a job in the Kingdom of Saudi Arabia, a land I knew almost nothing about. I lived and worked in Tabuk, a military city in the northwestern corner of the country with a mostly Bedouin culture. Because I worked in a hospital, and lived on a Saudi military base, I was able to closely interact with the Saudi people. I found them warm, and for the most part, welcoming. I was invited into Saudi homes and to their celebrations. Arab hospitality is famous, and I found it to be true amongst the Saudis and all Arab peoples I met in my travels.

Making the decision to go to Saudi Arabia on my own proved to me I could do almost anything I set my mind to. I soon found out that Saudi Arabia is a dangerous place; terrifying situations can blindside you in totally unexpected ways. I don't know where my courage came from while I lived there. I suppose I'd always had it, but only became aware of it in a land where every day required some measure of it. I had to dig deep within myself and find reserves of strength and determination I never knew I had. With that new-found courage I taught myself to swim so I could see the beauty of the Red Sea reefs. The swimming part was easy compared to overcoming my terror of deep water. But I freed myself from that fear too, and I saw those beautiful reefs with my own eyes. It was all worth it.

Looking back, I recognize my years in Saudi Arabia as some of the richest of my life. Time spent there was an unexpected treasure that had little to do with money. Living in the Middle East gifted me with a lifetime of memories. Since Saudi Arabia is a firmly closed country, even today, I feel greatly honored to have had the opportunity to live in the Kingdom. But this is not a feeling shared by all expatriates who work there. For most it is simply a means to an end, an avenue of quick money. I have friends still working in Saudi Arabia and they confirm that very little of what I write about has changed.

Saudi Arabia remains to this day a land of mystery and contradiction. It is an astonishingly beautiful desert land of great age. Whether perusing the slick malls of a modern city or sitting awed in the dusty silence of a centuries-old tomb, the land and its people felt inconceivably ancient to me. I was surrounded by history far older than the Bible.

I refer to my time in Saudi Arabia as the best and worst of times. It was a magnificent adventure in every way. Many Western expats sought out their own countrymen on arrival in the Kingdom and scoffed at anything Saudi, Islamic or Asian. Those same people had little respect for the beliefs and traditions of their multinational co-workers or those of the Saudis. But I stepped out of my comfort zone and built friendships with those from different backgrounds. I came away with a new understanding and respect for other cultures, religions and traditions which enriched my own life. I found that as humans we all share a common bond with similar hopes, fears and worries. My experiences gave me a certain maturity that only travel can provide.

On the other side of being an expat in Saudi, life can be difficult for most and impossible for some. Some days I had to literally take life one minute at a time. Unexpected dangers skulk in dark corners. Life there is in a constant state of flux and change. People you grow fond of, friendships that are made, often end when those people decide to leave at the end of their contract. Sometimes they get caught breaking a rule and are deported before you have a chance to say goodbye. Other friends and colleagues decide, for whatever reason, to do a "runner" (leaving on vacation with no plans to return and no notification to the employer). I did my share of grieving for colleagues when terrible things happened to them far from home. Some ended up forever broken or even dying in the horrific car crashes endemic to Saudi. Staff changes in the workplace are constant and adaptation to new personalities can be a daily struggle. Life isn't quite real; you know you are there temporarily and have no financial responsibilities in-country. Then there is the complete unpredictability of the Saudi administrators and the Saudi government in general. Senseless new rules and restrictions are sprung with no notice or warning. What was permissible one day becomes forbidden the next. The only thing certain about life in Saudi Arabia is uncertainty.

Unless you have lived in the Kingdom you cannot possibly imagine how life really is there. It is at once a monarchy, theocracy and dictatorship. The land and its people are a paradox.

From outside the country, Saudi Arabia is one of the most difficult places in the world to visit. Tourist visas are occasionally granted on a very limited basis to organized tour groups of four or more individuals. Foreign tours are co-managed inside the country by a Saudi tour operator to make sure the group sees only what the government deems allowable. However, tours of any land cannot begin to give a traveler the experience of living and working in another culture. It is unfortunate that so many expatriates live in the Kingdom for years, but never leave the safety and comfort of their compounds to see the beauty of Arabia. What riches they miss: astonishing archeological sites, the marvels of the Red Sea, the grandeur and mystique of the desert. I am so glad I took the opportunity to experience these wonders while I could.

I believe that Saudi society in its present form cannot endure. With the ever-expanding effects of social media and myriad means of communication Saudi Arabia cannot possibly isolate itself forever. After a short-lived revolt in Saudi in 2011, the government scrambled to satisfy Saudi citizens. The youth, the largest majority of the population in the country, have too much time on their hands because of high unemployment. King Abdullah has drastically raised the wages of Saudis, and the drive to get rid of expatriate labor and hire Saudis has surged forward. Though more and more Saudi women are gaining higher education and entering the work force, they still cannot drive nor gain any meaningful independence unless their male guardian approves it. How can any country move forward when half the population is repressed in an already oppressed society? Just recently King Abdullah named thirty Saudi women to sit on the Shura council, an advisory body with limited powers. But their appointment has little meaning, window-dressing meant to convince Saudi people, and the world, that Saudi Arabia is progressing with women's rights. None is fooled.

The Saudi government has blanketed the Kingdom with billions of dollars to contain social pressures and keep its citizens quiet. For now. Given its long-term social problems it is a temporary fix to buy time and secure the loyalty of its people. And then there is Saudi Arabia's dependence on just one resource, oil. The government has chosen not to invest in anything else, leaving the country vulnerable both economically and politically.

For most Saudis working to attain personal goals is a foreign concept. It is not their fault. Since the influx of oil money, the Saudi people have been provided with everything they need by their government, resulting in a welfare state. A huge obstacle to progress is *"wasta"* (privileged influence.) It is the way business is done in the Kingdom, a system firmly rooted in Saudi society where royal and business venality is common practice among the thousands of Al Saud princes.

In fact, there is widespread resentment of the hypocrisy of the royal family. In their own country, the royals display adherence to the strict Wahhabi form of Islam in Saudi Arabia. But outside of Saudi Arabia they live alternate lives in lavish homes, spending indecent amounts of money on profligate lifestyles. In their own country members of the royal family are above the law. There are thousands of members of the Al Saud family, all supported by the Saudi government with monthly stipends.

And then there is the "Commission for Promotion of Virtue and Prevention of Vice" (the "Mutawa" or religious police) who fight any meaningful changes, especially those involving women or anything they perceive as Western-influenced. The younger generation of Saudis is losing patience with these rigid government-approved extremists who are increasingly seen as interfering in personal lives. The religious police harass people and cause mayhem over anything they construe as inappropriate. Very recently the Saudi government announced a plan to limit the powers of the Mutawa. I have doubts about reforms actually being enforced, but if so, then I will be happy for the Saudi people.

The current ruler, King Abdullah, is a respected monarch relatively moderate in his views. But he has made few meaningful reforms during his tenure. He is in his late eighties and in poor health. Crown Prince Sultan, Abdullah's half-brother, passed away in 2011. Prince Nayef bin Abdul Aziz, the 78-year-old full brother of King Abdullah, was subsequently named Crown Prince, but passed away in June 2012. Prince Salman bin Abdul Aziz, the 76-year-old half-brother of King Abdullah, is now Crown Prince. Saudi youth are restless and desperate to see comprehensive modern changes to their country. But there is little possibility of this until the current line of elderly Al Saud kings have passed on. There is widespread speculation amongst Saudis about future succession; who will take the throne once the old guard is gone?

Given the Kingdom's own unique problems, in addition to the unrest and major political changes occurring in neighboring countries, and throughout Middle East as a whole, if ever there was a country ripe for its own explosive revolution it is Saudi Arabia.

I will always be in love with the Middle East, especially with those ancient things that endure in spite of fast food restaurants and luxury cars. There are still the Bedouin, the traditional desert people. While at work I occasionally encountered elderly Bedouin folks in the hallways, come to visit their family members in the hospital. In the breeze of their passing I caught the rich scent of smoke from their wood fires, the wooly aroma of the sheep and goats they herd. Somehow they clung to their old way of life in the modern world around them. And I yearn for the spice markets exuding the exotic scent of frankincense and myrrh.

Saudi Arabia is a country with controversial policies and human rights issues that raise strong emotions in many. The treatment and exploitation of Asian workers in Saudi and all over the Gulf are very real. My book, however, is not meant to be a criticism of Saudi Arabia or the Gulf countries. It is about the people I met, my personal observations, and my experiences as I lived them.

I invite readers to share my adventures with an open mind. For anyone familiar with Saudi Arabia, they know things happen there that happen nowhere else on earth.

In the heat of a still evening, dust hanging motionless in the air, an orange sun falling below the horizon and the Muslim call to prayer drifting over the city, I fall in love all over again.

The Middle East

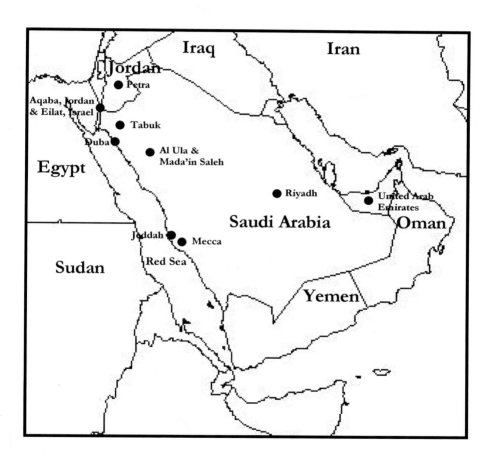

Into the Unknown

The beauty, and sometimes the terror, of life is that it can change drastically in a moment. On an April morning my life took a sudden turn. A turn that would transform my life profoundly and change the way I looked at life and the world around me. Forever. I bought a Calgary Herald newspaper that morning, a quick read over coffee.

After a heartbreaking divorce my life seemed to have no purpose or direction. I had a good job with great co-workers, but it offered no advancement in my profession. I was struggling financially. Something had to change. I could no longer bear the unremitting sameness of my everyday life. Yet I had no idea how I could break out and find a new life.

With no specific intent in mind, I scanned the classified ads. There, leaping off the page at me was a bold, full-page advertisement **"Medical Transcriptionists for Saudi Arabia"**. I felt my stomach drop, my face flush with hot emotion. Could I possibly be qualified with only one year of transcription experience? I'd had no thoughts of changing jobs, much less running off to a country I knew nothing about. Yet I was intrigued, tantalized by the unknown. Saudi Arabia. I felt certain the ad had been placed for a singular transcriptionist, me. With courage fueled by the heat of the moment I picked up the phone and called the overseas recruiter in Toronto.

"Yes, you're qualified," the recruiter confirmed. "Would you like to send us your resume and formally apply for the position? We happen to have one of our staff passing through Calgary tomorrow; could you arrange to meet with her at the airport?"

The following day I drove to Calgary airport with butterflies in my stomach. The recruiter had provided me with flight data and arrival time, but I knew nothing about who I was meeting other than her name, Caroline. I had been asked to hold a sign with my name on it so that Caroline might find me easily. I stood at the designated gate and waited anxiously. My mouth was dry as dust and my hands trembled with both fear and anticipation. Though fit enough, I was heavier than average and worried this might affect my chances. Out of the disembarking crowd a young, willowy blonde woman walked toward me with a smile on her face. We introduced ourselves and Caroline did her best to put me at ease. We settled in a little restaurant in the airport and she offered to buy me lunch. She laughed when I said my mouth was too dry to chew or swallow anything. We discussed the plan over my resume and the interview was successful. I wished Caroline a good trip back to Toronto. She parted with, "I know how nervous you are about your decision, but don't worry, we'll take care of you." Within the week I was offered a job in a hospital in Ta'if in southwestern Saudi Arabia.

My entire world turned upside down in a space of two days. My friends were horrified. My parents, who lived in a town outside of Calgary, were terribly upset. My father was struck silent, dumbfounded by my decision. My mother cried over the phone, "What are you thinking?" I often asked myself that same question. Plans proceeded in a dizzying blur throughout April. I had stepped far out of my comfort zone. I was terrified, often breaking into cold sweats. But I was determined to stick with my decision and gave myself no time to think. My flight was scheduled to depart Calgary in late August. I began my preparations, packing my apartment and selling off items. There seemed no way to prepare myself emotionally because, of course, I had little notion of what to expect.

Then Saddam Hussein invaded Kuwait. I felt bitterly disappointed, but so uncomfortable with the political situation I couldn't go forward. I postponed plans to go to Ta'if and fervently hoped the war would end soon.

14

Now I had time to think about my decision. It took a while, but I finally admitted to myself I really craved a drastic change in my life. At that time the song by the Irish band U2 defined how I felt about my life in general, "I Still Haven't Found What I'm Looking For". Only years later did I fully realize that my decision to go to Saudi Arabia was all about running away, searching for something I could not identify. Only years later did I understand that what began as an escape from my life had developed into what was then and is now my eternal thirst for the journey. My heart and soul long for distant horizons, new people, new cultures, even the mystery and danger of traveling off the beaten path. I discovered that no other feeling compares with the exhilaration of arriving alone in a foreign city where I know not a soul and have no knowledge of the local language. It is only then I feel most alive.

While the war waged on I decided to do some research on the country I was headed for. I learned that the Kingdom of Saudi Arabia involves much of the Arabian Peninsula, and is divided into two regions, the Hijaz in the west and the Nejd region in the east. The royal family makes its home in Riyadh in the east, the most religiously conservative city in Saudi Arabia. Traditionally the Hijazi people have always been more liberal than the Nejd people. In 1932, Abdul Aziz ibn Saud took control of these areas, unified the many tribes under the name of Kingdom of Saudi Arabia, and was proclaimed King. Before unification, the tribes of the region made war and raiding their neighbors a way of life. I learned that my destination is an ancient place; archeologists believe that human habitation on the Arabian Peninsula dates back some 20,000 years. I'd long been interested in archaeology and so reading about the history intrigued me. I hoped that I might be able to see some of the ancient places I read about.

Christmas came and went. Would this inconvenient war never end? Through those long months I agonized. Should I give up the Saudi idea entirely? Ultimately I remained faithful to my commitment. The Iraqi government announced acceptance of the UN resolution in January and the conflict ended. I phoned the recruiter the following day and resurrected my application. The Ta'if position was filled, but I was offered another position in Tabuk (northwestern Saudi Arabia) at Northwest Armed Forces Hospital.

Now certain of my departure, I dealt with the innumerable details of leaving my country, bank accounts in order, bills paid, will prepared, notices given, friends visited. It seemed each detail checked off the list produced ten new ones. I purchased clothing appropriate for the plunge into an ultra-conservative society: long sleeves, long skirts, high necks, and comfortable shoes. I bought everything in cotton for extra comfort in the heat I would encounter.

Family and friends continued their campaign of dissuasion. My co-workers often asked me, "Are you sure you want to do this?"

My days were spent in terror, my nights sleepless. I knew I wasn't a confident person, but still I remained resolute. My resolve was tested repeatedly. Just prior to departure, my dear friend Chris was diagnosed with AIDS, one of the earlier cases in the city. I'd known Chris since I moved to Calgary. In spite of our close friendship and my knowledge of his lifestyle, his diagnosis was devastating just when I was about to leave on my grand adventure. He'd always been there for me throughout our friendship and my guilt at leaving him was agonizing. For a short time I had decided to stay and see Chris through his fatal illness but he reassured me, "You've got to live out your adventure. I know you'll carry me in your heart." I remember meeting him and other friends for supper shortly before I left. We'd chosen a bright, lively Caribbean restaurant to buoy all our spirits. I hadn't seen Chris for a couple of weeks and I was shocked into silence at his rapid decline. We were all cheerful for his sake during supper, but I went home and cried for hours. I did go to Saudi, but leaving Chris behind is still an emotional issue for me.

Chris passed away a year later in August while I was in the Kingdom. The news came to me in a letter from a mutual friend named Sandi. For the next few weeks I moved through life in a fog of grief. I was again mindful of the importance of the new friends I would make in Saudi. They helped me through it.

My move to Saudi Arabia required a leap of faith and I found courage I didn't know I had. Over the years people have asked me what it felt like to leave everything I knew and go off alone to a place like Saudi Arabia. I tell them it was terrifying, like falling off the edge of the world.

Three weeks before my thirty-fifth birthday, my parents met me at the airport for my flight from Calgary to Chicago. It was difficult for them to see their only daughter launched into the unknown. Their apprehension was clear. I saw the tears in their eyes as I walked through the gate; it was gut-wrenching for all of us. I felt literally sick at my stomach as I sank into my seat on the aircraft. Tears rolled down my face and I wondered if I was embarking on the most dubious decision of my life.

But I was soon caught up in the emotion of my journey. I changed planes in Chicago's O'Hare airport. It was daunting in its size and complexity, but I knew London Heathrow would be more so. I began to worry. How would I negotiate such a place? Queasy with a mix of terror and excitement, I boarded the KLM flight to London. When I reached Heathrow I was amazed at the ease with which I found my way around. The airport personnel were friendly and helpful. My angst had been totally unnecessary. On stepping into the enormous airport, a thrill of anticipation coursed through me. Here was a place I had never been nor even imagined I would be. The crossroads of the world, Heathrow besieged my senses with unfamiliar smells, snatches of foreign languages, exotically dressed people. I was especially struck by the exhilaration I felt at my utter aloneness in this new place.

In Heathrow I connected with Saudia Airlines, Saudi Arabia's national airline. While waiting at the gate, I saw two American women I soon found out were also headed to Tabuk. They were easy to spot since most of the other waiting passengers were East Indians, and a great number of beautifully-dressed, exotic-looking women and men. At the time I hadn't a clue these gorgeous people were Saudis. I was puzzled. This flight was headed to Jeddah so where were the black-clad women and men in long white robes I had expected to encounter? I didn't know that Saudis who traveled outside their country often dressed in Western-style clothing.

A tall, red-headed woman approached me and asked where I was headed. When I said Tabuk she smiled and introduced herself, "Hi, I'm Trish from Sacramento, I'm going to Tabuk, too." When I told her this was my first trip to Saudi, she said "Oh, I know exactly how you're

17

feeling—terrified! This is my second trip to Saudi Arabia, so I'll help you along the way."

Minutes later a petite dark-haired woman approached us and asked us our destination. She introduced herself as Ann and exclaimed, "Imagine that, I'm going to Tabuk, too! I'm a nurse from Calgary." I knew right away that Ann was a character; her big brown eyes sparkled with mischief.

Our flight boarded and we were greeted by mostly Asian female flight attendants. They were dressed in elegant uniforms, long-sleeved tops in turquoise that extended to the knees with loose trousers in shades of teal and green. About the neck they wore loosely gathered, diaphanous scarves in brilliant blues and greens.

As the plane left the ground in London, a cadenced male voice came over the aircraft public address speakers. I had to ask Trish, seated across from me, what this was. She said, rather disdainfully, "Oh, this bunch is praying for a safe flight, you'll find they're always praying." Though Trish became a friend in Saudi, I was always troubled by her attitude. I found the same mind-set widespread amongst Western people living in Saudi. They complained about everything Saudi: the religion, the lack of what they considered conveniences, and especially about the Saudis themselves. Yes, life proved to be difficult in the Kingdom, but it seemed to me that many could not step out of themselves to experience another culture. Why then did these people choose to go to Saudi Arabia? Money, only money.

That graceful prayer was my first taste of Islam. The fluid voice was exotic and strangely haunting, an appropriate introduction to the land I was en route to. We were served dinner a couple of hours into the flight. I looked with eagerness at the meal before me, rice with nuts and raisins in it, and savory pieces of roasted meat scented with an unknown spice. This was accompanied by warm Arabic bread and a silky white pudding. The pudding was studded with pistachios and exuded a delightful fragrance that I later learned was cardamom. In fact, the scent of cardamom came to represent all that the Middle East is to me. I thought if this was the type of exotic food typical of Saudi, I'd be eating well. Trish, on the other hand, I noticed pushing the food around her plate. "I'd rather have a cheeseburger," she said.

I'd been fortunate to get a seat near the galley. An emergency exit door was located directly opposite the galley so there was a large open space between my row of seats and the row ahead. After my tasty meal, I stretched my legs out and slept. Opening my eyes some hours later, I was greeted by a huge protuberance of white-clad buttocks staring up at me from the floor. An enormous Saudi man, dressed in a traditional white robe, was bent over in prayer directly before me. I looked around the cabin and saw a sea of black-clad figures. What had happened while I was asleep? The doe-eyed women in chic clothing who boarded the flight in London had disappeared. Trish told me that just outside of Jeddah, Saudi Arabia, the Saudi women withdrew to the tiny aircraft restrooms to transform themselves into these black-shrouded figures. I had just begun my adventure but already my senses felt overloaded with new experiences. What other enigmatic mysteries awaited me?

After a thirty-two-hour trip we finally landed in Jeddah. The plane stopped on the tarmac and a huge bus approached the plane. To my surprise the bus rose slowly on hydraulics and attached itself to the exit door at the rear of the plane. The flight attendants herded all the female passengers into the bus, where the intense heat and stifling humidity made me catch my breath. The blasting air conditioners in the bus did little to cool the crammed, sweating bodies. I watched out the window as another bus arrived to pick up the male passengers from the front door of the plane. My first taste of Saudi gender segregation. Our bus lowered itself to ground level and slowly made its way to the nearby terminal. As we approached what appeared to be a blank grey wall of the terminal, the vehicle again rose on its hydraulics. Like magic a door slid back in the wall and we were offloaded into a customs hall. Apparently the bus containing the male passengers had been taken to another door for we did not see them again.

Ann, Trish and I were immediately singled out by young male customs officials, strutting and self-important in their tan uniforms. One arrogant youth with protruding teeth and squinty eyes demanded, "Give me your passports!" We did, and he herded us into a tiny, airless room, slammed the door shut and left. I hadn't the courage to get up and check if the door was locked too. The three of us sat exhausted and disoriented.

Our luggage and passports disappeared with the customs staff. It was a terrifying moment in a totally foreign environment. My stomach knotted with anxiety. Thoughts raced through my head. What if they lost my passport? Were we going to miss our flight to Tabuk? After some thirty minutes, Trish, with some Saudi experience, got up, flung the door open and stomped out of the room. We heard her shouting at someone regarding our passports. Ann and I, totally intimidated, simply waited. I had never felt more helpless. I had tears in my eyes and Ann said to me, "We'll be okay, don't let them see you cry."

Trish reappeared with a different man, a dour young Saudi male garbed in traditional long white robe and red-checked cloth headdress. It is called a "ghutra" and Saudi men take pride in the number of artful ways they wear it on their heads. The white robe is called a "thobe" (Saudi male dress is also their national identity.) The young Saudi man said not a word to us. But he held up our passports and beckoned us to follow him. The three of us walked through a narrow corridor where we saw our suitcases being ransacked. The customs officials seemed to be enjoying themselves, smiling as they rooted through our belongings.

Trish told us, "Stay calm. This is a game for these guys. They're supposed to be looking for pork, pornography or anything else which offends their culture, but really they're being assholes and trying to intimidate us."

The officials soon tired of their game. All they found was a high-fashion magazine in Anne's baggage which they promptly confiscated. The magazine, its cover displaying a beautiful and scantily-clad woman, was shoved into a box containing what appeared to be many other Western-style magazines. Wearing a sober expression our escort told us, "These magazines will be burned. They are forbidden in our culture." But I imagined they were quite likely prized possessions that were carried home for close examination. We put our belongings back together and our young Saudi escort herded us into another overheated, sodden transport bus. He instructed Ann, Trish, and me to sit together on the plane to Tabuk. Our handler, still holding our passports, sat nearby and watched us closely. The outspoken Trish asked Ann and me, within earshot of our handler, "Where the hell does he think we'll escape to, thirty thousand feet above the desert?"

I was often alarmed at the conduct of many of the passengers on domestic flights in Saudi. Just as the plane was touching down on the runway almost everyone except the Western passengers were up and grabbing their belongings from the overhead bins. Lines and wait times could be long at Saudi immigration so most wanted to be first off the plane.

I witnessed this scene many times: mobs of Arabs and Asians, men and women, climbing over each other to be first to get out of the plane and through customs. This while the plane rocketed down the runway with the engines reversed and braking. Some people fell and others were knocked about by the deceleration. The buckled-in flight attendants screamed and shouted at these passengers to sit down, but none paid attention. When the plane finally came to a stop they bolted for the exits though the stairs had not yet been rolled up to the aircraft door. When the door opened, there was another rush down the stairs. I once witnessed a woman fall down the last couple of stairs. Her husband rushed to help her while the other passengers literally stepped over them and kept going.

We usually had to board a small bus to be transported to the terminal. These same impatient folks jockeyed for position in the bus and were already clambering for the doors before the bus came to a stop. They fought to get out and be first in line. It is not a generalization to say that Arabs must be the most impatient people I have ever met. This applied to any form of waiting, whether it be while driving, standing in a queue, or attending a doctor's appointment. Nobody wanted to wait. The Saudis were the worst; it was a standing joke amongst Western expatriates that if the Saudis ever learned to queue they would be dangerous.

In Tabuk the plane lurched to a stop on the tarmac. It was the dead of night. We were allowed to descend via the traditional roll-up stairs. I walked through the aircraft door and was slammed by a wall of heat so intense I felt faint. The scalding air was suffused with pungent but fascinating odors. Dust, jet fuel and what I came to know as the smell of heat. Yes, dire heat has its own scent. The dry, torrid heat of the desert is dusty, but with a clean and sterile feel. The clammy summer heat of a seaside Arabian city is syrupy-sweet with the aroma of decay, the air saturated with salt. It settles on your shoulders like a wet cloak.

Ann, Trish and I trailed our escort, and passports, into the small, shabby-looking airport. The faded linoleum floor was dirty and exhausted from the feet of thousands. Standing everywhere were uniformed soldiers with automatic weapons. I knew Tabuk contained the largest military base in Saudi Arabia, but I was alarmed by the guns. I felt dizzy with fatigue, heat, and the strangeness of my new surroundings. But for a moment my terror disappeared, replaced by a tingle of excitement and anticipation of new adventures.

Our escort guided us through Tabuk customs without incident and our passports were finally handed back to us. In Jeddah we had all handed over shiny new passports; what we got back in Tabuk bore no resemblance; our passports now looked as if they'd been through a grain harvester, thrashed and macerated with rubber stamps, ink smears and grubby fingerprints. Anne and I were shocked by their appearance. "What the hell happened to our passports between Jeddah and here?" Trish grinned, "Well actually they look pretty good. I've seen worse."

Outside the airport, our care was transferred to a smiling, diminutive Filipino man named Joy who drove a tiny van. I thought the van might split from the pressure of the three of us and our luggage wedged into the miniscule space. Joy would deliver us to the military base which houses the Northwest Area Command of the Saudi Army and Saudi Air Force. The base would become my home for the next two years. Northwest Armed Forces Hospital, located on the base at the eastern edge of Tabuk, has three hundred and fifty beds and serves the Saudi armed forces and their families in the northwest sector of Saudi Arabia. Dark though it was my senses were assaulted by newness as we drove through Tabuk. Sand and more sand, date palm trees, unfamiliar architecture. I was surprised by the wide, well-paved city streets; perhaps I had expected tracks in the sand. Joy seemed to slow the van every half mile to negotiate a steep speed bump. Why were there speed bumps on a main thoroughfare? I would understand their purpose later after I had seen how Saudi males drove.

When we reached the military base entrance we saw three men dressed in khaki uniforms slouching against the walls of their guard shack. I felt a little thrill of fear when I noticed they too held automatic weapons. Joy stopped the van, stepped out and handed the guards our paper work. The bored guards ordered Ann, Trish and me out of the vehicle as well and proceeded to pull out the luggage Joy had so carefully wedged into the van. The men leered at us as they began opening our suitcases and throwing clothing and personal items on to the dirty road. They were clearly enjoying this because they smiled as they examined every item. I was absolutely furious. Trish roared at them in broken Arabic, "You're not supposed to do that! It's none of your business!" They merely smiled and went on with their ransacking. Our driver Joy did not interfere. He'd seen it all before. Finally the guards tired of their game and we three women were left to sort out our belongings, now heaped in a rumpled pile near the guard shack. We re-packed our suitcases and Joy patiently restored our luggage to the tiny van.

Later I learned Trish was right, the guards had no business going through our bags. Officially their only job was to check our passports and papers. I soon found out that everybody entering or exiting the base was required to run the security gauntlet. It never became easier. For example, employees rode in a large bus to get downtown, and every time we returned to the base, the guards would board the bus to check everyone's papers. Sometimes they searched all the women's purses just for the hell of it. They leered at the prettier women and asked us stupid questions in broken English. Sometimes they would hold us up an hour or more. The guard's ongoing harassment was their sole entertainment in an otherwise tedious job. We soon found out it was a wasted effort to complain about our treatment to the authorities. They simply did not care.

Once through security, Joy drove through the military base. From what I could see at that time of night the base seemed vast. The myriad streets were dark and quiet. And yet more of the speed bumps, these so lofty we were tossed about in the van as we passed over each one. We passed by the hospital where we would work and pulled up in a small parking lot before a high cinderblock wall. A dilapidated guard shack stood near a tiny entrance in the wall. Two sleepy Saudi guards sat propped in metal chairs against the shack, piles of cigarette butts testament to their boredom. They too held automatic weapons. Joy spoke to them in fluent Arabic and once again our passports and papers were examined. One of the guards grunted and lurched to his feet, motioning us to follow. We clambered out of the van and passed through the narrow entrance. We entered a vast yard-like area covered in sand and a few scrubby bushes. To the left and right of us were six identical, rectangular buildings with two stories each. The sandy yard and buildings were surrounded by the high cinderblock wall. The guard led us into one of the buildings which contained a large inner courtyard lit by bright lights. The two longest sides of the building were lined with two floors of apartments. Each end of the building was clad with yet more cinderblock. I noticed a stately tree in the courtyard, its branches lined with fronds of tiny leaves and fluted mauve flowers. I later learned this beautiful subtropical tree was called a "jacaranda". I followed Joy and the guard up the wide stairs to the second storey where the guard unlocked the door to my apartment.

I was met by a blast of chillingly cold air conditioning, a huge relief from the outside heat. I was surprised by the luxury of my accommodations, a fully-furnished one-bedroom flat with full bath, galley kitchen and dazzling blue carpet. It was one of four hundred and fifty flats in the six apartment blocks. Some six hundred single women representing thirty different nationalities lived within the walls. We had a curfew and the entrance was locked at midnight. No unauthorized male dared enter here. Just to have a maintenance man come to our apartment required extensive paperwork. To discourage any illicit activities, even the servicemen were accompanied by an ever-vigilant female chaperone. Nevertheless, it was well known that some of the girls brought their boyfriends onto the female compound late at night dressed in the full Saudi female regalia, including veil and gloves. We were never sure if the Saudi guards knew and just turned a blind eye. But this was a risky move. Discovery by the Saudi authorities would have almost certainly ended in deportation for both the man and woman involved. Probably arrest as well. Then there was the risk that a neighbor, noticing that the Saudi "woman" the girl was bringing into her apartment didn't look quite right, would alert the guards.

Alone for the first time in hours, I stood in my living room, the roar of silence in my ears. I was far too exhausted to sleep. I had never experienced such a long trip and aside from fatigue, I felt dirty and dehydrated. I dug through my suitcases for a towel and dragged myself into the shower. I luxuriated under the cool water for ages, sluicing off the grime of travel. Someone had left food for me in the tiny refrigerator, and I realized I was ravenous. I could not recall the last time I'd eaten. Cold roast chicken, bread and butter, boiled eggs and milk had never tasted so delicious. Around 5:00 a.m. I at last lay down on the narrow bed, thinking I could not sleep.

The next thing I heard was pounding on my door. The sun was up and I knew it was Friday morning, the Muslim holy day when nobody worked. I stumbled out of bed and peered through the curtains. It was Ann and Trish waiting to come in, looking as dazed and tired as I felt. "We have coffee, wake up!" Anne cried.

Ann came in holding a tray with three ceramic mugs of hot, fragrant coffee, provided by a kindly neighbor. She set the tray down on the huge coffee table in front of my couch and we silently savored the strong taste of the coffee. We discussed our recent adventures and agreed that our respective apartments were nicer than we had expected. We asked one another what we really wanted to see and do now that we were in Saudi Arabia. I knew what I wanted to see first, "I just want to get out in the desert. My recruiters told me how beautiful it is so that's tops on my list." Ann said the first thing she wanted to do was learn to scuba dive. She'd heard about the world-class diving in the Red Sea. Trish had been to Saudi Arabia before and lived in Ta'if, a city of about half a million in the southwest part of the country. Trish described the city, "Ta'if is beautiful because it's located in the Asir Mountains, good climate year round. And a fair bit of rain. Tabuk looks pretty boring. I don't think it's got much to offer but heat and desert." (I would soon learn that Trish was not the most positive person I'd ever meet.)

Trish and Ann continued to yawn, and after about twenty minutes they left with the empty coffee mugs. All of us longed for more sleep. I knew I should try to stay awake so I would sleep that night, but I could not.

I slept most of Friday, but was awakened in late afternoon by a faint tap, tap, tapping at my door. What small and feeble person could possibly be calling on me? I opened my curtains and saw nobody. But the tapping continued. I looked all around and finally down, and there was a brilliant green praying mantis on the other side of the glass, his muscular front legs tapping against my front door. Later I saw large, black ants everywhere I went, striding about busily in their quest for food, while furry little spiders with stripy legs watched from dim corners during the heat of the day. These interesting creatures were my first taste of the amazing variety of insects and other critters which populated this country.

I found my apartment comfortable and it contained everything I needed. But I found it increasingly difficult to cope with the kind of insect life that made themselves at home in my flat. Sure, the ants, furry little spiders and mantises were kind of cute, but they tended to stay outside. The vile cockroaches were an entirely different story. I'd never even seen one until I lived in Saudi Arabia. While the hospital maintenance staff sprayed our apartments frequently during the summer heat, no amount of chemicals completely eradicated the cockroaches.

During my first week in Tabuk I made a simple supper of scrambled eggs and toast. I went back to the kitchen for a second helping, but the leftovers had already been claimed. There sitting in the frying pan on top of my scrambled eggs was a massive shiny brown insect, at least three inches long. It twitched its antennae and stared smugly at me. It seemed to have no fear. So this was the infamous cockroach, right here in my own kitchen. I fought revulsion—should I kill it with a heavy object or spray it with Pif-Paf, the popular bug spray available everywhere in Saudi and the Gulf? I couldn't bear the thought of throwing it to the floor and stepping on it. I might remember the crunch for the rest of my life! I decided on Pif-Paf and sprayed the critter until his death throes ceased. Scrambled eggs and cockroach landed in the garbage. My appetite was gone.

I don't remember how many cans of Pif-Paf I used during my time in Saudi. A clean house did not mean a house free of insects. Cockroaches were a fact of life. As my revulsion for them grew stronger, at one point I seriously wondered if I could continue to cohabitate with such creatures. Then I thought how ridiculous it would seem if I arrived home to tell friends and family that I'd left Saudi because of cockroaches. I had to stay, but to this day the sight of even the smallest cockroach makes my skin crawl with disgust.

When I awoke on Saturday morning I knew the full meaning of "jet lag." The time difference between Calgary and Tabuk was ten hours and seventy-one hundred miles, ten time zones of fatigue so crushing it was an effort to even move. My system was shocked and dehydrated from the heat. I drank bottle after bottle of water. I felt nauseated, excited and disoriented all at the same time. I wondered what I had got myself into. What would this day bring?

Strangers in a Strange Land

That same Saturday morning, the first workday of the week, Joy, our smiling Filipino driver, picked us up in his tiny van and delivered us to Human Resources where we were scheduled for orientation. There we found three other lost-looking souls who had arrived two days before us. Patrick, a quiet Irish doctor with a round boyish face; his comical wife Jane, a British nurse with a face of porcelain perfection, and Andrew, a tall British male nurse with a beaky nose.

In the first few minutes of our acquaintance Jane pulled me aside and whispered about Andrew, "I've dubbed that one The Great Spotted Twit. He's an arrogant git!" I came to love the word "git", often used by the British to describe anyone incompetent, stupid or foolish. The Twit was later deported because it was found he was not a nurse at all. Jane was a great nurse, but her true calling was that of a comedienne. Jane knew every Monty Python skit ever produced. Her pixie face wore an ever-present look of mischief, and she would bring us all life-saving laughter during those first days.

We were given a hospital tour and shown our respective departments. I was assigned to do transcription in the surgery department. In my bleary state I was pleased to find the hospital spotlessly clean. The polished marble floors gleamed and the many tall windows sparkled. Dark-skinned, diminutive men, all dressed alike in blue belted jumpsuits, scurried about busily. These men, most of Bangladeshi or Indian descent, cleaned the windows, wrangled floor-polishing equipment often heavier than themselves, pushed brooms endlessly and cleaned up messes left by the Saudis. Joy told us these fellows were the lowest in the labor class and treated with disdain by the Saudis. As time went on I noticed that some of the Western staff did not treat them much better.

I would often see Saudi men, and sometimes groups of covered Saudi women, seated on the floor in groups near the elevators. They would sit for hours laughing, chatting and drinking from huge thermos carafes of coffee. Like a human roadblock, the groups of Saudis had to be stepped over by everybody using the elevators. This concerned them not at all. They also ate a great variety of food while they relaxed, everything from candy bars to trays of rice and meat brought by their servants from some mysterious source. Large garbage bins were numerous and conveniently located, but when the Saudis left they chose to leave their detritus scattered on the floor. Dregs of coffee, leftover rice, fruit peelings, candy wrappers and even soiled disposable diapers remained behind. The silent army of Asian cleaners would suddenly appear as if out of the walls and clean up the mess within minutes. My heart went out to them.

Orientation consisted of information similar to what was provided by the Toronto recruiter. My benefits included tax-free wage, free housing, free medical/dental care, recreational facilities, guided tours, and transportation. "What's not to like?" I thought to myself.

We were also given a tour of the recreation center, a large building situated right across the street from the hospital. The center was provided by NWAFH administration and reserved exclusively for use by non-Muslim hospital staff. It was comprehensive, with cafeteria, movie/book library, hair salon, television room (showing pirated VHS movies twenty-four hours a day), large swimming pool, outdoor patio, gym, and activity room. The recreation center was the number one social gathering place for hospital staff at lunch time. We could find out everything going on in the expat community.

Saudi culture and its restrictions were explained in detail by the Human Resources staff. Western men cannot wear shorts or sleeveless shirts in public. Public display of affection, even between married couples, is offensive to the conservative Saudis. Public events are always segregated by gender. We were warned of the death penalty for crimes such as murder, drug trafficking and homosexual acts. Particular attention was paid to acceptable behavior for females in public. The list was long and strictly enforced by the religious police (Mutawa). Trish told me about the Mutawa even before I got off the plane in Tabuk. "You'll know a Mutawa when you see him. They wear ankle-length thobes, have scruffy beards and carry long sticks. As far as I'm concerned they're thugs and bullies. They have their own version of modesty, and they'll whack you if it doesn't meet their standards."

Women were told not to wear makeup on the job, though we did anyway. The women in our group were even cautioned against loud laughter in the vicinity of males for fear we might "tempt" them. Riding in a vehicle or in the company of a male without benefit of marriage is strictly forbidden. Single women caught in the company of a single man not her relative would lead to deportation. And most alarming, I, a female, would not be allowed to drive in the Kingdom.

These same rules apply to this day.

Most important was the issue of ladies' abayas, the long black cloak we were required to wear everywhere outside of the hospital. An efficient Filipina named Cherish displayed her handmade abayas to us. We tried them on. Here I was at last in the infamous attire I'd seen on the plane, and heard so much about.

The abaya was capacious, a black circus-tent of a garment with long sleeves, the hem sweeping the ground. Like mist, the cloud of delicate black fabric settled upon me. I felt lost in its unfamiliar folds. My fingers caressed the delicate fabric and I commented to Jane, "Perhaps this won't be too bad." I thought I might actually enjoy stepping out in this Saudi fashion statement. Jane grimaced and scoffed, "I wouldn't be caught dead in the bloody thing." Later I would find the abaya a stifling pressure cooker in the stunning force of one hundred twenty degree heat. Jane eventually took the abaya with her everywhere. She kept it tied round her waist until she spotted a Mutawa and would then wrap herself in the garment.

All hospital staff was required to wear specific uniforms. Female nurses were issued white pant suits with the top reaching the knees. Non-technical female staff wore a tunic-like white shirt and an ankle-length brown skirt. I was issued three shirts and three skirts; I would come to loathe the shapeless, mud-brown skirt I had to wear every day.

On Sunday, my first full workday, I found myself parked in front of an ancient computer in the surgery department. Trish, an experienced secretary, was assigned to the Medical Education department. Ann, a nurse, ended up on a surgical floor. I was introduced to my British supervisor, John, a nervous racehorse of a man who fueled his days with cigarettes and coffee. He supervised the entire medical records staff, including transcriptionists. The director of the medical records department was a Saudi military man, Zafer al Amri. It was soon apparent that Zafer knew nothing about running a medical records department. The first time I met him he was slumped in his huge office chair, a stubby little man dressed in an unkempt green uniform. Heavy glasses with soda bottle lenses kept sliding down his long nose so that he had to constantly push them back up. Until the day I left Tabuk, Zafer never once met my eyes, so shy was he around women. John ran the department single handedly because Zafer usually could not be found (most days he called in sick or simply didn't show up.) The records department itself was a disaster zone and I knew it would never pass muster in the Western world. I was accustomed to relatively organized records in Canada, so I was horrified by the haphazard mess I encountered. Shelves, desks, every flat surface, were covered with patient charts. Small pathways meandered between wobbly stacks of dusty charts occupying the floor. Innumerable clerks milled about with no clear intent. How could the place be such a mess with so many staff present?

I had no experience in surgical terminology or with foreign accents. I was horrified the first time I listened to a Saudi surgeon dictating. Entire paragraphs passed in a blur; I didn't understand a single word. At first I really believed I wouldn't be able to do the job. How would I ever adapt to new medical terminology when I couldn't even understand the dictating physician? But I was determined to perform the job I'd been hired for.

Adding to my frustration and confusion was the fact that almost every dictation on a Muslim male involved the name Mohammed. I once went to the Radiology Department looking for a young Saudi man named

Mohammed who organized tours for hospital employees. The department receptionist physically showed me five different Mohammeds there in Radiology, none of them, unfortunately, the one I was searching for. I would encounter this situation repeatedly. Had I known Mohammed's Saudi tribal name it might have been easier to locate him. Most Saudis have numerous names. Suppose there was a man named Mohammed Saad Abdullah Haql Al-Rashidi—the first word is the individual's actual name, second word is the father's name, third word is the grandfather's name, fourth word is the place where he was born and the last word is the tribal name. Some Saudis used all their names, varied combinations of all, or just two or three, but never consistently. A man named Mohammed (the most common name among Muslim men, Fatima being the most common among Saudi women) might decide he wants to be just plain Al-Rashidi that particular day and the next day perhaps one of his other names. I got used to it, but in the beginning Saudi names made me crazy.

I met my two co-workers: Jan, the lead transcriptionist, an abrasive, loud American woman of about fifty years with bleached, jagged hair, and Nelia, a thirty-something soft-spoken, pleasant Filipina.

Jan's first comment to me, in the presence of Nelia, was, "Keep an eye on the Filipinos, they're sneaky." Jan said it with a half-smile, but it was soon apparent the department crackled with racial tension. I was stunned, but when I glanced at Nelia to gauge her reaction her face was expressionless. A dreadful start to a new job.

I soon realized nothing could have prepared me for life in Saudi. Those first weeks were psychological and physical torture. The brutal heat plundered my meager energy. No air conditioning seemed cold enough. I sweated miserably indoors and out. Heat rash made my days and nights wretched. My soul cried to get on a plane and go home. But when I phoned my anxious parents I told them, "I'm just fine. It's a very interesting place and my job is going well." They didn't need extra worries.

I was encircled by tension in the surgery department. I was overwhelmed by the shock of a culture and country so different from Canada there were no comparisons. I felt as though I was trapped in an inescapable bad dream, suddenly surrounded by a different religion, myriad languages and women shrouded in black. During the first few days I often ran from the department to weep in the privacy of a bathroom near my office. My entire being was disoriented and dazed. For weeks after arrival I was sure the sun was rising in the west and setting in the east. Trish encouraged me to hold on. "Believe me, you're gonna get used to it. My first time here I thought the sun was rising in the west, too!" And like some warped version of the novel "1984", repression of the populace was a palpable reality felt everywhere. My sense of being watched was ever present. After the freedom of my own country I felt suffocated.

But life carried on, and I put one foot in front of another, one day at a time.

One of my first tasks on arrival in Tabuk was to visit a grocery store to stock up on everything from cleaning products to basic foodstuffs. We were fortunate to have a fully-stocked supermarket just behind the hospital, recommended by the staff conducting orientation. The majority of customers were Saudi military personnel/families and hospital employees. After our first day of orientation, Trish, Ann and I walked to the market. It was a wonderland of exotic foods. Colorful tropical fruits I could not identify. Strange cuts of meat (did that label say "camel"?) and fresh locally-made cheeses. I gazed at refrigerated metal trays containing olives of all colors and sizes. Cans and bottles of imported delicacies lined the store shelves. I filled my basket with edible new experiences. Trish and Ann ransacked the shelves in their search for American breakfast cereal and pancake syrup. I heard Trish squeal with delight from the next aisle, "Oh my God, they have Wonder Bread!" She ran over to show me her wondrous find, the precious loaf clutched to her chest. I gazed suspiciously at the bread, "It doesn't look very fresh Trish. There's some mold on the edges." She didn't mind. "I don't care if it's centuries old. It's Wonder Bread!" she cried happily. Trish and I later flew to Jeddah a couple of times for weekend getaways. There she would spend considerable time searching grocery stores for everything from canned tamales to Doritos chips. If she found her beloved Wonder Bread, no matter its condition, she filled a suitcase with it. I never understood her need to eat sliced white bread when there was literally a bakery on every corner producing fresh Arabic bread. She had no interest at all in trying any food she deemed "foreign."

I witnessed another bizarre paradox unique to Saudi Arabia. While in the grocery store a grinning Indian clerk led me to the back of the store and pointed out some odd items taking up a number of shelves. He shuffled his sandal-clad feet and smirked at me, "Surely Madam wants to make use of these fine items," as he pointed at empty glass bottles with rubber stoppers, plastic tubing, gigantic bags of white sugar, yeast and grape juice. In my innocence I failed to grasp the clerk's intent. I later mentioned the mysterious items to a co-worker. She had a laugh at my expense, "You mean you don't want to make your own wine?" So the ingredients were meant for home wine production, blatantly displayed in a country where alcohol is supposedly forbidden!

Though I didn't really care if I had wine or not, I decided I should at least try to brew a bottle just for the heck of it. The result was disastrous. I'd been told to add a pinch each of yeast and sugar to a bottle of grape juice and seal it for a week or so. I followed the instructions and waited for my bottle of wine to magically distill. A few days later I came home from work to an overpowering smell of yeast. My bottle of wine had exploded all over the tiny kitchen! Glass shards and sticky grape juice were stuck to every surface. I spent my entire evening scrubbing the kitchen. I chalked up my experiment as one more interesting experience.

I did drink an occasional glass of wine with Patrick and Jane who were far more competent in their wine-making skills. They lived in a huge echoing white marble villa provided for Western-trained physicians. These houses had five or six bedrooms and were originally designed for populous Saudi families. Patrick used one of the many rooms to brew his wine. It was the best home product I ever tasted in Saudi; Patrick somehow made white grape juice taste like the best Chardonnay.

I found there were two seasons in Tabuk, hot and cold. Cold like I would never have believed. The summer temperatures were like nothing I had ever experienced, nor even imagined. I arrived in Tabuk in June and the summer heat was just beginning. It was not unusual to reach 110-125 Fahrenheit, but fortunately the heat was as dry as a gin martini. Once acclimatized, I didn't mind the hot weather. The short walk to and from work in the searing stillness did not bother me.

The hotter the weather the louder the cicadas. I enjoyed them most on Thursdays when I finished work around noon. During the searing heat of summer this curious insect is common in the Middle East. I've since seen others of the species in the United Arab Emirates and in the southeastern United States. They roost in trees and produce an extremely loud vibrating noise with their abdomens; they are especially flamboyant in the hottest part of the day. In the still, shimmering heat of midday the steady drone of their thousands of voices in unison is nearly deafening, but also strangely hypnotic.

One hot summer day I was lying by the swimming pool at the hospital recreation center. Suddenly I heard a clatter and whirring above me. To my shock a massive winged beetle zipped past, whirly-birding above the pool like a helicopter on reconnaissance. I was part horrified and part fascinated that this immense creature, whatever its name, could fly under its own power. I saw the insect a few more times and was always amazed by it.

The sameness of the summer weather and the weeks of cloudless blue heat eventually made me feel a little detached from reality. It became a joke of sorts when we didn't see a single cloud for weeks on end. I often walked the short distance to work with a new British friend by the name of Gabrielle, a tiny, middle-aged woman. Day after day, we'd peer at the bright morning sky and she'd sigh with disgust, "Oh bother, another sunny day…." I longed for clouds, any kind of clouds. I yearned for a ferocious freight train of a storm, anything to relieve the monotony.

Very little rain falls in Tabuk, but severe thunderstorms can occur in the fall and winter months. Tabuk was the first place I ever experienced thunder and lightning in winter months. I witnessed my first violent electrical storm around Christmas and thought the world had gone mad.

The cold season, fall and winter, came on slowly and the heat receded a little each day. Finally clouds appeared, too. By November, I found it hard to believe how cold it was. I could see my breath and going downtown required a sweater and jeans under my abaya. Gloves too. "Why didn't somebody tell me how cold it gets here?" I whined to Trish,

"I can get all the cold weather I want back in Canada!" Trish grinned at my discomfort, "Bet you never dreamed of having to wear winter clothes in the desert; people just assume it's gonna be hot all the time." The windows of the old transport bus that took us downtown were often rimed with frost.

That winter it snowed heavily in Jordan, just next door to us. I could see a dusting of snow on the distant hills around Tabuk and scarcely believed that either. There is an urban myth about one's blood thinning while living in hot countries for extended periods of time. I actually came to believe it. I felt chilled all the time that first winter in Tabuk. Worse still was the fact we had no heat in our apartments. Staying in my flat required layers of clothing and a heavy blanket wrapped around me to be comfortable. By some miracle I stumbled upon flannel sheets downtown and they felt wonderful in the cold of night.

I began to adjust to my new surroundings with help from Jane, Trish, and other new friends. By then I'd also met Anya, an ethereal Irish pixie, and Vicky, a comical, blue-eyed blonde from Alabama. Vicky was delighted to call herself an Alabama redneck, but she was at heart a kind and tolerant person. She often told me about her and her "daddy" going hunting for possums and other critters in the backwoods of Alabama. Calling me up to go shopping with her, she'd shout in her southern twang, "C'mon Bubba, let's go shoot somethin'!"

My thirty-fifth birthday fell on July sixteenth, three weeks after I arrived in Saudi Arabia. That same morning I was feeling down because no one knew it was my birthday. At lunch Jane issued an invitation, "You look like you need cheering up. Come over for tea tonight. I'll even perform your favorite Monty Python skit." When I walked into Jane and Patrick's house that evening, a large group of people sprang out and yelled "Surprise!" And what a surprise it was! The ensuing party lifted my spirits more than anything else had since I'd arrived. Jane invited a lot of people, the friends I'd already made and many new faces as well. She even made me a lopsided little birthday cake with brilliant pink icing. Some of the guests brought me little gifts: hair decorations, music cassettes, brilliantly-colored scarves and the like. That night I found out Vicky's birthday was on July 17th and Anya's on July 18th, so it was wonderful to celebrate our birthdays together. It was either Vicky or Jane who'd gone to the trouble of finding my birth date. I was deeply touched.

Almost every workday for lunch Jane and I went to the recreation center. Sometimes Patrick was able to join us. The cafeteria menu often featured British food preferences I'd never tasted. A great favorite was chips, beans and eggs – French fries and canned baked beans with a fried egg on the side. The cooks were pleasant Pakistani men who tried hard to please their customers.

Having lunch at the recreation center included an ongoing soap opera of other people's foibles. The daily lunch was a must-attend event. Some went early to get a good seat in the cafeteria. Even in the largest Saudi cities expatriate communities are relatively small and can, unfortunately, be quite cruel. Tabuk was no exception. But we also learned about things we needed to know, such as a gratuitous rule change by the hospital administration or the Saudi government. Or who has got themselves into trouble and onto a deportation order.

One recurring drama involved a local "Don Juan," a British anesthetist named Dr. Smith-Jones. He regularly wore shirts open to his navel and a surplus of gold chains round his scrawny neck. He could get away with this look at the recreation center, but covered the outfit with a white coat when working in the hospital. Dr. Smith-Jones often wore white patent loafers with loud clicky heels like tap shoes. When Jane heard his shoes she laughed, "Aw, there's our favorite cretin in his gigolo heels!"

This character always seemed to have a new woman on his arm. One time he captured a naïve young Irish lady just arrived to work in the hospital. Maureen was frail-looking, but quite beautiful. She had magnificent auburn hair sparked with copper, jade-green eyes, and the renowned Irish skin so fair it appeared translucent. She appeared enamored with Smith-Jones. We thought that Maureen must be blind to find anything attractive about this man. "What in hell does she see in him?" I enquired of Jane. "Bloody fool must have hidden talents, very well-hidden!" she giggled. Even the other hospital physicians sniggered at Dr. Smith-Jones.

Every day Maureen arrived for lunch before her beau and sat at an empty table. The sappy look on her face made us question her sanity. Finally Dr. Smith-Jones slithered into the cafeteria, a slight weasley-looking man at least twice Maureen's age. His alcohol-ravaged face featured a bulbous nose, crimson with broken veins. His thin, sand-colored hair was carefully distributed into a comb-over that did little to hide his shiny pate. He swaggered in his crushingly-tight black trousers and a lavender satin shirt with most of the buttons undone. Peeking out of the lavender shirt was an abundance of grey chest hair and a pile of the treasured gold chains. Smith-Jones grinned at his lady love with a picket fence of long yellow teeth and lecherous intent. Jane chortled through a mouthful of chips, "Bloody hell, there's a sight to put you off your food!"

One day Dr. Smith-Jones and Maureen had a vicious one-sided argument in front of everyone in the cafeteria. She shouted about his latest infidelities as he looked about the room. He'd already lost interest in Maureen and sought a new conquest. Throughout the time I worked in Tabuk Dr. Smith-Jones had a series of affairs, usually with very young women. Jane and I continued to wonder what attracted women to him. Our best guess was money, that he had somehow accumulated wealth while working in Saudi. It was common for pretty young women to come to Saudi hoping to "catch" a doctor, no matter his personal proclivities. But Jane and I didn't think Smith-Jones could have had much money put away since he was usually in the throes of a hangover or on his way to getting drunk.

One day Jane commented, "I've not seen that wanker Smith-Jones lately." In fact he just disappeared and no one seemed to know where or why. I suspect his drinking and lascivious ways finally caught up and he was deported in the dead of night. It happens.

I still felt homesick from time to time, but I knew I was adjusting to my new environment. I had no responsibilities for the first time in my life, no rent, utilities or other bills. I only had to show up for work. What a freeing experience! Moreover, I found myself falling in love with the beauty of Saudi Arabia. Though I hadn't seen much of the desert at this point, I would gaze out my apartment window in early morning and see the flat emptiness with a few low hills in the distance. When I was finally able to experience the desert firsthand, I was fascinated by it. While potentially deadly, it was nonetheless beautiful and ever-changing.

At the same time I was growing to love the enigma of Saudi, the cohabitation of ancient and modern. The remote past always just below the surface. At last I felt settled enough to look forward to adventure.

One of the most important things for an expatriate is contact with loved ones at home. There was an issue that greatly concerned my family and friends because they had difficulty reaching me by telephone. The Internet and new cell phone technology were not yet allowed in the Kingdom so there were few choices for communication with the outside world. My flat had a telephone; it could be used for incoming calls as well as outgoing calls, but only within the compound and hospital. My family and friends had to call the main hospital switchboard and then hope to be connected to my flat. Getting the hospital switchboard to answer was a challenge in itself. Connection to my flat was a miracle. My best friend in Calgary expressed her frustration when she tried repeatedly over many nights to contact me. For obvious reasons she felt terribly isolated from me. When my friends and family were able to reach me in my flat, the switchboard operators made no secret of listening in on our conversations. We often heard them breathing and eating.

For my own international calls I had to wait in a queue at the hospital switchboard. Staff was allowed twenty minutes for each call. If I had to make more than one call, I would finish the first and return to the back of the queue to wait for my next chance. The single international line was located in a stuffy little phone booth with foam padding on the walls. It had the appearance of providing some privacy, but anyone on the outside of the booth could hear every word being said inside. In letters I warned callers to be cautious of subject matter during our conversations (i.e. anything negative about the Saudi government, how we made wine over there, etc.)

It was easier to communicate by mail, though there were problems with that too. My letters home contained more detail than telephone calls, but I still refrained from specifics. Mail going out of Saudi Arabia was screened. Every day started with anticipation, the hope that a letter might arrive that day from family or friends. I received a letter from my former co-workers in Calgary asking me how I liked the package they'd sent me. What package I asked? Apparently they sent me a "care package" with carefully selected items: my personal favorites such as peanut butter, cheese spread, and the much-loved Canadian snack food, Cheezies. My precious package never reached me. I felt sad, not so much for the food items, but for the fact each co-worker apparently included a small note or card for me. I asked my Mom to purchase and send me a medical dictionary. She spent a considerable amount of money on the dictionary and postage, but it too lost its way. During my third week in Saudi, I made the naïve mistake of sending my mother a little pair of gold earrings. She never got them. By this time I'd learned about the horrifying Saudi postal system. Items were picked out of the mail by postal workers as they liked. A co-worker received a box of lovely Belgium chocolates from home. She was amazed they'd got through to her until she opened the actual box. To her dismay, some chocolates were left in the box, some with bites taken and then rejected by the taster. Obviously letters were the only thing we could send or receive safely.

On a Thursday evening I was in the laundry room on the ground floor of my apartment block. I hated using the communal washers and dryers because they were grimy inside and out. The washing machines were often broken and the dryers did not work at all. But there was no other option and I usually started my laundry by wiping the washer drum with bleach. As I stood fuming in front of a washer pulling out sopping wet clothing because the spin cycle hadn't worked, an elegant woman strolled into the room. Seeing me struggling, she smiled, "I can help you get that up the stairs." The beautiful woman introduced herself as Fawzia, an Egyptian nurse from Cairo. I gazed at her swan-like neck, long black hair and coffee skin. I thought, "This is what the legendary queen Nefertiti must have looked like." I believe Fawzia would have looked stunning wearing a flour sack. I had already met many fun-loving Egyptians at work. Fawzia was no exception, prone to break out in a belly dance routine at any moment. She helped me wring the water out of my clothing and then lent a hand with hauling my wet laundry upstairs. She even helped me hang it on the clothesline in the corridor outside my apartment door.

Of course, I invited Fawzia into my apartment for coffee and we ended up talking for hours. I found out she lived just down the hall from me and had lived and worked in Tabuk for six years. Fawzia worked at a clinic affiliated with the Saudi Air Force which was located off the military base. I judged her to be about thirty years of age, so I found it odd she was not married. I worked with many Egyptian women in their early twenties who came to Tabuk to save money for marriage.

Fawzia's story was a sad one. Her father arranged a marriage for her in her early twenties with a dashing Sudanese army captain. Though she would have been his second wife it did not matter to Fawzia for she fell in love with him during their closely supervised courtship. The captain seemed to adore her. He had a first wife who gave him children. Fawzia's role would have been a "love wife", a woman of pleasure and beauty for her husband. Unfortunately, Fawzia's father passed away before the marriage could take place. Her mother then broke the engagement because she did not like the captain's mother. Fawzia fatalistically accepted the situation, "I must respect my mother's wishes." I thought her mother was incredibly selfish, but this was a cultural issue I was not qualified to judge. Every time Fawzia went home to Cairo to visit her mother, she met secretly but chastely with her captain. She continued to love him, and he her, but when I finally left Saudi Arabia, Fawzia still hadn't been allowed to marry her great love.

Our friendship blossomed and Fawzia became one of my most loyal and trusted friends in Tabuk. I learned a lot from Fawzia during the next two years. Through her I came to understand and appreciate Egyptian culture and her Muslim traditions. She taught me the worth of friendship with those outside my own culture and belief system. I knew there were some who made fun of my friendship with Fawzia. We overheard two German nurses who lived in our apartment complex whisper a comment to each other as we passed them one evening, "There she goes with her Gyppo Mozzie pal. Why can't she find a friend amongst her own kind?" Of course they meant me. They felt sorry for me because in their minds the only friend I could find was dark-skinned and Muslim. Sadly, I met all too many Western people like them, those who would never seek a friendship with anyone they considered "different" from themselves. I met a few Irish expatriates who made friends with only those from their own county in Ireland! There was an Irish compound in Tabuk whose residents, when they threw a party, made it clear they would not welcome anyone from Northern Ireland.

When next I saw Trish she told me Ann had found an older American boyfriend within the first week of her arrival. After that I saw Ann only at work. As far as we knew, she had moved with her man to a downtown flat. I was amazed at the number of women who found boyfriends right after their arrival and moved in with them. How well could they know these men? And living together without marriage, as we've noted, is a risky situation in a country where females are forbidden to even speak to unrelated men.

For my part, I was in a big hurry to try everything at hand, a course of action which would later result in my hospitalization for a serious illness.

Market of Delights

I felt ready to explore Tabuk. I told Fawzia I was planning my first trip downtown to the "souq" (market). She offered to accompany me, "I would like to come with you since it is your first time. I will show you around and I think my Arabic will help too." Fawzia wore an abaya, but no voluminous scarves; she sported a stylish pouch-like hat with a wide headband that held her hair back. It covered only her hair and ears; her beautiful face and graceful neck remained on view.

For our own safety, the hospital administration warned female employees against taking taxis. Some taxis were driven by Saudis, but many by rugged, fierce-looking men from northern Afghanistan. These men came from a part of the world where women were kept behind walls all their lives, so I doubt they had very much respect for us worldly, independent Western women.

The hospital provided a wheezing old school bus, the only transport option available to single female employees to go downtown. The air conditioning rarely worked and the bus was usually over-crowded with sweating bodies. Before the religious police began to implement more rigid rules, the hospital administrators allowed males and females to ride on the same bus. The ancient vehicle ran back and forth from the hospital to the souq every hour from 5:00 to 11:00 p.m. There was one drop-off point downtown and from there we walked the couple of blocks to the main souq. As time went on and new recruits kept arriving to work in the hospital, the bus became standing room only. It rarely ran on time.

Apparently it did not occur to the transport department to add another bus to the route. Finally we women began to use taxis within Tabuk, but always in a group of two or three. Poor access to transportation was just another way for the hospital administrators to control the movements of Western females.

The souq was a Casbah of sensory overload: a long paved, open mall, disappointingly modern to my eyes, lined with tiny shops selling everything from foodstuffs and tents to abayas and veils. Innumerable little alleys branched off to older and more interesting parts of the market. In the heat of summer, the odor of the souq was almost unbearable. As Fawzia and I stepped on to the open mall, she saw my nose wrinkle. "What on earth is that smell?" I asked in frank distaste. She smiled mildly "You will become used to it in time. It is summer now and smells much worse. Winter will be better." And yet I was intrigued by the odor, an aroma thick with mystery. I would learn this smell was a heady brew of everything from heat, humanity, and open sewers to cardamom, freshly-baked bread, and heavy oriental perfumes beloved by Saudi men and women. To my amazement I would come to love it as the essence that embodied the Middle East was for me.

But more alluring sights and smells beckoned over the disagreeable. Fawzia watched me and smiled at my excitement. I peered into every shop: here a store with shelf after shelf of delicate glass bottles filled with exotic perfumes, there a ladies' store displaying blue-sequined stilettos and bizarre clothing creations. Women and little girls' garments were overdone with frills, sequins, and a variety of trimmings. Loud colors prevailed. No changing rooms were allowed in the shops. It was considered indecent for women to undress in public, even behind a curtain or door. We bought selected items, took them home to try on, kept what we liked and returned the unwanted for refund. A cumbersome way to purchase clothing.

Dozens of fabric shops displayed upright bolts of brilliant textiles, like pillars of light in the shop windows. I love bright colors and fell in love with fabrics many of my friends considered bad taste. Shopkeepers tempted my hungry eyes, spilling their samples over the counters: patterns of brilliant flowers, sumptuous glistening silks, shiny satins with sequins and sparkles, rich creamy velvets embellished with beads. I never dreamed I might own silk at such affordable prices. I asked Fawzia, "Why is everything so brightly colored and patterned?" It should have been obvious to me. Fawzia explained, "For women who cover themselves in black all their life, color is very important." Yes. I would witness this at the first Saudi wedding I attended, the transformation from a shapeless black figure to an exotic sparkling creature. The extravagant colors and embellishments were a life-giving transfusion of vibrancy for Saudi women. The women wore gorgeous, expensive silks and satins to weddings, but even their everyday dresses were patterned and colorful. I would often see brilliantly-colored clothing peeking out from under a black abaya.

The gold shops took my breath away. I had long been a connoisseur of fine jewelry but I found my equivalent of jewelry heaven in downtown Tabuk. I was drawn to it like a moth to flame. Trays and racks of gold in shop after shop, every window displaying yet another gold mine of wonder, obscene quantities of glorious, glittering fantasies in 18-, 21-, 22- and 24-karat gold. One shopkeeper reached under his counter and slammed a brick of gold down in front of me, enjoying my shocked look.

Gold is the dowry of Saudi women, precious metal given in marriage by their husband and families, theirs to keep even in the event of divorce. Fawzia pointed out the designs unique to Saudi. She also showed me other exquisite designs from Bahrain, Oman and the United Arab Emirates. I was surprised to learn that a lot of the gold is mined in Saudi Arabia. There are large deposits of gold, silver and copper in a mountainous region north of Jeddah in western Saudi Arabia. Remains of mining activity have been found there dating back to 900 BCE. Some archeologists suggest it may be the actual site of the legendary King Solomon's Mines.

I just had to try on some gold. I slipped a delicate 22-karat gold bangle around my wrist and Fawzia smiled, "The gold looks very nice on your fair skin. I can bargain with the owner and get a good price for you." It was my first major gold purchase and I sighed with pleasure. The gold felt warm and buttery on my wrist, and I understood "gold fever." The 18-karat gold did not interest me for it was too pale for my tastes. I wanted only the heavy yellow 22- and 24-karat gold. The yellow metal had no fixed price. It was weighed and the customer charged by gram according to that day's gold price. But bartering could be used for a gold purchase. Other than groceries and certain items of fixed price, most everything for sale in Tabuk, and much of the Middle East, can be bartered for. Fawzia haggled for my bangle. She and the shopkeeper shouted in Arabic, waving their hands and gesturing in ways I did not understand. It seemed as if they were angry with each other, but negotiations ended with a smile and an agreed price. Fawzia told me prices were automatically inflated for Western buyers.

This was fun! I soon learned some Arabic and became proficient at bartering, shouting in Arabic and waving my hands.

Then it was time for Fawzia and me to get back to our compound before the midnight curfew. A surfeit of gold-shopping had barely taken the edge off my gold hunger. I knew I'd be back downtown soon to wander the gold shops. My eyes kept gazing at the elegant bangle on my arm and I thought it was the most exquisite thing I'd ever owned. As we settled in our seat on the bus Fawzia looked over at me and smiled, "I can see you will be buying much more gold. It is beautiful, but you know it is also a sensible investment. Next time you come to my flat I will show you my own gold collection. I keep some here to enjoy, but most of it is in the care of my mother in Cairo." When I finally saw Fawzia's huge collection of gold jewelry she kept in Tabuk I wondered what the collection in Cairo consisted of.

Thereafter on almost every trip downtown, whether by myself or with friends, I had to visit at least one gold store. I soon had a favorite shop called Bani Yas. In many gold shops the clerks tried to fondle the hands and arms of Western females trying on jewelry. I did not have to worry about this at Bani Yas; the shop owners, Reza and Ali, were from Iran and always treated me with respect and dignity. Every week they brought in new and interesting jewelry designs from all over the Middle East. When I'd walk in the door Reza or Ali would bow and smile, "Welcome, Madam. We have most beautiful things to show you today." They would sit me on a stool with a cup of hot mint tea and then bring out their trays of new designs. My tea glass was kept topped up while I tried on delicious rings, necklaces and earrings. They were good businessmen and I was a good customer.

The gold jewelry was amazingly affordable and as time went on I purchased more gold, building my own dowry. Saudi women bought and traded gold on a regular basis, and it was common practice to trade old jewelry designs for new. One evening while sitting in Ali and Reza's shop considering the purchase of a particularly expensive necklace, a shocking incident of wealth occurred right next to me. A Saudi woman entered the shop carrying an overnight case while her male escort stood outside. She was completely shrouded in black except for her eyes. She hefted the case on to the counter and opened it. To my astonishment, the case was filled with gold jewelry, most of it bright yellow 22- and 24-karat. I was literally gobsmacked (British slang for astonished) that one woman could have so much gold. The woman pushed the pile of old jewelry across the counter to Ali and he weighed it while she chose new pieces. Then the bartering began. I continued to stare through the entire transaction, mesmerized by the glittering piles of wealth. I thought I might appear rude, but the Saudi woman glanced over at me and her lovely eyes crinkled in a smile.

Every time I went downtown I made a new discovery. The deeper I explored its labyrinthine depths the more wonderful treasures I found.

One very special shop in the souq both dazzled and offended me. It was a massive store located several blocks off the main street, sandwiched in between a modern bank and an abandoned three-storey villa. What treasures to behold. I spent literally hours amongst the huge stock of exquisite items on offer. A full one-quarter of the store was given over to fine rugs and carpets. I ran my hands over seductive, finely-worked silk carpets from Iran and China. They felt supple and soft like fine suede. Wool "Kalim" tribal rugs from Turkey and Iran, worked in brilliant colors. Exotic perfume oils, scents of the Orient. Little boxes of ebony and sandalwood inlaid with mother-of-pearl, turquoise and semi-precious stones. Exquisitely-worked Damascus steel sabers in hand-made silver scabbards. Silk jackets from Kashmir, intricately embroidered with tiny pearls and metallic threads. Heavy old silver Bedouin jewelry. And, yes, horse clothing! Tasseled leather bridles with silver dangles, and wool saddle blankets in vivid hues. But what offended me was that Saudi apparently had no import laws on endangered species, for dispersed throughout the store were items that saddened me. Spotted cat skins (perhaps leopard). Elephant tusks and various other articles made of ivory. Traditional "khanjar" and "jambiya" (types of daggers from Oman and Yemen respectively) with handles carved from rhinoceros horn. The store owner, a middle-aged Saudi man, was always polite to me but somewhat aloof. Perhaps because he never made any money off me. As many times as I visited the store I never bought anything since most of the luxurious objects were well beyond my budget.

Long after this experience I saw other products from endangered species, and heard of experiences with actual exotic animals when I later went to work in the United Arab Emirates (UAE). There wealthy royal family members are able to purchase endangered species with ease. I met a young Syrian man, the brother of a nurse colleague. The young man worked for the grandson of the President of UAE, Sheikh Zayed Al Nayhan, and loved to entertain us with stories of his experiences with the royals. In the course of his duties, he was often required to attend meetings at different palaces and villas in the city of Abu Dhabi. During a meeting with some Sheikhs at one of their resplendent villas, the group took a break. My young friend went in search of a restroom. He told us he opened a bathroom door and two young cheetahs bounded out of the little room like spotted rockets and raced through the villa in delight! He said he was astonished, but being an animal lover he immediately went in search of the beautiful creatures. He found them gamboling about in the "majlis" (living room, a place to receive guests) where he'd been meeting with the Sheikhs. The little cheetahs, probably four or five months old, playfully leapt over the seated men who smiled indulgently at their antics. My friend later told me, "I wondered why the couches in the majlis were in such terrible condition. You don't normally see tattered furniture in such a luxurious setting." Now he knew why, as he watched the cats chew and wrestle with the furniture. Sometime later one of the Sheikhs told my friend that the cheetahs had become too big and raucous to handle. They could never be returned to the wild so they were donated to a local zoo. Fortunately, the zoo was more of a game park, and a well-run facility.

In Tabuk a truly intriguing marketplace was the Bedouin souq, located on the outskirts of town. We were taken there on an outing organized by the hospital recreation center. Five of us, including Fawzia, Gabrielle, Paula (from Australia) and two Irish girls, Magda and Maureen, were driven to the site in the recreation center's small bus. It wasn't quite what I'd expected. Our little bus rolled up to what looked like a landfill, piles of garbage mixed with heaps of somewhat useful junk. Semi-permanent metal shanties housed yet more heaps and piles of refuse. I'd imagined a fantasy setting of tents and black-garbed tribesmen with camels and Arabian horses nearby. The reality, though disappointing, turned out to be fascinating. It was as if a gigantic garage sale had suddenly erupted from the sand. Mixed amongst the junk were treasures: old silver Bedouin jewelry inlaid with chunks of red coral and bright turquoise, camel blankets and saddles, water pipes, Arabian-style coffee pots, massive brass cooking pots big enough for an adult to bathe in. I bought an old brass-embossed coffee pot and two ancient copper serving bowls.

But the best part was the hospitality of the souq's residents. Here is where I was first introduced to Arab hospitality. Though these people obviously had little, men dragged tables and chairs from the little hovels they called home. Tea was called for and the hubbly-bubbly (water pipe) was prepared. Fawzia acted as interpreter. I'd been anxious to sample a water pipe and tried not to think of the possibility of tuberculosis or some equally frightening pathogens. I discovered I liked the hubbly-bubbly. The tobacco was strong and sweet with fermented fruits. As we were smoking a veritable herd of children appeared, climbing on our laps and touching our hair. Unfortunately no women came out to meet us. An ancient bent man came near, hobbling on a cane that looked as old as he. His cloudy eyes studied each of us closely and then he shook hands with all of us. I was amazed that this elderly Saudi man would shake a woman's hand. He obviously had an understanding of Western ways. These kind people appeared more interested in talking to us than selling us anything.

In my next letter home, I told my parents that their daughter had sat and smoked with the Bedouin. Who knew what I'd be doing next?

In the July heat of Saudi Arabia, I was amazed to find stores festooned with all manner of brash Western-style Christmas decorations. I wasn't too surprised. By then I knew how much the Saudis loved anything bright and shiny. Stores catering to mainly Saudi customers offered outlandish creations: plastic camel-shaped clocks sporting fabric roses, huge bouquets of silk flowers lit with fiber optic embellishments, fake-fur dashboard covers adorned with bunches of dusty plastic grapes and even velvet shoes with clear, hollow heels containing colored liquid resin in which tiny seashells floated. In my mind this was gaudiness unique to Saudi Arabia.

The hospital gift shop also contained merchandise dear to the Saudi heart. The shop was always a source of amusement for me. I stopped there every morning to buy the English language Arab News. The shop featured the same sort of gift items I'd encountered in downtown Tabuk. Islam forbids images of humans and animals, which is why Arabic calligraphy and design reached such heights of beauty. The gift shop owner, a pug-faced Saudi senior by the name of Ayoub, recognized my enthusiasm for his goods and was always eager to show me his latest acquisitions. The shop had no shortage of the usual garish and kitschy goods: billowing bouquets of silk flowers in colors not found in nature; huge coffee thermoses which no Saudi traveled without; cheap plaster "antiquities" that Ayoub claimed were recently unearthed by archeologists; plastic statuettes of palm trees, glittering with tiny battery-driven lights; shiny black polyester abayas tagged as "pure silk." And strangely enough, in spite of what I thought might be a forbidden image, oddly designed stuffed toy animals. Perhaps stuffed animals didn't count?

The strangest thing I ever saw in that shop was when Ayoub brought in a huge shipment of fox pelts. They were a bargain at only ten riyals (US $2.50). The furs resembled the sort of thing rich celebrities used to wear, perhaps in the "Roaring Twenties"; fox skins with legs and tail still attached, wound around some woman's neck with the beady-eyed head fastening the decoration with grimacing mouth biting the tail. I was startled on the morning Ayoub drew me aside and proudly displayed these new wares. He'd built racks across the ceiling which contained hundreds of dead-eyed foxes dyed in every color from black to hot pink. Ayoub was clearly eager to be complimented on what would surely be a bestseller. "They are very beautiful" I lied solemnly. He beamed at me and rubbed his hands together, "Oh thank you, madam, they are surely fine things."

Ayoub knew his market. The fox pelts were hugely popular with the Saudis. I felt I was going mad that day for I saw those foxes everywhere. On my way to the cafeteria about 10:00 a.m., I passed through an open courtyard. Foxes decorated the entire area. I saw colorful fur festooned over tree branches, lying in planters, sticking out of garbage bins. Little children chased younger brothers and sisters, slapping each other with their foxes. Myriad Saudi women proudly draped the brilliant foxes over their drab black abayas. I thought the brightly colored fur looked striking against the unremitting black. On my way home that evening I saw foxes lying on the hospital lawns looking trampled and dirty. Foxes also lay in the street, colorful splotches of fur driven over repeatedly, battered and forgotten. Apparently the silent armies of Bangladeshi cleaners, who came out only at night, collected all the foxes.

Not a fox in sight the following morning.

When I greeted Ayoub that same morning he was thrilled by the success of his fox pelts. Only a few were left for sale, "Oh madam, foxes very popular!" he exclaimed. I grinned, "Yes Mr. Ayoub, I saw them everywhere. You made many people happy with the foxes!" He was thrilled by my compliment. Sometimes I regret not having acquired one of the foxes for its tacky charm. But I'm glad I did not contribute to the murder of those innocent little animals.

One evening Fawzia wanted to stop in a downtown pharmacy. I was amazed at what was available without a prescription. There really wasn't anything we couldn't obtain: strong analgesics containing opiates, every type of sedative, muscle relaxants and birth control pills. I'd seen little evidence of birth control amongst the local Saudi women, so I guessed it was mostly expatriate women who purchased them.

Some pharmacists acted as proxy physicians for those who could not afford to attend a clinic or hospital. One main-street pharmacy was the most popular spot to bring maladies. The owner/pharmacist, a Turk I believe, held a sort of clinic. His patients exposed their afflictions, no matter the location, and the pharmacist would prescribe a treatment. It was said he would even perform minor surgeries after hours, perhaps lancing an infected wound or suturing lacerations. I tried to avoid this particular pharmacy at all costs. On one occasion I walked right into an examination in progress. I had no wish to repeat the sight of a foul, infected toe, propped on the counter where the pharmacist could have a closer look. The pharmacist was a repulsive, unctuous man who leered at any uncovered female face.

But the pharmacist provided an important service to the poorest of the expatriate community who had few other healthcare options. On any given evening the pharmacy was full of Afghan taxi drivers and street cleaners, the lowest of the labor class, who live in poverty at the very periphery of society. They wander the city streets of Saudi and other Gulf countries at all hours, diminutive Asian men dressed in orange jumpsuits and armed with a straw broom. There are many such people who exist almost unseen in Saudi society. The invisible minority who perform the dirtiest, lowest jobs that no one else will accept. A Saudi citizen has to sponsor and employ them, but nobody is certain where they sleep or how they eat.

All Things Delicious

Sometimes I had breakfast or lunch in the hospital cafeteria because food prices were reasonable. The cafeteria had two levels. While both men and women stood together in the cafeteria line waiting to choose their food items, the eating areas were segregated by sex, men on the ground level and women on the second floor. Particularly challenging was moving to the second floor balancing a meal tray and holding up a long skirt while climbing the flight of stairs. (The only time Western men and women were permitted to sit together in the cafeteria was during the holy month of Ramadan when all Muslims were fasting and did not enter the cafeteria.) Initially I could not comprehend the mysterious foods offered in the cafeteria, but I wanted to taste it all anyway.

On my very first morning of work I decided to check out the breakfast items offered in the cafeteria. While waiting in line I watched a server fill a bowl with some sort of loose brown substance and pour copious amounts of oil over it. What on earth were these people eating for breakfast? When my turn came I pointed at the brown substance and inquired of the server, "What sort of food is this?" He smiled at me, "Fool, Madam." Was this man insulting me? He saw my confusion and told me the dish, written "foul" in English, and pronounced "fool" in Arabic, was made with slow-cooked brown fava beans. It is the most popular breakfast item in Egypt and loved throughout the Middle East. I decided to risk it. The foul was served with good quality olive oil and chopped cilantro on top, accompanied by fresh Arabic bread. I found it delicious. I make it at home to this day. There were other breakfast items to choose from, most of them popular with British expats, like fried sliced bread, broiled tomato halves, beans from a can, and scrambled eggs. But there was no sign of bacon or other pork products. After all, I was in a Muslim country where pork is forbidden. Almost all lunch and dinner dishes seemed to consist of rice topped with some sort of meat, usually chicken or lamb. The expatriate staff referred to the cafeteria's daily lunch special as "roadkill and rice".

There are plenty of American fast food chains in Saudi Arabia, but there are so many delicious local foods I couldn't imagine eating fast food. The one exception is the famous and wildly popular Al Baik chicken, a fried chicken chain originating in the Kingdom. It is a pressure-cooked fried chicken called "broast" in the Middle East, usually served with a creamy garlic sauce that is deliciously addicting.

I found all manner of enjoyable foods downtown. But it was the bread, flat fragrant rounds hot from a clay oven that won my heart. A staple of the locals, bread seemed to be made in bakeries on every street corner. They were always open on one side, no air conditioning, and I could feel the heat emanating from some distance away. I felt sorry for the bakers who worked right beside the ovens with an outside air temperature of 120 degrees.

Shortly after I arrived in Tabuk Fawzia introduced me to a bakery located near the supermarket behind the hospital. She wanted to show me how the bread was made. "You have never tasted bread like this before," she promised. "You will love it." As I watched I was mesmerized by the baker's speed and efficiency. He was a tall, green-eyed Afghan youth who smiled as I observed him at his craft. In one fluid motion, he rolled the dough flat, poked tiny holes in it with a wooden implement (to ensure even cooking), and, reaching into a round oven located in a wall, he slapped the dough against the oven wall. The ovens appeared to be lined with clay. Still I wondered how the bread dough remained stuck to the wall.

Sometimes a bakery's ovens were literally holes placed in the floor of the shop. In other bakeries the ovens were located in the walls. Huge cylinders of natural gas were lined up behind the shop to power the ovens. Within minutes the baker retrieved the bread from the oven with long heat-blackened iron tongs and threw it on a nearby table, one hot golden disk after another. Fawzia was right. The bread was heavenly, crisp and chewy on the outside, warm and soft on the inside. I often ate it with creamy feta cheese and slices of fresh tomato; I could not imagine a more delicious meal.

Propane is used for cooking in many homes and businesses in the Middle East. The first time I entered a private home in Saudi Arabia, I was astounded to find the propane tank inside the kitchen, a huge safety issue that made me nervous. The propane is delivered to private homes and smaller businesses in a unique way. A truck carrying dozens of propane cylinders makes the rounds of neighborhoods several times a day. The truck contains two men, one driving and the other with his arm out the window ringing a bell to notify householders. A servant or other household member will run out to the street, wave them down, and the men will come into the house, remove the empty cylinder and replace it with a new cylinder. They are paid on the spot.

Even more fragrant than Tabuk's bakeries was its spice market, an aromatic oasis. I would stand and inhale in front of a shop, realizing I was actually in the faraway places I had dreamed of visiting. The open burlap sacks and fragrant little hillocks of loose spices represented much of what travel means to me. Here was an international buffet of brilliant yellow turmeric, pungent black peppercorns, crystals of rock salt, blood-red sumac, plump green cardamom seeds, and curled sticks of cinnamon bark. And so many other spices I could never hope to identify. Along with the pungent and earthy street odors I learned to love, my favorite scent is that of cardamom. Before I started my second contract in Saudi, I went home to Canada for vacation. I shipped a box of gifts to my parents and in that box was a bag of fresh cardamom. When we finally opened the box thousands of miles away in Canada, the Middle East leapt out at me in the scent of cardamom. I said to my mother, "There, that's the smell of the Middle East!" Even years later the perfume of cardamom takes me back to the Middle East.

My favorite spice store was run by a wizened old man who finally cracked a smile on my third visit. When I asked him the names of spices in my broken Arabic, he soon warmed up and told me all about his products, much of which I did not understand. After that I bought all my spices from him. As the old man measured my spices and poured them into little paper cones, he called over the chai walla (tea boy). The old man sat me on a rickety stool in his shop and served me the hot, sweet mint tea that is so refreshing in the heat of summer. I found this same custom throughout the Middle East and was often served tea in shops. While in Jordan a few months later I was even invited to the shop owner's home to meet his family.

Chai (tea) walla (boys) are a holdover from British rule in India when the British military and their families had Indian servants to do their bidding. Though their profession or title would not be considered politically correct in Western society, these fellows are a fixture in parts of the Middle East. Most are grown East Asian men, but still referred to as a "tea boy." A Middle Eastern shopkeeper always knows how and where to summon these men. After they received the order, they would race off to some mysterious source. Within minutes they'd return with hot black tea accompanied by fresh mint leaves. I later worked in a hospital in the United Arab Emirates where some of the hospital kitchen staff were assigned as runners within the facility. The patients could order tea or food at any time from the kitchen and the runners would deliver it. The young men would also bring tea to the hospital staff if we asked. I got in the habit of ordering tea almost daily and an Indian or Bangladeshi man would deliver the tea to my office on a tray. These fellows made meager wages so I always tipped them generously, and on their special religious occasions made them gifts of money.

As fragrant as the spice stalls were, there were other little nooks where nothing but frankincense was sold. As a Westerner I associated frankincense and myrrh with the birth of Jesus and the Magi. I always assumed it was some mythical substance, a story from the Bible. I never imagined I would see the real thing. One evening Fawzia and I came upon a tiny shop containing massive burlap bags with their top edges curled down neatly. They contained some hardened substance of a translucent golden color. I stepped into the shop and was met with the most delightful scent. I asked Fawzia, "What is that gorgeous smell?"

She could not immediately come up with the word in English, but described it as best she could, "It is what you call the incense. This comes from a tree." After some research I found that it was frankincense, the hardened resin (sap) of a tree which grows in nearby Oman and Yemen. The precious resin has been traded and used in Arabia and North Africa for more than five thousand years. I thought it the most exotic item I had ever seen and brought bags of it home with me. The best way to release the scent of frankincense is to put a tiny piece on top of a lit light bulb. The resin melts very slowly and suffuses the room with the aroma. I also found myrrh available in the souq, but it is less common, and I found the scent less appealing than frankincense. Myrrh comes from Yemen, Ethiopia and Somalia.

I also noticed stores that sold nothing but honey, shelves lined with jar after jar of an amazing variety of colors of the substance, from viscous black to clear golden sunshine. In fact honey is described as a source of healing in the Quran, and is still a very important folk medicine in Saudi Arabia, and much of the Middle East. In modern times honey is known to contain antibacterial properties and other health benefits.

The street of butchers was a grim place to pass through, and I tried to avoid it. I'd grown up on a farm so it wasn't the butchering that bothered me. The sight of thousands of flies sitting on the fresh meat and on the hanging chicken corpses, the filthy wooden chopping blocks, hiding God-only-knows-what sorts of bacteria, were bad enough. Worse yet were the racks of blood-encrusted knives nobody seemed to bother washing, the coppery smell of fresh blood, and finally the butchers themselves, their once-white aprons stiff with accumulations of blood and offal. Many butchers displayed the feet and head of that day's victims lined up in front of their shops. Cow, sheep, or camel, the amputated feet and their glassy eyes stared up from the sidewalk.

Fawzia introduced me to a variety of restaurants in downtown Tabuk. If Gabrielle and I planned to eat downtown, Fawzia often accompanied us. Vicky said she could not afford to eat out. Anya absolutely refused to eat anywhere but in her own home or at an expat compound. She was terrified of illness.

On the mid to higher end was the Caravan Restaurant, perhaps equivalent to a Denny's or IHOP in the United States. The Caravan was located on the second floor of a downtown building. The owners had pretensions of elegance with several gaudy fountains in the dining room and dusty plastic flowers stuck in every cranny. The once luxurious burgundy carpet was downtrodden and heavily stained. All pretty normal for a Tabuk restaurant.

We liked The Caravan for several reasons. Their food was odd but usually tasty, it was relatively private and the delightful waiters always made us feel welcome. Each table was separated by cloth curtains so that Saudi families with women could eat in privacy. But we rarely saw Saudis in the Caravan. Almost their entire clientele was made up of expatriates of different nationalities, but mostly Westerners. Fawzia and I often ate at The Caravan. She had lived in Tabuk for so many years that she knew the waiters in almost every restaurant. Because of her familiarity we received extra special service at most restaurants we frequented. The Caravan served food which could not be categorized into any one type. The cooks were Arabs and Filipinos so the food was often a mixture of Filipino, Chinese, Arab and American influences. Anyone craving a hamburger would receive a fried piece of meat slid into a fresh piece of Arabic bread. They might find Filipino pancit noodles served on the side. Rice was prepared in a dizzying variety of presentations. French fries (what the British term "chips") were interpreted as thick sticks of pan-fried potatoes. I don't think I ever had a real French fry in the Kingdom. A co-worker told me she'd had genuine French fries at the one chain restaurant in Tabuk at the time, Dairy Queen. But I could not think of any reason why I would want to eat at Dairy Queen in a country where so many yummy new foods were available.

True to form, Dairy Queen was Trish's favorite restaurant in Tabuk. I saw her at work from time to time and asked if she wanted to join me for dinner downtown. Eventually I learned that if I wanted to see her over a meal, there was only one choice. She'd say, "I'm not gonna eat any of the local crap so meet me at Dairy Queen. At least I can get a decent burger and fries there." I'd usually gnaw on a fish sandwich while Trish savored her American favorites.

There was a downside to dining at the Caravan. It was a favorite place to raid by the Mutawa (religious police), mostly because single Western men and women were its chief customers. Co-mingling amongst singles was no more acceptable in a restaurant setting than anywhere else. But the staff of waiters at the Caravan was very protective of their Western clientele. By Saudi law, all businesses must close and turn off their lights for the Muslim prayer that occurs five times daily. Smaller businesses ask their customers to leave the establishment during this time. Before the publicly-broadcast call to prayer the Caravan restaurant staff went downstairs to lock their doors and turn off the lights. During prayer call customers would eat by candlelight. There were many times when we could hear the Mutawa pounding on the doors downstairs, screaming in Arabic to let them in. The staff ignored them and everyone kept quiet as a mouse. Eventually the Mutawa would give up and move on to victimize easier prey. But one night they surprised us by arriving between prayer calls. Gabrielle, Fawzia and I were enjoying a leisurely dinner when we heard the downstairs door crash open. Multiple feet pounded up the stairs. From behind a curtain somewhere in the restaurant a Western male voice roared, "MUTAWA!" The restaurant cleared like magic, chairs kicked over, dishes crashing to the floor. As the Mutawa flew up the entrance stairs with sticks in hand, we all fled through the kitchen and down the steep back stairs into the alley. It was a game we often played and we never knew if we would be able to finish our meals or not. As far as I knew, nobody ever fell down the back stairs in the rush. If they had it would have been a long tumble.

Other favorite Tabuk restaurants were the Pakistani, Indian, and especially the Lebanese/Turkish restaurants. I loved the Mediterranean food: grilled lamb and chicken, hummus, moutabel (eggplant dip), sliced fresh vegetables, pickles, and fresh Arabic bread. The Pakistani restaurants served fragrant "dahl" (lentil stew), fluffy white rice, and big round loaves of chewy Afghan bread. The Indian restaurants served all manner of curries, both meat and vegetarian, hot fruit chutneys, samosas (crisp deep-fried pastry triangles filled with either meat or vegetables), fragrant biryanis, and Indian bread fresh from the oven.

Gabrielle loved Indian food and some days she'd get a strong craving, "I'd kill for a samosa or two. Let's catch the first bus downtown after work and get some." I rarely needed convincing. We'd come home carrying a brown paper bag with crisply fried samosas, filled with curried potatoes and peas. We spent the evening at my place or at Gabrielle's, eating samosas and drinking cup after cup of tea.

Most restaurants, aside from The Caravan, strictly segregated men and women. The upstairs section was always reserved for families and single women. These second floor sections were not floors at all. Often added as an afterthought, wobbly little rooms were more or less suspended from the ceiling by sticks, plywood and nails. The floors of these rooms often tilted so alarmingly I was sure that one day we would plunge through the floor and land on the diners below us. Stairs to reach the shaky rooms were just as makeshift, little more than wooden ladders.

The best Turkish food was available at the Rooftop Restaurant. The first time Fawzia invited me to the restaurant, she asked me if I was afraid of rats or cats. "Before we go upstairs you must know about the rats and cats." What an odd thing to say. "Well, I love cats, but I admit I've never seen a rat. But what do rats and cats have to do with our meal?" Fawzia smiled, "Don't worry. Let's go upstairs and you'll see what I mean."

We entered the restaurant, which looked pretty normal for Tabuk. We climbed shaky, worn-out stairs and arrived on an uneven concrete-covered roof. A four-foot cinderblock wall went around the entire roof. Fawzia and I seated ourselves at one of the rickety tables and a harried-looking waiter rushed over to take our order. I looked around me, expecting to see almost anything at this point. "I'm really puzzled Fawzia. Rats and cats? Are you playing a joke on me?" She only smiled.

Within a few minutes our waiter clattered back up the stairs balancing a huge tray of delicious food: "shish tawook" (chicken kebab), hummus, eggplant salad, fresh vegetables, and fresh Arabic bread. Just as we began to eat, Fawzia silently pointed to the wall behind me. I turned and watched as one rail-thin cat after another lined up on the wall like soldiers in formation. The usual feral cats: lanky, stringy creatures with huge ears and mangy fur. Nothing unusual here. I'd seen hundreds of feral cats around our compound and downtown.

Then a few feet away a huge rat appeared and clambered cautiously on to the wall. He was followed by several more of his companions. All appeared plump and well-fed, apparently in much better condition than the nearby cats. The rats seemed to grin at us with their razor-sharp yellow teeth. I turned and stared at Fawzia in shock. She smiled serenely. I felt a little nervous about the rats, but eventually turned and continued eating.

The cats watched our every bite from one wall while the smaller audience of rats watched just as intently. I figured the cats and rats had some sort of agreement; if there was so much leftover food to eat it would never be necessary for the cats to hunt the rats. I soon learned not to leave my chair for any reason until the meal was over. Simply lifting a butt cheek off the chair was an invitation to the mob of cats. They'd race to the chair, climb over the diner's lap, on to the table and help themselves. The rats were more wary and waited until all the humans had vacated the table. The waiters moved swiftly to remove the leftovers. But they were never fast enough. Within seconds the table was covered with a squirming blanket of squabbling cats and rats. I'd never seen two species engage in such a way. But the food was great!

(Feral cats were also a big problem in the female compound where I lived. Armies of lanky, multi-colored cats with big ears roamed about freely. Everyone fed the cats out of sympathy for their difficult life, but once a month the hospital maintenance staff held a cat hunt. It made me sad because I've always loved cats. But it was necessary otherwise we would not have been able to step out our doors for the cats.)

My favorite place for take-out food was a little hole in the wall on the main street of Tabuk. They served the most delicious chicken and rice. The front window displayed freshly-roasted chickens with crisp brown skin. A huge vat of fluffy white rice sat near the chickens, rich with nuts, cardamom pods, cloves, cinnamon and raisins. The mixture was bought by weight. The clerk simply weighed my requested amount of rice and chicken, spread out a thick bed of clean newspaper, dumped my order on it and neatly wrapped it up for me to take home. I often made a special trip downtown just for the chicken and rice, it was so tasty.

One nice hotel existed in Tabuk, the Sahara. It offered an unusual eating experience for Tabuk - a buffet. The buffet and dining tables were set around a beautiful swimming pool that was never used. The Sahara was a place the Mutawa did not seem to bother with, perhaps because it was located far from downtown. We often went there in a mixed group of men and women. The buffet was billed as an international selection of food, but it was usually limited to grilled lamb and chicken, salads, fruits, and delicate Middle Eastern desserts. The food was fresh and well-prepared, and the surroundings were clean and attractive. More progressive Saudi families came to eat at the Sahara, but the women remained veiled. I felt sorry for the veiled women as I watched them struggling to eat in public, awkwardly lifting their veil just enough to take bites without revealing their faces to strange males. The Sahara even offered "Saudi champagne", a fizzy mixture of 7-Up and fruit juice served in champagne flutes. We went to The Sahara for special occasions such as "ma'salama" (goodbye) parties and birthdays.

The most difficult part of spending time downtown was the lack of toilet facilities. Squat toilets (consisting of a hole in the ground surrounded by white porcelain with a place to set a foot on either side) were available if you knew where to go, but the filth of most drove me to remain dehydrated while downtown. Dehydration was not difficult to achieve when dressed in a black polyester abaya in 120 degree heat. The toilet at the Rooftop Restaurant was the worst. We had to clamber down the rickety stairs from the roof, walk through the kitchen (where we tried hard not to notice the hygiene situation) and into a dark narrow hallway. At the end of the hall sat a filthy squat toilet barely hidden by a tattered sheet someone had hung from the ceiling. I thought it a good thing the corner was so dark. We would have lost our courage had we been able to see clearly the filth around that toilet. It took time for me to adapt to some of the hygiene horrors I encountered, but soon enough I was able to overlook most situations.

What's Really Under the Abaya?

In the coppery glow of an Arabian sunset, I stood with my new friends Vicky and Anya at the entrance to our compound. I'd arrived in Tabuk only a few weeks earlier and was still stunned by culture shock and heat. We sweltered in our black abayas as we watched a battered Chevy Suburban roll up beside us. Vicky waved at the driver and exclaimed, "Here's our chauffeur, the Captain." We were on our way to a Saudi wedding!

Captain Mohammed Ghasim was a member of the Saudi military and resident on the same military base where the three of us lived. Vicky knew his lovely wife Yasmin, who had kindly invited us to the wedding. She asked that we come to their home beforehand. We three young ladies stuffed ourselves in the middle seat of the Suburban, giggling with anticipation of our adventure. The Captain turned and greeted us in formal, almost stilted English, "You are all most welcome to come to my home today." I pulled the side door closed and we were on our way.

Vicky, of course, had met the Captain before but this was my first meeting. I studied him from where we sat. He was a handsome man of proud demeanor, his profile angular and chiseled. He said nothing more to us during the drive to his home. Since the Northwest Armed Forces military base was so enormous, it took some time to reach our destination. But twenty minutes later the Captain pulled up in front of a splendid white two-storey villa surrounded by a high wall, which is a common feature in the Middle East.

Yasmin met us at the door and welcomed us *"Ahlan wasahlan, ahlan wasahlan*, welcome," she said graciously in Arabic. "Welcome," we found out quickly, was the only English word she knew. We were glad Vicky had a good knowledge of Arabic. Yasmin, no more than thirty-five years old, stood before us dressed in a stunning, crimson-red Saudi dress with silver embroidery sparkling at the neck and hem. The brilliant red set off the waist-length raven hair and the exquisite cheekbones of this beautiful woman.

Yasmin led us through the cavernous villa with intersecting hallways of cool white marble. The house smelled of sweet incense and strong Arabic coffee. She directed us into a high-ceilinged room and left us to make ourselves comfortable. On the floor were Arabic-style furnishings: brightly-patterned bolster cushions and lush hand-woven carpets. I thought to myself, "Oh no, not a Western-style couch or chair in sight." I was not accustomed to sitting on the floor. Trying to preserve some modesty, I wrapped my dress around my knees and lowered myself gracelessly to floor level. A large pillow cushioned me as I fell the last few inches. Vicky and Anya giggled at my embarrassment. I scanned the walls from my floor view. I saw only a few framed forest scenes, curiously hung on thick wires at ceiling level.

A mouthwatering scent of baking emanated from the kitchen. We had hardly settled ourselves when Yasmin and her three daughters appeared to serve us coffee and warm, sticky pastries fragrant with honey and cinnamon. The coffee was served in tiny golden cups without handles, set on a matching tray ornamented with intricate Arabic calligraphy. Our hostess sat gracefully upon the carpet and smiled at us. The daughters sat beside her, mini versions of their striking mother, with the long black hair and pretty faces. The girls knew a few words of English, and we managed some awkward conversation punctuated with lots of laughter. Captain Mohammed, relaxing in another part of the villa, came into the room and indicated it was time to leave for the wedding. Vicky helped me get up off the floor while Yasmin and her daughters made themselves ready in a flurry of black silk abayas, black gloves and full-face veils. We were off to the wedding.

We again piled into the Suburban and proceeded through a crossword puzzle of streets until the Captain dropped us off beside a high wall in a dusty alley. Weary-looking date palms lined the wall, their thirsty fronds drooping in the evening heat. We scrambled out of the vehicle and stepped through a beat-up metal gate into a courtyard large enough to hold hundreds of people. Dozens of brightly colored carpets overlaid the deep sand covering the courtyard floor. Before us was a milling crowd of black-draped female figures, laughing and chattering with excitement. Saudi weddings were strictly segregated; females had their own party, while men met at another location. Not one uncovered face among the women, but I sensed, as they waited, their breathless anticipation for the coming event. I found myself caught up in their infectious enthusiasm. I grinned at Vicky, "I can't believe I'm at a Saudi wedding!"

Finally the big metal doors of the wedding hall were thrown open. We were carried along in a sudden rush of perfumed female bodies fighting to be first inside the building. The hall was set up like an amphitheater with rows of wooden seats descending, ramp-like, to a small stage. The air smelled stale and the rumble of central air conditioning failed miserably to cool the vast room. Yasmin, a wonderful hostess, led us to seats about mid-way up so that we would have a good view of the festivities.

On stage a group of female musicians was tuning stringed instruments unfamiliar to me. Yasmin told us the musicians were from Yemen. These Yemeni women were short, dark, and angular, distinct from the more attractive Saudi women. No males over seven years of age were permitted at female gatherings, so the Yemeni women made a good business playing at weddings and parties. I found their music odd and discordant to my Western ear, like a mob of tomcats caterwauling. And yet, as I listened, I was gradually captivated by a beautiful primeval rhythm within the music.

All of a sudden I witnessed a magical metamorphosis amongst the wedding guests. Around me the black-draped women threw off their abayas and veils, emerging like exotic tropical birds. "Plumage" was the word that came to my mind. The landscape of black blossomed into an explosion of color and motion. I found it hard to believe these vibrantly-dressed Saudi females were the same featureless women I had just seen in public. For the first time I realized that a majority of Saudi women were stunningly beautiful. I felt dull and colorless in my plain black, cotton dress. But Saudi women don't just love beautiful dresses and jewelry. Surprisingly, when I later traveled to Jeddah and wandered around the beautiful malls, I saw some of the most magnificent lingerie. Store after store full of beautiful, daring underclothing. I realized there was certainly a lot more going on under those abayas than I could even imagine!

Every type of woman filled the room, young and old, thin and heavy, short and tall. I could not help but stare at the teenage girls, so strikingly sensual for their age with doe eyes, glossy waist-length hair and, to my surprise, wearing revealing silk dresses. I commented to Vicky that these teenagers seemed shockingly precocious. "A lot of these teenage girls," Vicky explained, "are here to be exhibited as prospective brides. This room is filled with future mother-in-laws looking to arrange marriages for their sons."

Young mothers showcased their handsome faces and long black hair, their shapely bodies dressed in brilliant silk miniskirts and smart designer outfits. Audacious cleavage exploded out of dresses. Sleek skin peeked from dresses slit to the thigh. The nubile younger women wore heavy makeup, almost clown-like in its application. But somehow it suited their lavish outfits. Little girls dashed amongst their elders in ornate dresses with row upon row of frills, ribbons and sequins. Middle-aged matrons, bodies thickened by childbearing, were clad in more conservative dress but no less colorful. And ancient crones sat secure in their traditional dress of plain black and their heavy silver Bedouin jewelry. An unmistakable sensuality infused the room; the heady scent of expensive perfumes and sweet incense mixed with the body heat of hundreds. The hall was roaring with excitement, the loud and raucous women competing with the squawking chords of the Yemeni band. Hoards of tiny children added to the melee, racing and darting amongst the fashionably dressed ladies.

Almost all the women were wearing a wealth of gold. The jewelry left me speechless, genuine precious gold as far as the eye could see: ropes of ornate necklaces, heavy earrings, glittering piles of bangles dancing on arms. Many of the middle-aged women wore a heavy gold belt around their midriffs. I tried to imagine how much carat weight existed in the room.

I watched young women move down to the stage to dance. They swung their heavy black hair in rhythm with the slow movements of their supple bodies. No wonder female hair was considered so erotic in Saudi society; here was proof of its beauty. My reverie was interrupted by a Saudi lady passing me a large incense burner releasing the smoke of "oud bakhour" (incense made from an exotic wood). The rich incense was being passed amongst the crowd. I found the fragrance astonishing, an exotic, heavy mix of sweet, spicy and musky.

I watched the Saudi women waft the smoke into their hair, down their dress fronts and under their skirts. Vicky, Anya and I followed suit and the dress I wore smelled of the delicious scent for weeks after. I later asked Captain Ghasim about oud. He told me it was used only at very special functions like weddings. Later I was able to see a piece of oud wood and it was as beautiful as its smell. It was imported from India in small mahogany-colored pieces banded with gold graining. Oud was costly, I learned. The Captain told us that a buyer could expect to pay $200 to $1000 per ounce depending on quality.

Yasmin encouraged us to join the ladies dancing on the stage but we felt shy; I wanted only to sit and absorb the amazing sights, sounds and smells.

A sudden shout went up amongst the women and they fled around corners or threw abayas over their heads. Even the crones threw a black scarf over their heads. I hadn't a clue what was going on. Vicky, who'd been to other Saudi weddings, told Anya and I that the women rushed to hide or cover because strange men were in the vicinity. It was time for the wedding feast in the courtyard. Sure enough, as we returned to the courtyard, a troop of Asian men stepped through the gate carrying food. With one arm they hoisted vast trays of rice with a whole roast lamb or goat on top of each. The trays were placed carefully on the carpets over the sand and the men left as quickly as they had appeared.

Yasmin seated me on the ground amongst a group of elderly Saudi ladies. I inhaled the fragrance of the food before us, the mountain of rice studded with sticks of cinnamon, green cardamom, raisins and pine nuts. The rice shone with "ghee" (clarified butter), so liberally applied it pooled around the bottom of the tray like a golden moat. Perched on top was an entire sheep with head, eyes and teeth intact. Other food items were arranged around the tray: bowls of sliced vegetables, fresh Arabic bread and glass bottles of warm Pepsi-Cola and Orange Crush. (Everyone seemed quite happy to drink the warm soda without any ice.)

The old ladies took over my education on how to eat with my right hand. Their example looked simple: they grabbed some rice, rolled it in their hand to make a ball, pulled off a piece of lamb and tossed everything into their mouths. My attempts were dismal and more rice landed in my lap than in my mouth. I felt glad of the black dress I wore because the front was littered with rice grains and oily ghee. The old ladies cackled at my clumsiness. One wrinkled old soul felt sorry for me; she drew a gigantic soup spoon from her pocket and handed it to me. I was finally able to get the food into my mouth and it was delicious. I found the lamb tough and fatty, but flavorsome. The rice was richly luscious with aromatic spices and butter. I would later come to know that amongst expatriates this type of meal was known as a "goat grab."

I was surprised at how quickly the women ate. No sooner had they sat, than they got up and returned to the hall to continue dancing and celebrating.

Our midnight curfew drew closer and we had not yet seen the bride and groom. But just as we rose to leave, the bride and groom stepped into the courtyard. The wedding guests rushed to cover their faces again because the groom was not a close family member. I thought how confusing this segregation of the sexes was. In much of Saudi society, a woman's face can only be seen by her father, grandfather, brothers, sons or husband.

As the couple moved towards the wedding hall, the women began the traditional ululating. This trilling sound is made by rapidly vibrating the tongue against the back of the upper teeth while holding a high note. Women all over the Middle East make this sound at weddings, and sometimes funerals. I felt chills down my spine at this ancient female expression of joy. I turned my attention to the bridal couple. The bride's face was not covered. Her cheeks were flushed with happiness and she looked gorgeous in a Western-style white and silver gown. Her young groom was tall and reedy. I watched him steal shy glances at his bride as if he couldn't believe this gorgeous creature had agreed to marry him.

Suddenly I was jolted out of my reverie by Vicky. She grabbed my arm and pulled me along, "C'mon, the Captain is outside honking the horn. We can't miss our curfew." We rushed outside and piled into the Suburban once again. The Colonel drove fast and we made it to our compound just before midnight. I was disappointed at missing the ritual where the bride is draped with her dowry of gold, but I would attend another Saudi wedding later in the year and get to see the entire ceremony.

An Argument for Veiling...or Not

I became fascinated with the lives of Saudi women after I attended the wedding. Silent shapes robed in black, faces shrouded against curious gazes, hands enveloped in black gloves. It was a mystery how they navigated.

What I construed as their plight disturbed me. One day I witnessed a startling sight in the hospital. A fully-veiled woman walked while breast-feeding her infant. Her husband was several steps ahead of her. Suddenly the woman stumbled and fell, exposing both her face and bare breast. The commotion caused her husband to turn and rush to help her. His immediate concern, however, was not for his wife or infant, or even for the bared breast, but to cover her face as quickly as possible! I would thereafter see Saudi mothers casually baring breasts to feed their infants in public while their faces remained steadfastly covered.

Another time I saw a Saudi woman leaning against a wall in the hospital, sobbing and obviously struggling with some terrible grief. Her husband stood at a distance looking impatient and embarrassed with her emotion. I felt distressed by her pain. So I walked over to her, unsure of how she might receive my attention. When I put my arm around her she fell into my arms and cried her eyes out. We had no common language but her grief was clear. We shared the moment as two women who momentarily knew no cultural barriers.

I have often been asked, "Why do Muslim women who have immigrated to the West continue to cover themselves fully despite their new freedom?" Devout Muslim women don't suddenly start wearing revealing outfits just because they move to a Westernized country. I have come to understand, in the context of modesty, and no matter where she may live, it is because these women feel protected from the unwelcome attention of strange males. For many, veiling is also a cultural identity which sets them apart.

The all-encompassing shrouding of Saudi women continued to be a hot topic of discussion amongst us Western women. At lunch one day several of us had a lively debate on the subject.

I was initially convinced that Saudi men forced their women to cover completely, and I felt sorry for them. Uncertain of my own feelings, I asked them, "What do you ladies think about this veiling business?"

Jane, ever the outspoken one, said, "It's a load of rubbish, men keeping women under wraps. It's all about male control over women."

Vicky thought there was more to it. "I don't really think its nonsense," she said firmly. "Did you know that in the Quran, there is nothing mentioned about covering a woman's face in public? It says only that Muslim women should be modest in dress and behavior." She had obviously done her research. "Actually, veiling seems to have begun long before Islam. It was a time when Arabian noblewomen covered in order to avoid vulgar looks and behavior by men on the street."

"In that case," I added, "maybe when the strict Wahhabi form of Islam took hold in this country they started forcing women to cover up even more. My God, I've seen women here wearing black gloves, there isn't a bit of skin showing." Heads nodded in agreement. "I've read that Muslim women all over the Middle East may choose whether or not to veil their faces. Muslim women outside of Saudi seem to have a choice, but I don't see that Saudi women have much choice."

Nonetheless I was beginning to realize that the clothing did indeed provide psychological protection and anonymity to Saudi women. In an ultra-conservative society, it provided privacy in the presence of unrelated males and protection from sexual harassment. In fact, the degree to which Saudi women cover is more cultural than religious.

Jane again saw it differently. "It's the bloody men really," she sputtered angrily. "This Saudi lot has absolutely no concept of self-control."

What Jane said often held true. While I'd certainly go on to meet polite, intelligent Saudi men who treated me with respect, the majority of Saudi males seemed to lack any sense of restraint. That may confirm the Wahhabi Islam belief that uncovered women attract men so strongly they cannot control themselves when they see uncovered flesh. Nonetheless, we were angered by this uniquely Wahhabi view which places the blame for lack of male restraint entirely on the woman.

As Western women, when downtown, we were often stared at and harassed by Saudi men, even East Asian expatriate men. I always dressed in my abaya in public, but many Saudi men regarded us as little more than prostitutes. The first time a Saudi male sidled up to me on the street and whispered, "Seester, seester, I give you five hundred," I wasn't entirely sure what he meant. Saudi men, well-intentioned or not, always addressed Western female strangers as "seester" (sister). I told a female colleague about this and she laughed loudly, "You were propositioned! He wants to buy you for a little while and apparently he finds you worth five hundred riyals!" She was quick to add, "Learn to laugh about it, girl, because you're gonna hear it a lot during your time here." She was right. I would hear this proposition many times over the next two years and eventually I was able to find it hilarious. In fact, I found the financial offer varied anywhere from a couple of hundred to thousands of riyals, perhaps depending on the contents of the Saudi male's wallet and the level of attraction felt.

But more troubling to me was the fact that many Middle Eastern and Saudi men, as well as expatriate East Asian men, had the offensive habit of touching and groping at their crotches. This common practice was one of the first things I noticed when I arrived in Saudi. But unless they were being intentionally lewd, for most men it seemed to be an entirely unconscious habit. I have never understood this or the reason for it. When Gabrielle and I went downtown and saw yet another man groping his crotch she'd sigh and comment, "There he goes, checking to see if everything's still there!"

One evening, Gabrielle and I were in a crowded stationery store in downtown Tabuk. I sensed someone behind me and felt a hand travel across my behind. I turned to find a young Saudi man grinning at me, looking pleased with what he'd just done.

With all my strength I hit him with a roundhouse slap to the face. His expression was astonished as he fell into a book display, scattering books everywhere.

Gabrielle turned at the commotion and saw me red-faced and angry, the young man lying at my feet in a pile of books. She asked me with dry British formality, "Whatever are you up to?"

The youth scrambled to his feet and dashed out of the store. I knew he felt shamed in front of the other men and wanted to escape quickly. Gabrielle realized what had happened and we fell about the place laughing until we cried. Some Filipina girls in another part of the store started to clap and I took a deep bow, my anger replaced by humor. Nearby males of various nationalities simply stared at me. But I was on firm ground. In Saudi, women of any nationality are perfectly within their rights to use physical force if touched by a strange male.

At the same time I felt that Saudi males could not be entirely blamed for their behavior. American classics like MTV had reached some who'd never been outside their introverted country. For a young, repressed man with no factual or accurate knowledge of the world outside of Saudi, how would he view the scantily-clad Western women in the provocative music videos? All the women he'd ever known in his immediate family certainly never dressed or acted in such a way.

I did not wonder then that some Saudi men looked at Western women as purely sexual objects.

I soon discovered it was frighteningly easy to get into trouble even with the best intentions. Everything seemed antithetic to all I took for granted in my homeland.

Danger at Every Turn

There is no place on earth quite like Saudi Arabia. Danger is everywhere, in the relentless heat, the vast desert, befriending the wrong person or simply crossing the street. There is no room for complacency; to do so could get you hurt or even killed. There is no such thing as being too paranoid when living in Saudi. If a situation doesn't feel right then you best heed your intuition.

Because of the paradox that is Saudi Arabia, those who go to work there tend to think the Saudi authorities must be stupid and unaware. With the discovery of oil in 1938 the Saudis walked out of the desert into the Twentieth Century. They have never fully made the adjustment; one foot is in the ancient past and the other in the modern world. Expatriates joke about the Saudi authorities because of the often senseless and arbitrary decisions they make. The Kingdom is ostensibly a monarchy, but it is a dictatorship by any other name. Hence it operates like a dictatorship. Not one individual ruling with an iron fist, but the entire Saudi royal family who use the state-sponsored religious police to control the population. After being in Saudi for only a few days I felt like I was being watched. The Saudis authorities know what expatriates are doing; where you go, whom you see, what you talk about on the phone, and who your friends are.

But I grew to love the adrenalin rush that came with everyday life in Saudi Arabia.

A respiratory therapist, also from Canada, was appalled to discover that a Saudi co-worker was selling drugs to patients and employees right out of the Respiratory Department. Of course, she went to her Saudi department director to report the trafficking activity, a crime carrying the death sentence in Saudi. The department director took it to the hospital director, Lt. Colonel Ghasib, and suddenly the Canadian found herself under arrest. It was a situation of damned-if-you-do and damned-if-you-don't. She felt she'd done the right thing by reporting the trafficking.

But the hospital administrators decided to not only blame her, but make an example of her. She was thrown into jail for a few days, enough time for the expat community to hear about it, and then deported within hours of her release. This was not an unusual situation. Accusing a Saudi of any illegal activity would have caused the employee and the entire hospital administration to lose face, an unbearable situation for Eastern peoples in general. The Canadian woman was used as an example even though the authorities knew she was not guilty of any wrongdoing.

Other harsh realities sometimes overshadowed my new adventures. During my first week in Tabuk a young Canadian paramedic named Stephen took his own life. Or so we thought. His roommates came home from work to find him hanging in a closet. The news rushed through the expat community like a wild fire. All were shocked because the young man had been in Saudi only two weeks. Stephen was an attractive fellow and by all reports, well-liked by colleagues. But was it suicide? A variety of rumors surfaced. Trish whispered to me one day, "I heard that he couldn't save a Saudi child at the scene of a car accident so the parents murdered him in retribution." Jane shared another rumor, "I heard Stephen was secretly dating a Saudi woman, the family found out and killed both of them." It was Vicky, over coffee in her apartment, who introduced the most grisly rumor to Anya and me. "Have you ever heard of auto-erotica? It's a peculiar sexual practice where near-asphyxiation heightens orgasm." Thinking it through, I said, "Maybe his death was accidental; he went a little too far, passed out completely and ended up strangling himself." The rumors circulated for weeks. But perhaps Stephen really was carrying some sort of psychological burden when he arrived. The stress he encountered in the Kingdom may have pushed him to suicide.

It came as a shock to me when I realized how many unhappy, even unstable, people sought escape in Saudi. Some seemed to think that coming to a foreign country and making tax-free money would magically resolve the problems they'd run from in their home country. It was very evident that the expatriate population in Tabuk had its share of misfits who could not have fit in anywhere. This was clearly not a place for the weak of heart, or mind. I saw people literally break down, unable to deal with the unadulterated insanity that is Saudi. As a consequence, many people joined the expat party circuit, drinking dangerous home-brew and risking their jobs with blatant disregard for the rules. It's an odd phenomenon about Saudi expats that many seem to lose their normal inhibitions or participate in behavior they would never do in their own country. Aside from the drinkers, many also engaged in rampant promiscuity. I was always amazed at this loss of inhibition while living in one of the most repressed societies on earth.

The reality of Saudi Arabia is sobering: I cannot find another way to describe life in Saudi except to say that it is too vivid, too intense. A place where a very thin skin of civilization overlies a cultural mentality stuck somewhere in the seventh century. Where witchcraft and sorcery are real and genuinely feared by most Saudis; where the chief executioner, the one who beheads criminals, is a respected and revered figure. A place where I became attuned to thinking before speaking, my senses sharper, constantly on guard. Since I had no choice but to be self-sufficient and independent, I, too, had to face myself and my emotions more honestly than I ever had before. I could either be strong or go home and face my own demons.

The same week as Stephen's death a middle-aged man called Ed was deported to his home country of Australia. Ed specialized in maintenance and repair of intricate laboratory analyzers. He was also a recovering alcoholic who believed that by coming to the "dry" land of Saudi Arabia he could stay sober. But soon after his arrival in the Kingdom Ed discovered "siddiqui," or simply "sid" ("little friend"), a potent, and sometimes lethal, home brew distilled from potatoes, fruit or whatever was at hand. A gallon of "sid" cost five hundred Saudi riyals (US$130) on the black market. The brewing, a profitable business mostly run by Filipinos, took place on the single-male compound. The stills were moved regularly so not to be found in frequent raids by hospital security. Some described sid's effect as drunkenness magnified by something akin to being high on a mild drug like marijuana. The brew was hellishly addicting by anyone's estimate. Endless stories circulated of people blinded or dying of alcohol poisoning after imbibing excessive quantities. I tasted sid on only one occasion and thought people must be desperate, indeed, to drink such swill. To me the brew tasted like a combination of laundry detergent, ammonia, and rotten vegetables. The wretched Australian soon fell back into his alcohol addiction. Ed became prone to violence and was more often drunk than sober. After he tried to assault a co-worker, the hospital administrators decided to deport him. In fact, Ed's condition was so precarious an employee from the Australian embassy in Riyadh traveled to Tabuk to escort him back to Australia.

For me, falling ill proved to be alarmingly easy. Some weeks after arriving in Tabuk, Fawzia and I went shopping downtown. While there I wanted to try the famous Middle Eastern street food, the "shawarma." This delicacy involved a man with a long knife skillfully slicing chicken or lamb off a rotating spit of meat, tucking it into warm Arabic bread and dressing it with garlic-sesame sauce and sour pickles. What an irresistible taste experience. "I just have to try one of these," I told Fawzia. The wiser of us, she counseled me, "Perhaps you should not eat the shawarma yet. Your body must become accustomed to this new country." I later wished I'd heeded her advice. I admit I'd paused momentarily when I saw an open jar of mayonnaise on the shawarma stand. I wondered how long it had sat out in the heat. But stubborn, I ordered my shawarma and enjoyed every bite. Fawzia and I caught the bus back to the compound, satisfied with our evening expedition. Unfortunately, no matter how delicious, I would live to regret that food experience.

About ten days after my first shawarma, I developed a high fever and excruciating headache. I assumed I had a flu bug. I never considered the possibility of a third world disease. I'd had all the required immunizations in Canada, including typhoid, cholera, and hepatitis B. I naively assumed I had guaranteed protection from any "foreign" bugs.

I continued to feel worse, so fatigued and achy I finally visited the Employee Health physician. He took one look at me and admitted me directly to the hospital. Tests soon confirmed the shocking diagnosis of typhoid. How had this happened to me? Both Fawzia and I had missed the fact a typhoid epidemic was beginning a sweep across Tabuk when I insisted on eating that shawarma! I was started on intravenous antibiotics and fluids. By this time I felt truly awful, so sick I almost wished to die. Within the next month people all over Tabuk fell ill and local hospitals were packed with typhoid cases.

I improved over the next few days and was finally discharged home, weak as a newborn. I spent the next two weeks recovering in my apartment. There was no lack of care as my friends fussed over me. Fawzia, though I'd ignored her warning to postpone eating the shawarma, never said, "I told you so." She felt badly because she hadn't known about the typhoid epidemic that would eventually affect the entire city. I reassured her, "It's not your fault Fawzia. If I'd listened to your advice I probably wouldn't have got sick."

After I returned to work I continued to have vague symptoms. More antibiotics, including sulfa, were prescribed with no resolution. My "titer" (determination of concentration of the typhoid pathogen in my system) continued to climb. Further tests confirmed I was now a typhoid carrier, a dangerous situation for those around me. My friends gently poked fun at me, calling me "Typhoid Mary." I became frustrated because the employee health physician could not seem to resolve my situation. At last I demanded an appointment with the tropical diseases specialist, Dr. Neequaye, a native of Ghana schooled in Britain. He doubled my dose of sulfa to 2000 mg daily. "You're carrying two strains of salmonella typhi," he told me, "we must rid your system of both as soon as possible." When my titer doubled in one week, Dr. Neequaye finally prescribed the antibiotic of last resort, Chloramphenicol. This antibiotic is used mostly in third world countries. The range of possible side effects frightened me, including bone marrow suppression and in rare cases aplastic anemia which can be fatal. But what choice did I have at this point? I took the drug and the typhoid was finally eradicated from my system. Fortunately, I suffered none of the side effects. Dr. Neequaye told me as many as fifty percent of expats in Saudi are likely typhoid carriers who never become symptomatic and thus never treated. My parents warned me, "Don't come home on vacation until you're absolutely sure you're cured."

In addition to typhoid Saudi Arabia is rife with a variety of frightening endemic illnesses. Risk is greatest in the heat of late summer. The most common ailments are hepatitis A and amoebic dysentery, both food-borne illnesses caused by poor hygiene. But schistosomiasis (bilharzia) is a major public health problem in Saudi. It is a disease caused by parasitic worms present in fresh water sources where infected people have urinated or defecated. The eggs hatch and grow inside fresh water snails. The larvae are able to penetrate the skin of those wading or swimming in affected water. Without early intervention the disease becomes chronic and causes widespread damage to internal organs. Other diseases include bacterial meningitis, a major cause of death in young Saudi children. Proof of meningitis vaccination is now mandatory for all "Hajjis" (religious pilgrims) attending "Haj" (annual pilgrimage to Mecca in western Saudi Arabia.) There are occasional outbreaks of Rift Valley Fever, a viral infection. Malaria is a risk in Saudi Arabia's southwest Asir province, a relatively lush region when compared to the rest of the desert kingdom. Asir can see 12-20 inches of rainfall in a year. Along with its location on a high plateau the conditions are ideal for breeding mosquitoes. Other less common ailments are Dengue fever, avian flu and brucellosis (caused by drinking unpasteurized camel milk.)

And then there are the sexually-transmitted diseases. In Saudi Arabia statistics used to be very limited. At one time HIV/AIDS did not officially exist in the Kingdom. Eventually the Saudi government was forced to admit that HIV/AIDS is certainly present in the Kingdom. (Admitting to sexually-transmitted diseases causes loss of face because it suggests immoral behavior, forbidden in the Quran.) Unfortunately, this disease is commonly brought from other countries where it is generally known that Saudi men go for sex tourism. In a country where adultery and homosexuality are punishable by death it is considered a less risky option to travel outside for illicit sex. Unfortunately HIV is brought home to Saudi wives, and the cycle continues.

While I survived typhoid, an exhausting and sobering experience, I began to wonder how safe I was against any sickness endemic to Saudi. But mostly I worried about how fear of serious illness might possibly affect my decision to involve myself in further adventures. It is true, of course, that travelers must use caution when arriving in a third world or developing country. Bacteria endemic to the region are not usually those a Western immune system is familiar with. I used more caution after my bout of typhoid, but ultimately realized that possible illness is part and parcel of living in Saudi Arabia.

I decided I could not avoid future excursions for fear of illness or other calamity. There was too much yet to see and do.

A Cast of Characters

Because of my experience with obstetrics and gynecology transcription, I was eventually transferred to that department by order of Dr. James Hoey, the director of OB/GYN. My move happened suddenly. One morning my friend Gabrielle, who worked as the OB/GYN department secretary, called me in the surgery department, "You must come up here. Dr. Hoey wants to chat you up regarding the open transcription position here." I was up there in moments, hopeful I might finally escape the racial tension in the surgery department. Dr. Hoey was a tall, cadaverous Irishman of about sixty years with good humor written all over his face. Though strict with his staff he laughed easily and often. His wit was famous throughout the expat community. In my first conversation with Dr. Hoey, he introduced himself with a big grin, "I'm the poor bugger what got shot in the ass getting out of Iraq!" This incident apparently occurred when Saddam Hussein invaded Kuwait and Dr. Hoey barely escaped the country with his life. He made light of it, but in fact he was shot by a nervous Iraqi soldier and seriously injured. Iraq had a high-quality healthcare system at that time and many Western-trained physicians who'd held jobs there ended up in Tabuk.

It was a brief interview. Dr. Hoey had a quick look at my resume. "I think you'll do just fine with us here," he said. "It will be great fun to have a Canadian among our lot!" He called my supervisor, Jan, in the surgery department and informed her he needed me that same afternoon.

I breathed a huge sigh of relief. I hoped the OB/GYN department would be a more peaceful place than the one I was leaving.

My new office was perfect, a small room in a back hallway on the Labor & Delivery ward. I was happy to find out that I'd share the office with Gabrielle. She filled my workdays with laughter at her British slang and tales about her previous job in Riyadh. I liked Gabrielle because she genuinely enjoyed the Middle East and its people. She too made friendships with other nationalities. Gabrielle told me her mother was born in India during the final years when Britain ruled India. I was fascinated by the stories she told me about her mother's childhood. She would often say, "I'd murder for a cup of tea," and indeed she nearly always had a cup of tea in hand.

Gabrielle asked me what I really wanted to do while I was in the Kingdom. "Oh, I've just got to get to the desert soon," I said excitedly. "I've heard from so many that it's quite beautiful. And lately I heard about a wonderful ancient city in Jordan called Petra. I love archeology so I must try to see it." I asked Gabrielle what she liked best about Saudi Arabia. "Well, meeting so many people from different countries and cultures has been a wonderful experience," she said, "but I absolutely adore the desert and the heat. England can be so damp and dreary. You know the funny old saying that mad dogs and Englishmen go out in the midday sun? Well that's me!"

Gabrielle and I loved our office for its seclusion from the main stream. A large comfortable chair behind the office door was our spot to relax, chat or read the newspaper. When I arrived that chair was the only furniture in the room aside from Gabrielle's desk. John, my supervisor in medical records, acquired an ancient computer for me, but I had no desk to set it on. John didn't seem motivated to find me a desk. And the staff in Materiel Management told me they didn't have any spare desks. "What am I supposed to do?" I enquired of Gabrielle. With a crafty grin she told me, "Do what all the rest of us have to do, snatch and run!"

And that's how I furnished my office. I scoured the hospital for what I needed and simply grabbed it when nobody was looking. Eventually I appropriated a wobbly little table to set my computer on and a decent enough office chair. But I had to guard my own equipment as others might take it the same way I had!

Gabrielle and I often walked to work together. As we passed through the waiting room near our office we'd see our sleeping Saudi guard, either sitting up or stretched out on the couch reserved for visitors. He was a string bean of a youth, all gawky elbows and knees. Members of the Military Police were stationed all over the hospital, but our guy slept most of the time. He did not inspire a lot of confidence. What if we were suddenly and inexplicably attacked? He wore a sidearm, but Gabrielle and I doubted he knew how to use it. We often joked about his comatose state.

One morning we said to each other, "Let's take a photo!" Gabrielle took several photos of the guard and he didn't even flinch at the flash. On the rare occasions we found him awake, he watched us pass with dull, bovine eyes. We never heard the man utter a single word. This relaxed attitude also extended to the police force in Tabuk. They drove high-powered Volvo police cars which were almost always parked in an inconvenient spot such as an intersection or traffic circle. It was common to see the officer tipped back in his seat resting peacefully.

While hospital staff worked on ancient, obsolete computers, new ones gathered dust in a basement. Whoever ordered the new computers failed to note the lack of a systems specialist on staff to install or maintain the equipment. Worse still, the computers were configured for 110 volt while the hospital was wholly 220 volt. New state-of-the-art blood and chemistry analyzers sat silent in the laboratory. The machines could not be used because compatible processing agents were never ordered.

Obtaining basic office supplies such as scissors or tape was hopeless. After trying to order a pair of scissors from central supply, Zafer called me. "Chilly," he stuttered, "I cannot autorize (sic) your request, scissor too expensive. Go buy own scissor." I finally admitted defeat and bought my own supplies downtown.

Hospitals in the Middle East are organized on the British system. Lowest in the hierarchy of staff physicians are the junior and senior house officers. They perform duty rotations in their quest to choose a specialty. Next up are registrars, inexperienced physicians who have nonetheless chosen their specialty in a particular field of medicine. On the top rung are consultants, fully qualified and experienced in their specialty.

The staff of the OB/GYN department was a cast of characters. After Dr. Hoey arrived and organized the unit, the staff became close-knit. Many of the physicians asked Gabrielle and me to address them by their first name.

The "Sari Gang," so named by Gabrielle, consisted of three female physicians born in India and trained in Britain. Dr. Vijaya Chalasani and Dr. Usha Koneru, consultants, and Dr. Padma Prasad, a registrar, were valued as the most motivated and efficient of the department physicians. As females they shouldered the bulk of the workload. Modest Saudi women rarely tolerate a male doctor, especially in gynecologic matters. The Sari Gang glided about like delicate flowers, a white coat over their brilliantly-colored saris and waist-length hair in a neat braid. Gabrielle and I looked forward to seeing what color saris they would wear each day. Dr. Chalasani told me her closet contained no less than two hundred saris. This number is not unusual for Indian women who wear saris every day of their lives.

One of the first things I'd noticed about the ladies was the fact they all wore silver toe rings on the second toe of each foot. When I asked them if the toe rings had a specific meaning, Dr. Chalasani told me that all married Hindu ladies wear them. They wear only silver toe rings because to wear gold below the waist is considered disrespectful to Lakshmi, Goddess of Wealth. I knew I had to have some of those toe rings, married or not! From then on, when they returned from vacation in India both Dr. Chalasani and Dr. Usha brought me not only silver toe rings, but also silver anklets with delightful little bells that jingled happily when I walked. I also loved the look of the tiny diamond in their perfectly shaped noses. At one point I worked up the nerve to have my nose pierced. I loved the look, but unfortunately the piercing became infected and I had to let it close.

Eventually I bought myself gold toe rings and have worn them ever since.

There was another female consultant in our department who managed a remarkable deception. Dr. Huda, an Egyptian, was tossed out of the country shortly after I started working in the OB/GYN department. She certainly stood out in a crowd. Everything about Dr. Huda screamed drama and a desperate need to be the center of attention. She wore vivid theatrical makeup every day. Her long black hair was shellacked with hair spray to keep it in place. It was difficult to tell if Dr. Huda was attractive or not under the makeup. I don't know how she got away with the makeup and the outfits she wore. But it was rumored she was the mistress of a Saudi man high up in the military hierarchy. Dr. Huda was a short little woman in her late forties who compensated for her height with towering plastic heels. Her brightly-colored polyester outfits were straight out of the sixties. Clunky costume jewelry hung from her ears and draped her neck. Both arms sported stacks of plastic bangles that clattered with the slightest movement. And Dr. Huda was at least twenty years beyond carrying off the short skirts she favored.

When I first asked Gabrielle about this odd woman, she exclaimed, "Dr. Huda is a bit peculiar, but you ought to see her resume. She's attended top medical schools in both Britain and the United States. Did her residency at Oxford." I was surprised. "What the heck is she doing working in a small Saudi hospital with a degree from Oxford?" I wondered. "With those qualifications she could have any job she wanted, even if she does dress funny!"

When Dr. Huda was deported, a disillusioned Gabrielle told me the entire story about the woman. "I heard some of the consultants say they never saw Dr. Huda actually participate in a surgery. She spent a lot of time in the operating theater with junior residents, but only supervised and directed them. Everybody thought she was a great teacher because she allowed the junior doctors so much latitude." Apparently Dr. Huda was also careful to attend cases where she would be the only consultant present. Gabrielle said that several of the consultants and two residents finally became suspicious and approached Dr. Hoey. A stealthy and apparently quite lengthy investigation ensued. Eventually Dr. Hoey determined that the Egyptian woman had never attended a medical school in her life. Her only medical experience was gleaned from a job as a nursing assistant in Cairo. Our department was shocked and angered by the perfidy of this woman. How did she manage to stay under the radar for so many years? I was especially distressed by the thought of how many patients may have suffered because of her deceit and lack of conscience. She supervised major surgeries like hysterectomies and C-sections. Ultimately the no-longer-a-doctor was stripped of her job and deported from the Kingdom within hours.

During my two years in Saudi I would see a number of counterfeit medical personnel deported. On initial application with an overseas recruiter every prospective employee must be able to produce original education certificates and references. Obviously some people manage to slip past the recruiters with bogus credentials. By the time they reach Saudi Arabia they find the rules so lax they feel confident about continuing their deceit and collecting a wage in accordance with their so-called qualifications. Usually they are found out when fellow staff start to notice their lack of even basic skills.

A rarity graced our department, a young Saudi female junior house officer. Dr. Khawla Al-Khowair was a pleasant young woman of nervous disposition determined to become a fully-qualified physician. She remained completely veiled, except for her eyes, at all times. Occasionally she would come to our office, close the door, lift her veil and chat with Gabrielle and me. I hadn't been in Tabuk for very long the first time she did this. I was a little shocked. The action seemed so private. But showing her face to us, aside from the fact we were women, demonstrated Dr. Khawla's affection and respect for Gabrielle and me.

She would fan her face in a humorous way and grin at us, "It is very hot under here!" Gabrielle and I loved to see her face; suddenly she became human to us, not just another anonymous blacked-out figure. Though Dr. Khawla's skin was spotty, her flashing gazelle-like eyes and long black lashes were stunning. Saudi women who veil their faces often have skin problems, particularly in the summer. Accumulation of sweat and heat under the veils encourages growth of bacteria. Vitamin D deficiency is epidemic amongst Saudi women. They spend much of their life indoors and dress in black from head to foot while outdoors. In a country with so much sunshine!

Dr. Khawla wore her veil even in the operating room, but had contrived a way to wear the surgical mask over it. I admired Dr. Khawla for her determination to pursue a career in a country where many women were not even allowed basic education. She attended a university and was considered "worldly" by female peers. But each evening after work she was picked up at the hospital entrance by one of her brothers or her father. Of course, as a single female, Dr. Khawla lived at home with her family. She often expressed a desire to marry a religious scholar. Gabrielle and I, between us, questioned whether her education might ultimately be wasted. An ultra-conservative man would never allow his wife to work outside the home.

A few weeks before I left the Kingdom for good, a young Saudi female resident joined the department. Dr. Layla was also covered except for her eyes. She had a delightful fun-loving personality and would often ask me about Canada. But I'd never seen her face.

One evening I was doing laundry and passed a beautiful young woman coming down the stairs from the second floor of flats. She was dressed in very short shorts and a frilly little top that bared a band of taut midriff. The lovely girl greeted me by name and smiled, "Hello, how are you this evening?" I looked at her closely, but did not recognize her face or voice. Then she laughed mischievously, "It is I, Layla! Come from behind my veil!" I smiled back, "Well Layla, you had me at a distinct disadvantage!" I could not help but gaze at her stunning face, glossy black hair to her waist and a perfectly spectacular figure in her skimpy outfit. She was among women on our compound so she felt free to dress as she liked. A thoroughly modern young Saudi woman. We chatted for some time and I realized what a pleasant person she really was. I had to tell her, "Layla, you are truly a lovely woman, inside and out." She smiled at the compliment, "It is very kind of you to say."

Dr. Faisal, one of our young male house officers, knew we saw the young female residents without their veils. He would often try to ascertain details from me. He was especially curious about Layla when she arrived. He'd put on his impish little-boy smile and enquire, "You must tell me. Is she beautiful, is she ugly?" I would answer him sternly, "Dr. Faisal, you are very naughty. You know I can't tell you anything. Dr. Layla would be very hurt if she knew I described her face to an unrelated male." And so she would have been. To describe a Saudi woman's covered face to an unrelated male is almost as bad as that male actually seeing her face. Call Dr. Layla modern or not, it was her personal choice to cover and I respected her privacy.

A colorful assortment of people from other hospital departments drifted through our office every day. First to arrive each morning was Ravi, an underpaid member of the blue-jumpsuit army of Asian men who kept the hospital sparkling clean. He told us he was from Kerala in the south of India.

Ravi had a rather frightening look about him, and we suspected he suffered from some sort of thyroid condition. He was a slight man, rail-thin, weighing perhaps eighty pounds and not more than five feet tall. His huge brown eyes protruded in a permanently startled expression. A head of coarse black hair stood on end and his entire body trembled like a revved-up greyhound.

After a perky good morning to Gabrielle and me, Ravi proceeded down the hallway to a bathroom where he engaged in a ghastly routine. It sounded as if he was being throttled. He repeatedly cleared his throat with vulgar spitting barks, clearly prodigious in their content. This routine inevitably occurred about the time Gabrielle and I were eating a light breakfast. After about a week of enduring Ravi's routine Gabrielle grimaced, "The poor little sod doesn't even know how much it bothers us, but I can't stand it anymore." Reluctant to hurt Ravi's feelings but so repulsed by the sounds, we finally asked him to perform his ritual somewhere else. We attempted to explain the differences in our customs, that this was something we were unused to in public. I don't know if he fully understood, but he did go elsewhere for his morning ritual.

Few of the Housekeeping staff spoke English, but Ravi was completely fluent in the language. He was an intelligent young man who'd obviously received a decent education. What then, Gabrielle and I wondered, had brought him to Saudi to work under the terrible conditions he endured every day? Like so many Asians working in the Middle East, he was quite likely supporting an entire family in his homeland. But Ravi still popped up every morning to see us, always enthusiastic in spite of his lot in life.

Each morning also brought Rico from the mail room, a young Filipino man always excited about the amount of mail I received. Rico looked as if he'd stepped out of a professional laundry, his hospital uniform neatly pressed and his person carefully groomed. His good looks were marred only by a severe underbite. Gabrielle often told me, "Rico is sweet on you," but I never noticed his affection for me. So it came as a surprise when two years later, by then working in the United Arab Emirates, I received a letter from Rico expressing words of love. I was flattered. Rico was a pleasant co-worker in Saudi, but I had no romantic interest in him. Years after I returned to the United States, married my husband and returned to the UAE for a second time, Rico continued to send me love letters in spite of my dissuasion. He kept track of me via the Filipino grapevine, a network across the Middle East that knows all. Rico's letters continued to find me until I left the UAE for good.

But "The Boys" were our favorites, at least for Gabrielle and me. Less so with the department medical staff. They were three Saudi junior house officers, Dr. Mohammed Al Rashidi, Dr. Faisal Al Musali and Dr. Ahmed Bamukhayyar, none appearing over the age of twenty-five. Both slickly handsome, Mohammed and Ahmed invited female glances with their gleaming black hair and poetic brown eyes; while Faisal, his round childish face wrapped in a perpetually naughty smile, looked cherubic. The three lurked and shuffled about the hallways, giggling and avoiding responsibility. One was never seen without the other two. Personable young men though they were, it was hard to comprehend how these man-children would ever become competent physicians. Dr. Khawla was often disgusted with their antics because she worked harder than any of them. She had a lot more to prove as a Saudi female. "The Boys" sometimes watched cartoons on the lunch room television, the volume turned so loudly we had to shout at them. If Dr. Hoey found them so occupied, they would scatter like startled pigeons.

Dr. Faisal seemed least likely to ever succeed. Around the hospital he often appeared dazed, such that Gabrielle said he looked as if he had just fallen out of a cupboard somewhere. But most mornings Dr. Faisal looked as if his mother had sent him off to work, hair neatly combed, white coat buttoned, his face washed squeaky clean.

Dr. Mohammed appeared to be the bad boy of the group, but he was genuinely likable. A beautiful young man with a heart-stopping smile, he usually fell into work looking dissipated and sleepless. Gabrielle and I often commented on his fatigued state. His lips would curve enigmatically and he'd say, "I've had a long night...." Rumor had it that Dr. Mohammed kept a veritable stable of Filipina women for his pleasures. We were frequently discomfited by his critical candor regarding the Saudi royal family. Dr. Mohammed freely admitted that in all likelihood the wrong person might hear him someday, and he'd simply disappear on what he termed "the one-way helicopter ride." He said this with a fatalistic shrug, as if he best live fast while he had the opportunity. He probably did, we thought.

"The Boys" were completely irresponsible. One night Dr. Mohammed was asleep in the on-call room when an emergency C-section arrived in the emergency room. Calls from the switchboard and repeated knocks on his door produced no response. At last a senior consultant was called from his bed at home to deal with the case. When questioned the next day, by a livid Dr. Hoey, why he had not attended the patient, Dr. Mohammed shuffled his feet and looked down sheepishly, "I couldn't wake up. But it's no problem because someone else took care of the patient." Both Dr. Faisal and Dr. Bamukhayyar gained a dubious reputation for being found five hundred miles away in Jeddah whenever they were on-call. They knew they were on duty, but avoided it without any evidence of guilt.

These young men knew they could be careless because they were Saudis. Dr. Hoey would yell and shout at them to no avail. Their attitude could never be altered. For their entire lives they'd been handed everything by the Saudi government and as far as we could see, had little sense of accountability.

I usually enjoyed going to work. We had a lot of fun in our department, and I never tired of being amused and entertained by my amazing assortment of co-workers.

Everyday Life for Saudi Mothers

I found my department fascinating and soon became familiar with the reproductive lives of the Saudi women of Tabuk. Many of them have a difficult life, but their faith in Allah's will enables them to deal with a way of life Western women could not imagine. Most all Saudi marriages are arranged. Amongst more traditional families with limited education marriages occur early, as young as thirteen or fourteen. It was not unusual to see women in their late thirties having had twenty or more pregnancies. The numbers of children produced is seen as Allah's will. And the Saudi government encourages couples to have many children to enlarge their country's population. I remember transcribing a chart on a woman in her forties with twenty-six pregnancies, twenty living children and six miscarriages. She'd had a couple of twin pregnancies, but basically she had been continuously pregnant since an early age.

I could not imagine what it was like for Saudi women burdened with their multitudes of children. Exhausted mothers dragged themselves into the OB/GYN clinic trailing a horde of children, an infant in arms, only to find out another child is on the way. The husband stands by proudly, lifts his eyes to heaven and says "al hamdulilah" (thanks to God). The wife is likely thinking quite differently at that point. Dr. Chalasani told us that quite often Saudi women tried to find a moment alone with the doctor to plead for contraceptives.

Birth control is not forbidden in Islam. But if a husband agrees to his wife's taking an oral contraceptive it often results in failure. The women are given explicit instructions on how to take birth control pills, but the belief seems to be that if one pill works for preventing pregnancy, then taking the entire package at once should surely work over the long term.

Women with little schooling are difficult to educate regarding prenatal care. Some view modern medicine as illogical. Many women arrive at the hospital in advanced labor with no prenatal care. There are often complications and delivery can quickly progress to a Cesarean section. This procedure is seen as a great threat to Saudi families. It is generally advised that a woman have no more than three C-sections. This severely limits a Saudi woman's childbearing potential, thus her value within the family decreases. Some of our doctors spoke about performing C-sections on women well beyond their third pregnancy. After repeated C-sections there is a high risk of uterine rupture before and during delivery, most often resulting in an emergency hysterectomy. When a woman can no longer bear children, some husbands take another wife.

I remember Dr. Hoey talking about a case where a husband brought his wife to the hospital in advanced labor. When the attending doctor examined her, the infant was found to be a footling breech (infant is presenting feet-first). This is an emergency situation for both mother and child, and almost always requires a C-section. In this case the circumstance was explained to the husband. His wife had no voice in the matter. The doctors told the husband she required an immediate C-section to save the infant, and quite possibly the mother as well. The husband was infuriated and took his wife to another hospital. By then the infant had expired and a C-section still had to be performed to extract the infant's body.

The husbands usually stayed around during their wife's gynecologic exams, but most did not hang about while she endured labor. Often the wife would be dropped off at the hospital while he went off to drink tea with his cronies. Among younger Saudi couples, we would occasionally be treated to the sight of a husband pacing anxiously outside the labor room.

The one thing the husband is required to do is produce proof of marriage to the woman. Any female, Saudi or otherwise, arriving at a Saudi hospital in labor must be able to produce a marriage certificate.

Without the all-important piece of paper or at least provision of the name of the baby's father, it is assumed the female is guilty of the serious crime of "fornication" (sex outside marriage.) A Saudi Arabian girl found pregnant without benefit of marriage would in all likelihood be killed by her father or brothers to restore the family "honor" after she has delivered the infant. Other Muslim nationalities are usually thrown in jail, allowed to deliver the infant, and then either flogged or stoned to death. Sometimes the pregnant mother will deliver and raise the baby in jail, a punishment affecting both mother and child. Sentence time can be indeterminate. A woman pregnant by rape will not be treated any differently since there must be four male witnesses to attest to the actual rape. In places like Pakistan the raped woman goes to jail.

When Saudi women of any class came in to deliver their babies, the women and children of her immediate family moved in too. This seemed strange to me, compared to the sterile and rigid guidelines of most North American hospitals. At the same time I'm sure the custom provided great comfort to the new mother. Following delivery the woman and her baby were moved into a large room. Soon after, an army of Asian servants would begin delivering all the comforts of home. Female relatives arrived in droves accompanied by dozens of small children. The servants first brought huge carpets to cover the floor of the hospital room. Plates and dishes, baskets of fruit, incense burners, and huge varieties of food were then brought in and set on the carpets. Relatives came and went at all hours. The entire OB/GYN floor assumed a party atmosphere. For those of us who worked on the unit every day the general havoc was made worse by the multitudes of little children. While their mothers visited with the new mom and her infant, the children were allowed to run wild in the hospital hallways. It often became so disruptive the hospital administrators had to get involved. I found it hard to believe this was a hospital ward.

I was astonished by the flower bouquets sent by family and friends to the new mothers. I've never seen anything like them before or since. The displays were gorgeous in their colorful abundance, but exceedingly ostentatious (and I thought wasteful.) When the postpartum unit had a particularly high number of births within a day or so, the hallways took on the look of a meadow fantasy. Some of the floral arrangements were nine or ten feet tall and sometimes as wide. The incredible numbers of blossoms, every variety from roses to exotic tropical blooms, were arranged on strong wire stands to withstand the weight of the display. Sometimes a particular patient would receive several of these monstrosities. When every room on the unit contained a patient, the jungle of floral displays left little room to navigate the halls. The displays only added to the bedlam already created by visiting relatives and their unruly children. The scent of the many flowers in a contained space was often so cloying some of the nursing staff felt faint.

The hospital also contained a VIP wing where women from powerful families, even a royal Sheikha (chief wife of a Shaikh/leader/governor/royalty), delivered their infants. Most large hospitals in Saudi and the Gulf countries have a separate VIP section for these wealthy, pampered women. The obstetrics nursing staff dreaded the times when these women came in. They ordered the nursing staff about like servants, even though they brought along their own retinue of servants from the palace. On discharge they demanded members of the nursing staff accompany them to the palace to take care of the infant. The VIPs had British nannies and every other type of child-care service in their vast homes, but for the first few weeks of the infant's life they wanted a nurse twenty-four hours per day. Of course hospital administration was quick to satisfy their demands. Thus nurses were rotated to the palace leaving the hospital short of nursing staff. Royal family demands were never refused, no matter what the cost to the general public.

Assignment to a VIP household was something almost every nurse dreaded. Some Western nurses resigned after maltreatment by a Sheikha. They were often ordered to perform other duties besides caring for the infant. A young Singaporean nurse named Fan was given a one-month assignment in the home of a Tabuk VIP. She was told her one and only duty would be caring for the newborn infant. Now occasionally a nurse would come away from an assignment with a huge bonus, sometimes thousands of riyals. Fan hoped this might happen for her. Instead she ended up sleep-deprived for days on end, not so much engaged in child care, but by the lady of the house whose constant demands had little to do with her newborn. One night Fan was ordered to clean up a mess made by other children in the household. When Fan refused on the basis of the fact she was not a servant, the VIP mother slapped her viciously.

Fan left the house immediately, walked until she found a taxi and returned to her quarters at the hospital. Early the next morning she submitted her resignation and left as soon as she was able.

Motley Crew

The hospital administration was populated by multitudes of military officers. Many seemed irrelevant with no particular function or purpose in the hierarchy. The hospital director, known as "Sasquatch" to all of us, held the hospital in an iron grip. He was a hulking brute of a man, extraordinarily tall, at least 6'5", with protruding eyes and a sloping Neanderthal brow. His resemblance to the legendary creature Bigfoot, who is said to roam wilderness regions of the world, was uncanny. Vicky happened to be with me the first time I saw the director. The hair on the back of my neck stood up as he passed us. His appearance alarmed me so, that I could not help but stare. Though he was wearing a military uniform I whispered to Vicky, "Who or what is THAT?" "You mean you haven't seen our beloved Sasquatch yet?" Vicky whispered back. "That is the hospital director, Lt. Colonel Ghasib. All I can tell you is, don't ever get on the wrong side of that guy."

The hospital staff knew Colonel Ghasib was unbalanced. In certain moods he would storm about the hospital like an enraged buffalo, his great head thrashing about looking for petty infractions by staff. During a hospital-wide outbreak of bacterial pneumonia, he grilled the employee health physician, nicknamed "Dr. Panadol" (for his propensity to prescribe Panadol, the Middle Eastern equivalent of Tylenol) about the huge amount of antibiotics he was prescribing. Dr. Panadol was terrified of the Colonel and went so far as to ask the employees to fill their prescriptions downtown. (Hospital staff normally obtained prescription medications for free at the hospital pharmacy.)

Dr. Panadol's real name was Alastair Hughes, an elderly bewhiskered man rumored to be a retired British Army Colonel. I often saw the family at the swimming pool and felt sorry for his young wife and two small children. Dr. Hughes might have been frightened by Colonel Ghasib, but he was a bully with his family. He barked at them constantly. When Dr. Hughes decided it was time to leave the pool, the former British colonel organized his family in military formation and marched them out of the recreation center. I often wondered if he was abusive to them in the privacy of their home.

Dr. Hughes was not regarded as a competent physician. His peculiar diagnoses and questionable treatments were legend.

One outrageous diagnosis became famous in the hospital. People talked about it for months after. A young Lebanese man named Abdul worked as an interpreter on the surgical ward adjacent to my office. One day he presented himself to Dr. Hughes with concerns about chest pain and tightness, which he said started that morning. Apparently Dr. Hughes did little more than put a stethoscope to Abdul's chest. No tests. No medications. But he did send Abdul away with an outrageous diagnosis. The worried young man was told his chest pain was likely due to infected chest hair follicles! Dr. Hughes made no secret of the fact he hated Arabs and openly referred to them as "wogs." The unfortunate Abdul ended up in the emergency room two weeks later with a heart attack. After a lengthy hospitalization he was sent home to Lebanon.

Hughes was also a cruel bigot. Many young Arab female staff went to see him for severe menstrual bleeding and cramping. It was obvious to me that some of the girls suffered greatly every month. One day a young Egyptian woman Gabrielle and I were acquainted with told us about her humiliating experience at the hands of Dr. Hughes. "He is a cruel man," she said. "He gave me nothing for my pain, nothing to help the bleeding. He told me angrily to go downtown and buy tampons for extra protection." She continued tearfully, "We are young Muslim women and Dr. Hughes knows we cannot risk anything that might break our virginity. If we do not bleed on our wedding night it will be very bad for us and our family's reputations." Of course, whatever my or Gabrielle's personal opinion about this tradition was not at issue; we were angered by Dr. Hughes' lack of empathy and his open scorn for deeply-held traditions of another culture. After a few weeks the young women no longer went to see Dr. Hughes. They suffered silently.

Colonel Ghasib regularly patrolled the cafeteria to check on length of staff breaks. One evening he snatched security passes from several off-duty employees who were in the hospital after hours. He was trailed by a cringing assistant who gently reminded the Colonel that staff came to the hospital at all hours to use the long distance phone line or eat in the cafeteria.

In view of his erratic behavior, Christian staff was amazed when Colonel Ghasib arranged a "festive" dinner at Christmas. He authorized the hanging of banners in the cafeteria wishing us "Happy Festive Time." Christian hospital staff happily attended the dinner and even enjoyed the chewy, over-cooked turkey. But in the midst of our festive dinner the Colonel stormed into the cafeteria and ripped the banners from the walls. His face was twisted with rage. Apparently he'd changed his mind regarding anything festive. He roared at us, "All of you leave the cafeteria immediately!" The lot of us fled.

During a cold snap the Colonel went about the hospital snatching sweaters from employees, screaming about proper hospital uniforms. He seemed to miss the fact that staff was wearing cardigans over their uniforms because it was so cold.

On the lighter side, Colonel Ghasib had an obsession for what my female friends and I termed "lipstick and charming qualities" memos. Ghasib wrote the memos but the hospital's Director General signed and issued them. Female employees were frequently warned not to wear makeup to work nor display our "charming qualities." God forbid we should tempt any males. Most of us simply ignored the rules. I did not stop wearing my favorite red lipstick. We suspected Colonel Ghasib himself must occasionally have been tempted and hence the memo. The style of the English translation of the memos was written in the flowery beauty of the Arabic language, and distributed throughout the hospital at least once every couple of months. Below is an actual memo (verbatim):

"In the Name of Allah Most Gracious Most Merciful"

Subject: CIRCULAR

His Excellency, the Director of NWAFH and the
Rehabilitation Center

May Allah peace, mercy and blessings be upon you.

We have been informed that some female employees in the
hospital still ignoring the previous instructions issued by
this department, comprise, that they should not show their
charming qualities and not to wear any kind of cosmetics
such as dyes, make up powders, perfumes, jewelry, tight
clothes or alike.

Therefore, we would like to confirm that all female
employees should avoid wearing above-mentioned
cosmetics, and to inform all female employees that work is
not a place for beauty competitions or fashion shows, any
violation to the above-mentioned instruction will be
subject to disciplinary action.

All female employees should be informed of the subject
matter and to act accordingly.

Best regards.

Major General Dr. Abdul Hamid bin Mohammed Al-
Faraidi
MSH Director General

One week the Prince of Tabuk (His Royal Highness, Governor of
Tabuk Region) announced a visit to the hospital. Colonel Ghasib took his
duties seriously in any matter involving the royal family. Dozens of
massive flower bouquets were ordered and displayed in every available
space, giving the hospital the look of a greenhouse rather than a house of

medicine. An army of Bangladeshi laborers was deployed to help clean the entire hospital, polish floors, shine doorknobs, and wash walls.

Outside the hospital more extensive preparations were being made. The prince lived only five miles from the military base, but traveled with a huge entourage of lackeys and hangers-on. The prince and his cronies were transported in a clutch of limousines that snaked through the streets for miles, leaving substantial traffic snarls in its wake. The Prince of Tabuk was not to be inconvenienced or made uncomfortable on his short journey. Every speed bump on his expected route had to be removed. They were so numerous on the base that another army of Bangladeshi laborers was pressed into service. The poor fellows worked day and night to scrape off every noxious bump on the route. We expats watched all the ridiculous activity with great amusement. I personally looked forward to seeing a real prince. But in a startling change of mind, the prince decided not to visit the hospital after all.

Colonel Ghasib was furious. He stomped about the hospital throwing the bouquets of flowers into great piles to be removed by yet more laborers. The speed bumps were re-built within a week and all returned to normal. Such are the whimsies of life in the Kingdom.

The Colonel often sponsored what expatriates termed a "goat grab," like the one I'd attended at the wedding. With no advance warning all the department heads were informed their presence would be required that same evening. Dr. Hoey described a goat grab to Gabrielle and me in his uniquely humorous manner, "The lot of us, on the ground on carpets, enormous trays of oily rice with an entire cooked lamb or goat balanced on top. We eat with our right hand. (Eating with the left hand is forbidden in Islam.) The men all fall on the food at once, a lively event with chunks of meat and rice flying about. I've not ever heard such grunting and burping. And an infection control nightmare!" Western female staff were sometimes invited to the Colonel's goat grabs, but it was rumored they got the leftovers. Since I'd experienced such a meal at the wedding, I thought the elderly women I sat with on that occasion showed better manners than the men that Dr. Hoey described.

Colonel Ghasib had a talent for turning good work into catastrophes. One day he went on another rampage and fired all the Irish doctors.

Most large Saudi hospitals are governed by a recognized Western medical institution; Northwest Armed Forces Hospital was under the auspices of the Royal College of Surgeons in Ireland (RCSI). We heard the Colonel had some sort of argument with the Director of the Royal College, and on that note Colonel Ghasib fired all the Irish physicians. On his orders all the Irish doctors vacated the hospital and left the country within two weeks. Some of the physicians had been in the Kingdom for years and barely had time to pack their belongings.

The Colonel was also obsessed with a notion that the Mayo Clinic might become the governing medical body for NWAFH. Of course, the famous clinic, as far as anyone knew, had absolutely no interest in such a plan.

The action of firing so many physicians at once is representative of the way many matters are dealt with in Saudi Arabia. Neither Colonel Ghasib nor his underlings considered the future consequences of current actions, of what might happen when twenty-five doctors are suddenly let go. To no one's surprise the loss of staff created havoc in almost every hospital department.

Dr. Hoey was hired as director of OB/GYN about one year before Colonel Ghasib's purge of Irish physicians. Under Dr. Hoey's direction the department took on an air of professionalism. We took pride in the fact our unit was the most efficient in the hospital. Hoey made our department successful because he was outspoken and a strong decision-maker. It soon became obvious the Colonel did not like department heads who thought independently. Nor those who were outspoken. He preferred obsequious types who said "yes" no matter how it might compromise patient care. Colonel Ghasib blocked Dr. Hoey at every turn, meddling with important decisions and any attempts at further improvements in our department. The Colonel's ongoing harassment and interference eventually defeated our beloved department head. After almost a year of fighting the Colonel, Dr. Hoey resigned in disgust and returned to London. A few days later the Colonel began the purge of Irish physicians.

The Saudi government itself occasionally purged certain nationalities. This was the case after Operation Desert Storm. Countries sympathetic to Saddam Hussein, including Jordan, Egypt and the Palestinian Authority, saw thousands of their citizens booted out of the Kingdom. These nationalities often worked as translators in many different capacities. The loss of so many workers at once created a vast shortage all over Saudi Arabia. Most important, the precious source of income so many families depended on was abruptly cut off. Their sudden departure created more than just an inconvenience.

During Ramadan the Colonel often left Saudi on "recruitment" trips. He usually went to London, the center of it all for recruiting medical personnel. Many wealthy Saudis own properties in London where they can spend time outside of their country. There the men can openly drink alcohol, chase women, gamble and partake of various other vices. The stories of Saudi excesses outside of their country are infamous. They seem to feel that the laws of their host nation do not apply to them. It is common to see Saudi men and women shopping on the famous Oxford Street in London, some in traditional garb and others dressed in expensive Western apparel. Colonel Ghasib usually returned from his recruitment trips resembling a scruffy old tomcat after a particularly active spring. "I hope I never run into that wanker on a London street," Jane joked. "He gives me the bloody creeps." I wondered how much recruiting actually went on during the Colonel's trips to London.

For us expats getting in and out of Saudi was a job in itself, made all the worse by Saudi staff in the passport office. When my friend Donna organized a group to travel to Jordan, I had to find out if we required a travel letter from the hospital administration. Members of our group started weeks in advance to be sure our paperwork was organized.

Terrifying though it is, expatriates are not allowed to hold their own passports while working in Saudi Arabia. My passport, along with hundreds of others, was kept in the hospital passport office. In lieu of the passport, every expatriate is issued a residence permit (in Arabic an "Iqama") to be carried at all times.

As the director, Colonel Ghasib should have spent some time checking into the goings-on in the passport office. This department was entirely staffed by young Saudi males dressed in traditional thobes and gutras. They spent a large part of their workday relaxing on their department couches, drinking cup after cup of sweet mint tea. Some even dozed off from time to time. The first time I had to deal with staff in the passport office I realized they'd refined incompetence into a work of art. When I entered the department I saw several sullen young Saudi men lounging on couches drinking tea. There was no rush to serve me, nor anyone else for that matter. They stared at me, slurped their tea, and continued to sit immobile. I discovered I could get them off the couches by opening the little swinging door leading into their territory. This action usually summoned one to the counter, sighing and shuffling. I was often tempted to charge into their office and shout, "Get off your lazy arses!" After repeated dealings with this lot, I termed them sloths for their slow motion.

To see how the passports were kept in that office was a bad dream. The lack of respect for them was distressing. At every visit I saw great stacks of passports shoved here and there, in drawers, on shelves, their colored bindings forming a virtual United Nations of nationalities. Gabrielle once burst back into our office after a visit to the passport boys. Face flushed, she grabbed my arm and pulled me out of our office, "You've got to see this!" As we stepped into the passport office she pointed to a pile of navy blue British passports shimming up the collapsing leg of a desk! On the occasions I was able to see and hold my own passport, its appearance alarmed me. It was stapled, bent and mutilated by unknown hands. Not surprisingly, passports were often lost by the sloths, a nightmare I hoped would never happen to me. For Canadians, obtaining a new passport meant a trip to Riyadh. In fact it might take several trips to complete the process.

Travel letters are usually required from the Saudi employer for domestic travel. I asked one of the youths whether I needed one to go to Jordan. With a lazy yawn he said, "I don't know; go ask another Canadian." His gutra sat crookedly on his head and tea stains decorated the front of his thobe. I replied, "Do you really work here or are you just visiting?" The young man looked exasperated and said he would check for me later. I told him I'd wait and he could check now. With a long-suffering sigh he mumbled something to a comatose colleague and then disappeared through a doorway. I never saw him again.

Frustrated and losing my patience, I barked at another couch dweller. He mumbled "Canadian...no travel letter for Jordan." By then I'd spent almost thirty minutes in the passport department for the answer to one question. After expending such enormous energy, the sleepy youths poured another cup of tea and sank deeper into their couches. I found this kind of service in Saudi the rule rather than the exception. Sometime later, to their delight, the sloths were issued shiny new office chairs with wheels. After that they could be found having chair races in their department or rolling up and down the long hallway outside their department, clutching the ever-present tea glasses in their hands. The chairs were especially useful in that they no longer had to stand up at all. When we came to their counter they could simply roll over to us.

No matter our nationality, the boys in the passport office made us wait until the last possible moment for our passport. Every excursion outside of Saudi required an exit and a re-entry visa. The few days prior to leaving on a trip were filled with anxiety. No expat could be sure if the visas would get stamped into the passport in time. I haunted the passport office, harassing the sloths, "Is my passport ready yet?" Just hours before departure the usual answer was, "No madam, not yet." I was always lucky to obtain my passport in time, but some staff did actually miss their flights.

I still relate stories of the passport office to family and friends because the tales always garner looks of disbelief and then laughter. As frustrated as I was at the time, I can now giggle about the hilarious antics of those passport sloths!

Even with passport and papers in order, and a boarding pass in your hand, an expatriate could never be certain of getting on the plane. Consider my friends Jane and Patrick: midway through their contract they were excited about flying to London for a family wedding. They were at Tabuk airport, sitting in the lounge an hour or so before their scheduled flight. Jane told Gabrielle and me what happened next. "Some git of an airport official got on the PA system and announced in both Arabic and English our flight to London was cancelled."

At that time Tabuk had a small airport and the Saudia 747 aircraft bound for London was sitting on the tarmac right outside the terminal.

The reason for the cancellation soon became clear. Some Al Saud family member, probably the Prince of Tabuk, decided he needed the plane. This was typical of wealthy, powerful Saudis whose demands took precedence over everyone else. Jane and Patrick watched aghast as a long line of limousines pulled up to the aircraft and disgorged masses of Saudi men and women in traditional dress. Dozens of children milled amongst the adults. "There must have been a couple hundred of them," exclaimed Jane. "Had to be a royal entourage." Behind the limousines came multiple vans. "The doors of the vans rolled open and streams of Indian servants spilled out," she said. "Right away they started loading hundreds of suitcases and boxes into the cargo hold."

When wealthy Saudi or Arabian Gulf families decide to spend a few months out of their country, they take literally everything with them: servants, chefs, chauffeurs, specific kinds of kitchen equipment, blankets, bedding, even foods such as spices, cooking oil and different types of rice. As if none of these items were available at their luxurious destinations. When supplies ran low, a call would be placed to their homeland and a plane would be commandeered take them more of everything.

Jane told us the airport lounge was filled with other disbelieving passengers waiting to take the same flight to London. "I was so angry," sputtered Jane. "There we were with no flight. We had to organize another flight and Saudia staff was not at all helpful under the circumstances. Instead of getting to London a day before the wedding we ended up arriving in time to get off the plane and rush straight to the wedding." I think that experience finished Jane and Patrick. Jane said it was the last straw and they didn't sign another contract.

One day I had to deliver medical reports to the Translation Department, to be translated into Arabic. Finding the department the first time was a challenge for me. I found myself lost in a maze of corridors in a remote annex of the hospital. I thought perhaps I should have left a trail of breadcrumbs to find my way back. I finally stumbled into a hallway hazy with blue cigarette smoke, the floor a minefield of spent cigarette butts, the carpeting agape with holes. I felt as if I'd entered some parallel universe; surely such an important department could not look so seedy.

I peered around a corner into a dim, smoky room where I saw various figures in repose. The room was stiflingly hot, the blue wall-to-wall carpet beneath my feet crushed into oblivion. I looked about and every flat surface was littered with glasses containing dry dregs of tea and coffee. Teetering atop them were plates, crusty with dried-on food remnants. The foul air was permeated with the odor of idleness, cigarettes, stale food smells and perfume. Horrified by my first taste of the place, I thought it was probably a good thing it stay hidden.

A squat young Saudi man sat tipped back in a torn-up office chair, feet propped on his desk, a cigarette in one hand and a glass of tea in the other. He beckoned me with a wave of his hand. This was my first encounter with Bish-Bish Zahrani, the Translation Department director. I cautiously approached Bish-Bish and was at once struck by his astonishing green eyes and comical smile. Here was a man who was clearly pleased with his lot in life. He was surrounded by a hodge-podge of cronies who likely gravitated here for its relative safety from the demands of real work. None seem bothered by their noxious environment. One of his cronies deposited a glass of hot mint tea in my hand. I tried to dispel the thought of when the tea glass might have been washed last. But refusing the tea would have been discourteous. So I sat cautiously on the edge of an ancient arm chair, grimy with years of ground-in dirt, and Bish-Bish proceeded to tell me his story about being internationally famous. The room remained respectfully quiet during the story; I think everyone present had heard it all before. Bish-Bish didn't say what he was famous for, and I decided it was probably best not to ask.

Sitting atop a stool nearby, sniffing tiny sample flasks of perfume, was another young Saudi male with a crooked nose that took up most of his face. One hand held a perfume sample and the other a cigarette. I wondered why this guy had all these perfume samples at work. Not that any genuine work was being done in this room. I hoped the cigarette would not ignite the perfume. "Hello, I am Farhan." he said with a flirtatious smirk. I shot back, "So what's your job here?" Farhan pointed proudly to his chest, "I am number one assistant to Bish-Bish."

Farhan pushed one of the perfume flasks under my nose, forcing me to sniff the skunky stuff. I felt lightheaded in the miasma of Marlboro cigarette smoke and the stink of cheap perfume in the overheated room. Did they not have any air conditioning here? Bish-Bish pointed to another young man meekly seated on the floor in a gloomy corner. "This Ali, he is Egyptian," said Bish-Bish without any explanation of Ali's purpose in the room. In the eyes of his Saudi colleagues Ali clearly did not rate the use of a chair. I'd finished my tea and social obligations, and stood to leave. Bish-Bish and Farhan both shouted, "But you cannot go yet, we are enjoying your company." Nevertheless I pleaded a hectic schedule and handed the medical report I had come with to Bish-Bish. "No problem," he said, and I watched the report disappear into a chaotic heap of papers on his desk, the documents crinkled and ringed with coffee stains. I doubted the report would ever be seen again.

As I left the office I noticed against the back wall a white-robed figure stretched out on a worn, sagging leather couch. A curious thing. All my subsequent visits found the same white-robed figure, a male I assumed from his dress, on the same couch. I never saw him talk or move. But I knew the figure was alive because a cigarette was always clutched in one hand. Who he was, or what his function, I never found out.

I thought as I left the room, "God-awful."

I was not surprised that payday was also a chaotic affair. Hospital employees were paid once per month in cash. Unfortunately the hospital had no such thing as direct deposit or even a pay envelope handed to individual employees. Every payday a gigantic queue snaked from the door of the Finance Department all the way down the hall past other departments. Several employees from the National Commercial Bank arrived in the hospital dragging immense suitcases stuffed with cash. The Finance Department people began doling out the cash at 9:00 a.m., but most of us started lining up by 8:00 a.m. We made the best of the wait by gossiping and complaining about the mode of payment. There was one door into Finance, barely enough room for two people to be in the office at one time.

Most of the Westerners knew how to queue and, for the most part, were patient. But four Saudi women could always be depended upon to make trouble. I never did find out what jobs these women performed in the hospital. But when the four showed up the general mood became hostile. Every month it was always the same. I knew it was only a matter of time until I would have my own encounter with these vicious females. One payday I was just in the doorway to Finance when the largest of the Saudi females, an imposing woman, rudely pushed me out of her way and sailed to the counter for her pay. I pushed in front of her just as rudely and said she could wait her turn like everybody else. The huge woman sneered at me, "We are Saudis; we never wait."

I stood my ground until Farid, the Finance manager, came to clear up the altercation. He told me the hospital's Religious Officer had made it clear Saudis were never made to wait. (I don't know what the Religious Officer had to do with it). But nonetheless the four women had made so many prior scenes that Farid immediately conferred with the Religious Officer who finally changed the rules. Farid then informed the women they had to wait in line just like everybody else. Expats were slapping me on the back and cheering as I left with my money. The Saudi men behind the finance counter thought it was hilarious. All I'd wanted to do was make a point. I wasn't the only one who'd tired of these rude women. Later I would see them in the hallways, and if looks could kill I'd have died on the spot. I guess the women didn't know anybody important because I kept my job. People had been terminated for far less.

The same Saudi women not only disrupted payday. In the cafeteria line they argued with the servers over the choicest bits of food, holding up the line and intimidating all in their path. They reached the cash register, manned by a meek young Indian fellow who conscientiously calculated the cost of food heaped on their trays. When he quoted each the price of their lunch, they would laugh and throw a few riyals at him, always far less than the true cost of their food. They knew this meek little man would never argue with them. Once settled at a dining table, they ate little off their trays. I watched daily, dismayed, as they threw huge quantities of food into the garbage bins.

Later I learned the large woman who'd pushed me out of the doorway in the finance department had a breast reduction, apparently in a desperate bid to lose weight. From all accounts the surgery was botched. From then on I would often see her face creased with pain. She was obviously suffering, and I felt sorry for her, but her rude antics never changed.

As days flew by, I would meet a cavalcade of dubious characters, some eccentric and harmless, others who made my skin crawl. I love to people-watch so I was never without rich entertainment. Living and working in Saudi offered a never-ending variety of interesting people.

A World Apart - East Vs West

Bigotry, and a sort of caste system, exists amongst expatriates in Saudi. There is a definitive hierarchy based on nationality and religion.

First, salary in Saudi Arabia is determined by an employee's country of origin. At the top of the pay scale are those from first world Western countries such as Canada, United States, Britain, Australia, Western Europe and Scandinavia. (The term "Westerner" is applied to anyone who is not from Africa, the Near, Middle or Far East.) Next on the scale are educated East Indians/Pakistanis, Indonesians, Eastern Europeans, Central and South Americans, educated Filipinos/Asians and non-Saudi Arabs. The bottom of the hierarchy is made up of hundreds of thousands of unskilled Asian laborers from India, Bangladesh, Sri Lanka and some Far East nations. They fill the jobs no other nationality will consider: cleaners, servants and construction workers.

As a Western medical transcriptionist I was paid six thousand riyals (about $1700 US) per month. At the end of each one-year contract I received a bonus of one month's salary. I considered my wage fairly generous since I paid no taxes nor did I have any expenses in Saudi other than groceries and personal purchases. Many Filipinas are employed as medical transcriptionists, but at the time they were paid not six thousand, but only two thousand riyals per month.

The Asian labor class is the most visible minority in Saudi Arabia and the Gulf region. These poor souls are habitually subjugated and frequently mistreated. This holds with the Saudi and Gulf people's notion that Asians are somehow less than human. After all, Saudi Arabia did not officially abolish slavery until 1962. The Saudis talk about their Muslim "brothers and sisters", and yet a great many of these exploited workers are Muslims.

Asian laborers often live in appalling conditions. They are frequently housed in rundown old accommodations considered unsuitable for Western staff. Rooms meant for one or two individuals are fitted with rows of bunk beds to fit two or three times that number. Usually one bathroom and one kitchen are shared by many. Privacy is only a dream for most. And in a country where temperature can soar over 120 degrees Fahrenheit, air conditioning is sometimes non-existent.

A dreadful example of the less-than-human thought process has always stood out in my mind. I sometimes chatted with a Swedish physician who worked in the Family Practice clinic. As a woman Dr. Lindberg was often summoned to the local palace to minister personally to the Sheikha, chief wife of the Prince of Tabuk. Dr. Lindberg told me the Sheikha had once met her by chance and taken a liking to her. She demanded that Dr. Lindberg become her personal physician. Dr. Lindberg was not fond of attending to the Sheikha because she was a haughty, demanding woman, but the doctor had little choice and did not dare refuse her. The Sheikha employed a small army of East Indian men as her chauffeurs and servants. After several visits to the palace Dr. Lindberg shared some of her palace experiences with me. "The Sheikha's male servants are so beneath her notice she does not cover her face in their presence. A Saudi woman, especially a royal, would never reveal her face to a strange male," she said in a troubled voice. "It finally dawned on me that the Sheikha literally does not consider her Indian male servants as human!" Dr. Lindberg went on to tell me that many of the servants hadn't been paid in months. Verbal and physical abuse by the Sheikha and her retinue was a normal part of their day. Her army of servants was kept on duty 24/7, subject to the Sheikha's whims at any hour of the day or night.

There are labor laws in place in Saudi, but they are rarely enforced. Saudi and Gulf employers seem to have the attitude that Asian laborers are expendable; an endless supply can be recruited from poverty-stricken countries. I often saw laborers on construction sites wearing rubber flip flops. Even the bare basics of a hard hat and decent footwear are not provided by all employers. Accidents are common. While living in United Arab Emirates I saw laborers transported to and from the work site in long trailers almost identical to cattle haulers. Tourists who witnessed this appalling sight made such an uproar the UAE government felt pressured to make changes. The mode of transport was eventually switched to school buses. In 2006 the UAE government banned construction companies from expecting their laborers to work during the high heat of summer days. There is a law in place in Saudi Arabia and the United Arab Emirates whereby outdoor laborers are brought inside when the temperature reaches approximately 112 degrees Fahrenheit. In UAE the workers are to be given rest in a shaded place from noon until 3:00 p.m. from June to September. Nonetheless, UAE is still occasionally in the news regarding violation of this law.

Saudi Arabia is supposed to have followed suit, but only for the months of June and July. In the summer it is common to see construction laborers working long into the night. Few positive changes have been made for laborers in the Kingdom. There is little or no protection for the labor class and the Saudi authorities often turn a blind eye to reports of abuse. For a poor overworked laborer to complain would very likely mean the end of his job, and deportation.

Tragic stories about Asian maids are all too common. Thousands of women come from India, Sri Lanka and Far East Asia to work as maids and nannies in Saudi households. Because some of these women are literally prisoners in Saudi homes, they have few options when an employer turns abusive. Maids who become pregnant after rape by an employer are often arrested and charged with "illegal pregnancy." An incident in Tabuk involved a young Filipina woman I will call Maria. She was employed as a maid in a Saudi home. The woman claimed she was repeatedly raped by her male employer. One day Maria could bear it no longer and stabbed him to death with a kitchen knife. The unfortunate young woman was sent to a women's jail. Though she did not receive the death penalty Maria might suffer in that jail for the remainder of her life unless the Philippine government can negotiate a ransom at some point for her release. The problem is that Maria is just one of many Asian expats stuck in Saudi and other Gulf States jails. Pardons are often handed out during the holy month of Ramadan; maybe she'll get lucky. As might be expected prisons in Saudi Arabia and the Gulf States provide little in the way of services to those incarcerated. In some the food is so inadequate a prisoner must depend on family and friends for extra provisions, even for basic necessities such as soap and personal care items. I admired the Filipino community when they stepped up to take care of Maria. Every week a group of Filipina women visited her and others of Philippine nationality in prison, bringing food and comfort items.

In addition, the suicide rate is high among Asian maids in the Gulf region. The usual choice is by hanging or jumping from a high balcony. Some unfortunates survive their suicide attempt, but are permanently paralyzed or disabled. After an extended hospital stay, the Saudi authorities ship these women home to a family who likely depended on her wage for survival in the first place. Embassies often step in to assist in repatriation of the gravely injured, but usually the only financial support they can provide is airfare.

An Indonesian maid was executed in Saudi in June 2011 for allegedly killing her employer after years of physical abuse. The Saudis did not inform the Indonesian government of their decision to execute the woman. There was a huge uproar by both the Indonesian and Philippine governments whose countries supply a lot of the domestic help in Saudi. Both countries have long fought for better protection of their nationals in Saudi. After this incident the Indonesian government announced they would stop sending their citizens until the Saudis promised better regulations. The Saudi government made a promise to institute new rules, but at the same time, coincidentally, announced they would stop issuing work permits to Indonesian and Filipino domestic workers, and begin recruiting from other countries. Namely Ethiopia and Morocco. The announcement seemed a deliberate reprimand to the two Asian nations. How dare they make bold demands that their citizens should have better working conditions in the Kingdom.

The Saudis apparently do not feel duty-bound to improve the working conditions of Asians, nor even obliged to notify their foreign consulates or embassies regarding execution of their nationals. They are only Asians after all, an expendable commodity.

Filipinos, who make up the largest percentage of Asian expatriates in Saudi Arabia, are a cohesive community who are admirably supportive of each other. But there is another side to the Filipino community. Jane, Patrick and I often had lunch together at the cafeteria in the hospital recreation center. One day a middle-aged Filipino man loitered near our table. He looked like a shady character with a round, oily face and narrowed eyes that darted around like tiny nervous finches. He was obviously a man who felt it necessary to watch his back at all times. He sidled up next to Patrick and quietly said, "You need anything? I get you what you want." We knew then he was a member of the "Filipino Mafia," a procurer of all things illegal, for a price. Patrick politely refused the offer and we watched him scuttle over to a table of Irish girls to make his offer.

Although the Saudis thought they were in charge, in reality the Filipino Mafia ruled the hospital and its grounds. A large percentage of the hospital staff were Filipinos, most of whom had worked in the Kingdom for years. The Mafia controlled the "sid" trade (illegal home brew), drugs, loan-sharking, and even prostitution.

One evening Vicky and I wandered through the recreation center thinking we might get a movie from the library and watch it at my place. I pointed out a Filipino man whom I saw often. I asked Vicky, "Who the heck is that guy? I see him almost everywhere I go." Vicky whispered, "Y'all need to know about that guy. His name is Romy, and he's the big boss over all the Filipino Mafia in Tabuk. There's nothin' he don't know and nothin' he can't arrange. I've heard he'll even kill someone for yah if the price is right." I found out that Romy's real job was activities director at the recreation center, but the BMW he drove sure wasn't purchased on his salary alone. His appearance was not particularly memorable, a short, chunky man with greasy unkempt hair. He was always friendly and laughed often. But the first time I was close enough to meet his eyes a chill trickled down my spine. His eyes were cold, flat and ruthless, like a shark's eyes.

Their Mafia's so-called "captains" also exploited their own people. A lot of Filipina women supplemented their meager hospital salary doing anything from house-cleaning to hair-dressing and sewing. These women were in turn controlled by under-captains who collected a percentage of their extra earnings. I hired a young woman named Celeste to give me a pedicure and haircut every month. She charged fifty riyals to do both, a bargain for me. When I asked her if she sent most of her earned money home, she said, "I try, ma'am, but first I must pay my supervisor her share." The "supervisors" took at least fifty percent. I was appalled and asked Celeste, "Could I give you extra as a sort of tip that you can keep for yourself?" Celeste's eyes widened in fear, "Oh, no Ma'am, if my supervisor finds out I kept money from her I will have big trouble." If anybody, Westerner or otherwise, wanted a special favor, legal or illegal, we all knew which Filipinos to ask. I never asked for anything, for I did not want to put myself in a position where I was beholden to such villains.

When Westerners go to work in the Middle East it seems like a holiday, a good time where the job is simply a sideline. The money is tax-free, vacation time is generous, and travel to exotic locations is an inexpensive option. But for many Asians, life in the Middle East is not much above slavery. There is little joy in their lives. They work longer hours for far less pay. Area attractions are nothing more than a fantasy for want of cash to enjoy them. Western staff enjoys four to six weeks of vacation every year in addition to a free yearly air ticket to point of hire. And the ticket can always be bartered and used for a different destination. Asian labor receives a free air ticket once every two to three years. A long time to be separated from family.

As a Western employee I enjoyed decent housing, sometimes shared with another Western female, but usually a single accommodation. At NWAFH all single females of all nationalities lived on the same compound. But Asian women were placed two or three in an apartment meant for a single person. Western employees are recruited by head-hunting firms to whom the employer pays an exorbitant fee. But Asians and their families pay huge fees to recruiters who then find employment for them in the Middle East. A family might save for years to send even one family member abroad. That person often becomes the sole monetary support for their family. If a family cannot pay the fee up front, the worker is hired into what amounts to indentured servitude. The recruitment fee is deducted from the salary they receive at their new job. Thus many start new jobs already deeply in debt; it might take years to pay off the fee.

I thought it strange that Saudi Arabia is the only Gulf country that collects and retains the passports of all nationalities including Westerners. But almost all employers throughout the Gulf region hold the passports of Asians. Asian laborers and maids often abscond from their employers, usually because of horrific work conditions. Many haven't been paid in months. But without passports or identification, they cannot leave the country. Thus they drift around the country picking up illegal work where they can. Every couple of years some governments in the Gulf region announce a general amnesty for these essentially stateless people. Thousands gather at a central point where the authorities pack them on airplanes and deport them to their home countries.

Lists of absconders are featured every day in the newspaper classified section. Since the employers still hold their passports the photos and identification numbers can be published. The hope is that someone will recognize them and alert the authorities. The published information also prevents absconders from formally applying for other jobs.

These stateless workers are sometimes found dead with no form of identification on them. A particularly grisly custom in the Gulf is the means of identifying them. The government authorities photograph the deceased and post it in the newspaper, hoping someone will be able to identify him. The dead are photographed as they are found, some with bloody, injured faces and others in early stages of decomposition. On any given day I could see the face of a dead man in the newspaper.

Sometimes Asians arrive only to find the job they were hired for is not the job they end up in. Even educated Asians hired for healthcare or technical jobs might find themselves working as a maid or laborer. The wage they'd been promised might be arbitrarily cut or not paid at all.

Many Western expats hire cooks, gardeners, drivers and housekeepers from the local population of expatriate Asians. These poorly-paid men and women are eager to find a second or even third job to bolster their income.

I hired a young Sri Lankan woman to clean my apartment every two weeks. Ranjani was a petite forty-something woman with curly black hair and a gracious manner. She worked in the hospital laundry for one thousand Saudi riyals (about $260 US) per month. While that same amount of money may have gone far in Sri Lanka, she was impoverished in Saudi. The hospital provided one free meal per day to Ranjani's class of employee. For many this was the only meal of their day. The poorly-paid women went shopping in groups, buying up bulk lots of vegetables, fruits and fish and dividing the cost amongst them. Most, if not all, also sent money to families in their home countries so they had little to live on in Saudi. I overpaid Ranjani because I could afford to and she and her family needed the extra money. Sometimes we would go together to the grocery store where I would ask her to buy everything she needed so I could pay for it.

Physicians are recruited from many countries. To work as a consultant in Northwest Armed Forces Hospital a physician had to hold a degree from a recognized Western medical school. Most consultants at NWAFH were Irish, British, European and Canadian. Few were from the United States. There was also a large number of East Indians and Pakistanis educated in Britain. All consultant-level physicians were paid the same wage, no matter their nationality. Clinical department directors usually received a little extra each month. House officers and registrars were mostly expat Arabs, Pakistanis and East Indians. They could work as a resident without a Western education, but could not advance beyond residency status without the Western degree.

Of course, the Saudis sit at the top of the Muslim heap in their position as host to foreign workers. I personally met Saudis who were humble, kind and interested in me as an individual. But many Saudis feel culturally and even religiously superior to all other nationalities. You'll find that Saudis are especially proud in the Nejd (eastern) region where the tribes pride themselves on their pure blood lines. And yet because of their country's enormous wealth, many Saudi Arabians see themselves as different, better, with a sense of prerogative.

"Saudization" (referring to jobs filled by Westerners being turned over to Saudis) is increasingly widespread in the Kingdom. A Saudi will agree to a desk job or administrative and professional employment, but they will never take a job that involves physical labor. I recall a young Saudi man hired as a file clerk in Medical Records. One of his duties was to roll a cart through wards and departments to collect patient charts for re-filing. But he refused to push the cart, feeling such a duty far beneath him. The young man was not fired or punished, simply re-assigned to another department where cart-pushing was not required. Gabrielle and I often laughed about what we considered every young Saudi man's dream job. "Give the lot of them a desk, a rubber stamp, a phone, and a tea boy. It's all they want or need." That was Gabrielle's philosophy.

Few Saudis have a work ethic as a Western individual understands it. The Saudi people are not entirely at fault; their own government has made them what they are. Because of their country's oil wealth, they have been given everything they need. Few Saudis have ever had to work hard to realize a desired achievement. "The Boys", the three would-be doctors in our department, illustrated a good example. The Saudi government has looked after them all their lives, and so they lack any concept of responsibility. Another major problem is that all too often jobs are handed to Saudis based on "wasta" (personal connections). The better the connection, the better the job. Education or experience to perform the actual job is not a consideration. Thus many Saudized business concerns become mismanaged disasters in short order.

A prime example of this is an ophthalmology hospital in Riyadh, a facility heralded as the world's best when it opened in 1982. A friend worked there for many years. She watched as the hospital was gradually Saudized. Certainly there are well-educated and motivated Saudis on staff (a good number of Saudi physicians receive their education in Britain, Canada or the United States), but they are hugely outnumbered by those holding jobs by benefit of wasta alone. Over the years the hospital has slowly deteriorated to a level where it now barely functions. Of course the Saudis would never admit this for fear of losing face.

Recently the famous Johns Hopkins University became affiliated with the ophthalmology hospital. Their apparent goal was to provide better patient care and develop new treatments and procedures. The Western staff in the hospital hoped for positive changes, but unfortunately the plan has failed miserably. The individual sent from Johns Hopkins is little more than a figurehead occupying an office. The Saudi administrators can point to him and gain face from his auspicious Johns Hopkins presence, but neither he nor the famous university behind him has the power to make any significant changes.

As long as Saudis refuse to perform jobs they feel are beneath them the Saudi Arabian government will be forced to continue importing Asian labor to fill those jobs.

All That Is Forbidden

I knew before I went to Saudi that any relationship between a single man and woman, platonic or otherwise, was strictly forbidden outside of the hospital work environment. Western expats found ways around the rules, but we all knew we'd be punished if caught. In most cases a Westerner would be deported for drinking alcohol, having a relationship with the opposite sex, taking photos of women or public buildings, and myriad other infractions as decided by Saudi authorities. Those deported were expelled from the country within hours minus wage or bonus. However, for Asian expats the consequences of illegal activities could be much worse. Asian males and females caught in association without a marriage license could be flogged or even imprisoned. They would eventually be deported, but not before the authorities made an example of them. It is not just Saudi Arabia where Asians must be wary. The same applies in other Gulf countries.

In Saudi Arabia Western expats learn quickly how to circumvent the rules regarding unrelated men and women mixing outside of the hospital or recreation center.

Single male staff of NWAFH, aside from Asians, lived on another compound named Briga, some five miles from the military compound and hospital. Briga was also home to non-physician married couples. The accommodations consisted of crumbling old prefab houses with one family or else two to three single men sharing one house. Since single women were forbidden to visit single males in their home, a lengthy process was involved to visit a single male in Briga. Or just to get into Briga at all. A single woman required a letter of sponsorship from a married couple living on the compound. The couple provided a written invitation to their own home, but of course many single women were actually visiting their boyfriends living on Briga.

The single woman was required to present the written invitation to the hospital security department. The head of security, Captain Ali Al-Suaida, was another administrator with a frightening countenance and fearsome reputation. Like Colonel Ghasib the hospital director, he was tall with cold reptilian eyes that seemed to look right through a person. It was common knowledge that the captain and his minions were ruthless when they mounted surprise raids on Briga searching for illegal alcohol stills. Those caught red-handed were of course deported, but not before they were savagely beaten by the captain and his thugs. The arrestees were often roughed up again after the security department turned them over to the police at Tabuk jail. On the occasions I was invited to Briga for a genuine visit with married friends, I presented myself and my invitation to the hospital security office. Those seeking a security pass were never asked to take a seat in the presence of the captain. I was made to stand in front of his desk while his cold eyes looked me up and down as if to discern my true intentions on Briga. Under his ice-cold gaze I felt the hair stand up on the back of my neck. I shivered and thought of how awful it would be to get caught in a compromising situation by this brute. The captain never refused to sign my requests to visit Briga, but others told me a signature, or not, depended on his mood that day. Once his signature was obtained he issued a security pass to present to the security personnel at Briga.

I am sure the security people knew exactly what was going on. Certain married couples on Briga were known to sponsor just about any single woman who asked. But there was great risk to both the sponsoring couple and invited female. I, like any single woman, had to ride the small transport bus to Briga. On my arrival the security personnel would demand the security pass the second I stepped off the bus. All single women were herded into the tiny security hut and grilled about their visit. Even after they examined my security pass, whoever was on duty would bark, "Whom are you planning to visit, what will you be doing, will you stay overnight?"

Some of the guards, always young Saudi men, were flirtatious. But most were rude and made it into a game of harassment. Everyone knew the danger of being caught with a single man; usually deportation for the single woman, the sponsoring couple, and the boyfriend. I never met any male who I felt was worth the risk. But, no matter the intention, everybody was treated to the same grilling.

There was another way that single men and women could actually live together. "Tabuki marriage," possessing a fake marriage license, was big business. Those with their own computers who could turn out a realistic-looking license charged whatever the market would bear. Five hundred riyals (about US $135) was the norm. A friend of mine did such a brisk business she put a down payment on a house in Canada. She inherited the "business" from a departing expatriate. But this was another risky activity; getting caught meant immediate deportation at the very least. The authorities could legally request proof of marriage from any couple riding in a car together or just talking on the street.

Genuine or bogus, marriage certificates had to have an Arabic translation attached. There were always Arab expats who wanted to make a bit of extra money to perform this service. Some Western expats, and rarely Asians, sought a Tabuki marriage so that they could live together as man and wife while in the Kingdom. Many men who arranged such marriages for themselves, often a British or American man and a Filipina woman, already had wives in their home country. In most cases the legal wife did not want to live in Saudi. Some visited their husbands only once and decided they could not possibly live in Saudi long term. I was always curious how these men managed their double life. Surely some legal wives knew about the other "wife" in Saudi, but tolerated the arrangement as long as their husband sent home his paycheck. Tabuki marriages rarely ever led to legal marriage outside of the Kingdom.

I remember an acquaintance named Grace, a statuesque redhead from Australia, met a British man, Tony, in Tabuk. They appeared to genuinely fall in love. Tony had a wife and four children in London, but he was a Catholic so divorce was not an option. So Tony and Grace arranged a

Tabuki marriage. They spent a lot of time figuring out how they could ever be together in the real world, but there seemed no solution. By all reports Tony refused to divorce his legal wife. The entire expat community knew of their situation and sympathized because Grace and Tony were very likeable people. When I left they were still living together in Tabuk, but knew some day they would have to part. Grace accepted the arrangement because she obviously adored Tony.

For others I think they simply could not bear to be alone. Filipina women who agreed to a Tabuki marriage hoped their Western "husband" might divorce his legal wife and take her back to his country. I felt sorry for the Filipinas because many came from poverty-stricken backgrounds. How could I judge their hope to meet a man who would marry them and take them to a better standard of living? But the Tabuki husband would eventually go home to his legal wife and leave the Tabuki wife behind. Some of these abandoned Filipinas went on to arrange another Tabuki marriage. Each time they hoped to be taken to their husband's homeland. I found most Tabuki marriages rather tragic arrangements.

A middle-aged German doctor named Dr. Holst had an arrangement that astounded all. He maintained a Tabuki marriage with Lynn, a lively, attractive young midwife from the island of Grenada in the southeast Caribbean. Once a year Dr. Holst went home to Berlin to visit his legal wife and family. Later in the year the doctor would meet his family at an exotic holiday location with Lynn in tow. She almost always accompanied the doctor and his family on these vacations. One big happy family! Lynn had a husband in Grenada whom she visited once a year. I don't know if her husband was aware of the Tabuki marriage arrangement, but it was certain the German doctor's wife knew.

Then there was Sylvia, a pleasant, attractive redhead from Vancouver. A nurse, she was middle-aged and worked with a young and dazzlingly handsome Egyptian man named Abdu. Abdu, who worked as a nursing aide/translator, set out to woo Sylvia, and she fell madly in love with the young man. Abdu was almost half Sylvia's age. Within two months the couple went outside Saudi and married legally. Of course, I wondered how the marriage was going to work given the age difference. Soon after her marriage I ran into Sylvia on my way home from work. I was surprised to see her wearing a "hijab" (headscarf), which is worn by Muslim women. I genuinely liked Sylvia and we stopped to talk. I asked her about her whirlwind romance and marriage. She glowed as she told me, "Abdu is such a wonderful man, so kind." She fussed with her headscarf and seemed a bit flustered about wearing it. Her eyes teared up as she told me, "I love Abdu and made a decision to convert to Islam. Some of my co-workers have been pretty cruel, even having the nerve to tell me I'm stupid to marry Abdu."

"You don't have to justify your decisions to me, Sylvia. You love Abdu, and you're obviously very happy. That's all that matters." I gave her a hug and smiled, "Congratulations on your marriage, Sylvia. I wish you and Abdu all the happiness."

I truly hoped their marriage would work.

A few months later Sylvia and Abdu resigned, and he returned with her to Canada. Apparently Abdu was anxious to get started on his 3-year residency requirement to obtain his Canadian citizenship. A couple of years after I left Saudi I ran into a Canadian I'd known in Tabuk. She told me that Sylvia's young husband had literally disappeared in the middle of the night. Sylvia was heartbroken after she realized Abdu had married her to obtain a Canadian passport. The marriage she took so seriously had been a sham. I felt angry and sad for Sylvia. But here again was a case of an individual, a young man, coming from a poverty-stricken family in Cairo. Abdu likely felt this was his one and only chance at a better life.

A mysterious young woman worked as a nurse in the hospital. Margrete was Dutch, strikingly beautiful with waist-length blonde hair, blue-green eyes and a tall willowy figure. She kept herself aloof and did not socialize with anyone in the hospital. When I saw her downtown she was always alone. Margrete traveled to Jeddah every weekend without fail. One particular hotel in Jeddah had a remarkably liberal attitude in allowing single women to stay, probably the only hotel in Saudi that did so at the time. Staff from the hospital often traveled to Jeddah for weekends. Many saw Margrete going in and out of the hotel with wealthy-looking Saudi men in luxury cars. I saw her twice at the hotel myself. Others glimpsed her at elegant private parties in Jeddah, always escorted by one or more affluent Saudi men. The rumor was that

Margrete was quietly engaged in high-end prostitution. Every Thursday afternoon I saw her at our compound gate waiting for airport transport for her weekend flight to Jeddah. Margrete always looked breathtaking in sleek designer clothing and spectacular jewelry. I never saw her wear an abaya except when she went downtown.

Trish and I once saw Margrete in Jeddah climbing into a long black limousine with a stunningly handsome, middle-aged Saudi man. "She's just a common hooker," Trish said in a disgusted tone. I preferred to think of Margrete as a courtesan if indeed that was why she traveled to Jeddah every weekend. It was certainly a dangerous sideline she engaged in, but after seeing the sort of Saudi men who accompanied her, men of great power and influence, I'm sure she was well-protected. Margrete likely returned to her homeland a very wealthy woman. It is fairly common to hear about beautiful young women traveling to the Gulf to make their fortune as the mistress of a wealthy man.

One day an American Muslim woman named Sandra arrived to work as a secretary in the hospital. Fawzia met Sandra shortly after she arrived in Tabuk. She told Fawzia she'd converted to Islam shortly before coming to Saudi. Sandra was probably about fifty, but looked much older in an unkempt way. She was a large angular woman who favored outsized long skirts and long-sleeved sweatshirts no matter the weather. She wore a variety of headscarves in the same dull colors as her clothing. As the months passed Sandra began to cover up more and more. She began wearing her abaya to work and leaving it on all. day over her uniform. Then one evening she climbed on the souq bus completed blacked-out: a voluminous abaya, black gloves and a huge black headscarf that covered her head and shoulders. But what shocked me was the square of thick, black, gauzy material which covered her entire face. Fawzia was with me that evening. I looked over at her, "Is that Sandra?" I whispered. "Yes, I think so," Fawzia whispered back "I recognize her glasses." Indeed Sandra had placed her clunky old-fashioned glasses on top of the veil covering her face and eyes. Most Saudi women looked glamorous and exotic in the same outfit, but poor Sandra looked ridiculous, especially with the addition of her eyeglasses. I felt a stab of pity for her, and even more so later.

Fawzia and I often utilized the services of Selim, a Turkish tailor downtown. Almost all tailors working in the Middle East are Turkish or East Asian males, many of whom are exceptionally talented. Most have a working knowledge of written and spoken Arabic.

Selim was a kindly, older man who'd lived in Tabuk for many years. As a tailor his Saudi work visa did not permit his wife and family to accompany him. Suddenly we began to see Sandra more often at the tailoring shop, but we assumed she was having clothing made. A few weeks later Sandra simply disappeared. The story eventually surfaced that she and the Turkish tailor had formed a romance, or as much of a romance as could be carried on when all they could do was talk through his store window. In Tabuk women were not allowed to enter tailor shops because, of course, measuring meant males touching females.

Apparently the Turkish tailor asked Sandra to marry him. They were an unlikely couple and could not have known much about each other. They didn't even have a language in common. She accepted. Apparently the hospital administrators caught wind of the impending marriage and put a stop to it immediately. Sandra was deported for "lascivious behavior." The Turkish tailor was punished by having his bi-annual leave cancelled. He would not be able to leave the Kingdom for four years. The expat community, in their cruel way, thought the entire situation was hilarious. But I found it very sad, two lonely people in want of companionship.

Though I had the attention of several men, I was not interested in pursuing a relationship in Saudi. But the man who put in the greatest effort to woo me was a Saudi, Captain Farid. He was an acquaintance of Fawzia and she had known his wife and family for many years. The captain told Fawzia he was contemplating immigration to Canada. She thought it might be beneficial for him to speak with me, as a Canadian. Perhaps I could provide him with some useful information. Fawzia called me beforehand and alerted me to the possibility of the captain dropping by our office.

As it happened, I was alone in the office when he dropped by. I looked up from my keyboard to see a man in his forties standing quietly in the doorway. I guessed this was Captain Farid. I would not have called him handsome, but his angular, even features, crisp black hair and proud military bearing leant him a courtly presence. He smiled at me with brilliant white teeth, "Are you Chilly?" His English was heavily accented, but precise and formal. "Yes I'm Shelly. And you are Captain Farid?" He stood straighter and stepped forward to offer his hand. "I am Captain Farid and I am happy to meet you. But please to call me Mohammed." I was momentarily surprised at a Saudi man offering to shake hands with a woman, but I grasped his strong brown hand in greeting. After he introduced himself I invited him to sit down. As is traditional in the Arab world, the captain and I first engaged in the customary flowery greetings and common polite questions on both sides, like "How is your family's health?" Though an Arab may be a complete stranger to you, part of his or her formal greeting will always include a polite inquiry about the health of your family. Had I been male I could have asked after Captain Farid's children's health, but to ask about his wife's health would be considered very rude.

Then we talked about what Canada had to offer a prospective immigrant. But it soon became apparent to me that Captain Farid had forgotten all about Canada. He was interested in me. Many Saudi men do not consider their wives an impediment to affairs with other women. The captain was obviously seeking a bit of fun. I felt uncomfortable, but treated him politely.

Fawzia told me he had powerful connections within the military and perhaps even with some members of the royal family, so I knew I had to tread carefully. Soon Captain Farid made his proposal, "I have a small farm near Tabuk. I would have honor if you would visit my farm. It is beautiful with many trees. All my friends come there to enjoy." I'd heard a lot about these farms and that they had little to do with actual farming. Other female friends and acquaintances told me about similar invitations from Saudi men. Their main purpose was a place for Saudi men to bring their lady friends and partake of alcohol and drugs. Numerous Saudi men attended these parties and some of the things I'd heard were disturbing and frightening.

A free-spirited British girl we all called "the little hippy"—her name was Angie—had attended many of the farm parties. Jane knew Angie well and sometimes she sat with us at our lunch table. She explained the circumstances in her comical British vernacular, "There's plenty of hooch and drugs at the farms so you got to be careful. These Saudi blokes are so repressed. When they get hold of alcohol and drugs they go bloody starkers. Lose their inhibitions like." Angie's voice dropped to a whisper, "Went to my fella's farm last week to smoke some kif. Lots of expat women about. Next day I hear things got out of hand after we left. Couple of Aussie girls got passed 'round by some crazy drunk Saudi boys."

I had no idea if the Captain had such atrocities in mind. He came across as an educated and intelligent man. My natural instinct was to avoid any close relationship with a Saudi man, no matter what he seemed. To allow myself to be taken to the desert by a strange Saudi man, to a place where many unknowns, and perhaps dangers existed, was something I would never do. If the worst happened, a woman had no recourse. She could not go to the police or even to her consulate. By engaging in precarious behavior, she brought trouble upon herself.

Mindful of the Arab male ego and his possible high connections, I told Captain Farid diplomatically that he seemed a nice man, but I was not interested. I told him I did not wish to create problems for myself in Saudi Arabia. His ego was unable to accept my decision and so the wooing began. For the next two weeks gigantic, ostentatious flower arrangements arrived daily at our office. I felt I would die of embarrassment because I couldn't tell anyone but Gabrielle and Fawzia where the flowers were coming from. "The Boys" surmised the situation immediately. They thought it hilarious and spent much of their time trying to find out who my admirer was. I had Fawzia speak privately with the captain in order to make the point that I was not interested. Fawzia felt bad, conceding, "I did not know this would happen."

I didn't want to make her feel worse, but privately I thought she should have suspected this from a Saudi male, especially one with some power.

But the Captain continued his pursuit. He saw his flower arrangements were not winning my heart so he changed tactics. Jewelry began to arrive in abundance. Dazzling sets in plush velvet boxes of necklaces, earrings, rings—and bracelets to match—in heavy 22-kt gold. Oh how I wanted to keep that gold jewelry for its sheer beauty, but I knew I could not. Gabrielle was impressed, "Bloody hell, take the lot of it and do a runner!" Fawzia patiently had every item of flower and jewelry returned to the Captain by means unknown to me.

In the back of my mind was the fear of further problems such as deportation or worse. It is not unknown for Saudi men rejected by Western women to exact revenge. This was easily done by fabricating a situation; one word in the right ear and you could find yourself on a plane the next day, or even in jail. After all, who would the authorities choose to believe, a Saudi man or Western woman? I was nervous and stressed during that time. After about a month Captain Farid finally gave up his pursuit. Fawzia had finally convinced him I was not going to change my mind. He left me alone, probably because of our mutual friendship with Fawzia. After that I had to watch for the captain in the hospital because a chance meeting might reignite his rejected ego.

Many women engaged in affairs with Saudi men and accepted the gifts they gave, especially the gold jewelry. I thought the high risk of things going wrong was not worth any amount of gold jewelry.

Constraints of the Ancient Past

For all its glossy veneer of modernity Saudi Arabia is still a tribal-based society. Traditional nomadic Bedouin are less common now, though some still live an ascetic and difficult existence in the desert, abiding by their ancient code. Others have settled in towns and live in the desert for only part of the year. In the summer months it is common to see beautiful, spacious villas with traditional Bedouin tents set up in the courtyard where the men gather in the evening for coffee, conversation, and smoking hubbly-bubbly. The Saudis came from the desert; it is in their blood and genetic makeup. They are never far from their roots.

Fortification of family and tribal connections remains the strongest reason for arranged marriages among many Saudis. Girls from traditional families have little choice in the matter of their future husband. As is common in Saudi in general, marriage between first cousins is highly valued and encouraged. Sadly, these closely related marriages often result in babies born with multiple anomalies and rare syndromes. Many young women know from an early age which first cousin they will marry. But even engaged, they may meet only once or twice under close supervision. Some brides and grooms may not see each other until the actual marriage ceremony. Sometimes the girl's father arranges a marriage with a considerably older man. This may be the fate of a girl considered troublesome by her family. Perhaps she talks back. Or perhaps an elderly man with two or three wives might wish to marry a young girl to give him more children in his old age. Saudi Arabia has no law regarding minimum age for marriage for women. Just recently a seventy year old Saudi man allegedly paid a $20,000 dowry to the parents of a fifteen year old girl he wished to marry. Apparently the girl ran away soon after the marriage. I've often thought that brides must sometimes get a shock to find out what sort of man her father has chosen for her.

In Saudi Arabia and much of the Middle East a young bride must absolutely be a virgin, not so much for the moral symbolism as for the actual intact hymen. Of course there can be a variety of physical reasons why a virgin may not bleed during her first sexual experience. Some women are not even born with a hymen. But for many families, if a bride does not bleed during the wedding night's consummation she is not "pure." Her groom will divorce her immediately. Her family may even kill her over the shame they feel.

In the last few decades traditional Bedouins have come to a cautious acceptance of modern medicine. But a combination of tribal customs, ancient Islamic practices and pre-Islamic spirit beliefs makes them a challenge to treat with modern medicine. Like many aboriginal peoples in the world, the Bedouin have a long tradition of healing with plants and herbs; severe mental conditions are often treated with readings from the Quran. Modern medical care in Saudi Arabia became a reality only after discovery of oil. Before then the Bedouin people relied on traditional healers for all manner of treatments. Many still do. Even today many traditional Saudis remain dedicated to the old-style healers. Some illnesses are treated with methods such as hot irons applied to different parts of the body, often causing severe nerve damage. Individuals are immersed in the sea to the point of near-drowning. Sometimes electrical charges are applied to the part of the body believed to be causing the illness.

The practice of FGM (female genital mutilation/female circumcision) has been banned by the World Health Organization. It is a practice believed to prevent women from feeling sexual desire, thus making them faithful wives. It is especially prevalent in regions of Africa among both Muslim and non-Muslim populations. Though FGM is practiced in parts of the Arabian Peninsula and other Gulf countries, the current actual numbers are unclear. The physicians Gabrielle and I worked with in Tabuk sometimes shared stories with us. The gynecologists and pediatricians were occasionally approached by ultra-conservative parents who wished to have their young daughters circumcised. Such a procedure would not be permitted in a Saudi hospital. Unfortunately, the family would then to go to someone outside the medical community, usually an elderly woman with a razor blade and no concept of hygiene.

A fairly common occurrence in Saudi is that of women breastfeeding children not their own, a wet nurse. Saudi cultural tradition says that a man cannot marry his wet nurse, and neither a man nor a woman can marry his or her wet nurse's biological children or any other children she has nursed. Anyone who has shared a breast is seen as family. Marriage between a man and woman who shared breast milk is considered incest. Breast-milk kinship is considered as good as a blood relationship.

But who your wet nurse was in infancy can reap great benefits in adulthood. Dr. Nabila and her husband arrived in our department shortly before I left Tabuk for good. Both were young Saudi medical students from Jeddah who'd been assigned a two-month rotation at Northwest Armed Forces Hospital. She was a happy-go-lucky and liberal young woman whose concession to modesty involved only a long skirt and loosely wrapped headscarf. Her husband, Mohammed, was modern and relaxed with Western staff. He was one of the few Saudi males I ever met who had a sense of how to dress in Western fashions.

Nabila was happy to share details of how her lot in life was dramatically changed by one small event. She'd been born to a low-ranking family, but by chance she was breastfed by a woman who also nursed a prominent member of the Saudi royal family. As a result of her royal connections she enjoyed lavish privileges. Dr. Nabila and I took a liking to each other and struck up a friendship. One day she came to the office, her cheeks flushed and a big smile on her face, "I am going to Jeddah next weekend for a wedding," she began. "The sister of my friend Princess Badriyah is getting married, and I would be honored if you would attend the wedding with me. Of course, your airfare and expenses would be paid for."

"Oh no!" I was shattered. "I would love to come with you Nabila, but unfortunately I'm leaving Saudi Arabia that same weekend!"

When an expatriate leaves Saudi Arabia for good, the flights and exit visa are already in place and cannot be changed. No doubt Dr. Nabila's connections could have fixed this with a flick of a royal wrist, but I also had firm plans on return to Canada. I have often imagined what the weekend might have been like, the guest of a young woman with high royal connections. A royal wedding celebration must be quite amazing. The fact that I could not attend the wedding was a great disappointment.

A rather bizarre aside about breast milk and kinship involves a *fatwa* (a legal pronouncement in Islam) issued by a Saudi Islamic scholar in 2010. In a country where everything is sexually segregated, the scholar came up with what he considered a practical solution. An unrelated man might be permitted to drink a woman's breast milk (though not from her breast) and thereby become related to her. Thus he becomes a relative of the family without breaking any segregation rules. Saudi women were apparently not consulted regarding this idea.

It made little sense to me that Saudis consider it incestuous to marry someone who was breastfed by the same woman, and yet despite the high rate of serious birth defects, it is traditional to marry first cousins. In some regions of the Kingdom more than half of marriages are between first cousins. The Saudi government now has a program where closely-related couples are counseled about the risks of genetic defects, and blood tests are mandatory. Nowadays more educated Saudi families are aware of the risks, and are pulling away from the tradition. But marriage between first cousins is still prevalent. The only disabled children I ever saw in public were those with Down syndrome. Saudi families with severely disabled offspring are often deeply ashamed and quietly care for these children in the home. Since Saudis have large families, when a genetic defect turns up in more than one child, many parents see it as God's will.

A strong belief in magic is still a part of everyday Saudi life. Superstitions, spells, curses, love potions, charms, and "evil eyes" are all very real to even the most modern Saudis. Last year the Saudi government announced they would start recruiting Moroccan women as domestic help in the Kingdom. But there was a swift outcry from Saudi women who are fearful about bringing these women into their home. They believe Moroccan women practice black magic and might place spells on their children. They also say that Moroccan women are too beautiful to have around their husbands. At last report Saudi labor officials backed down, at least temporarily, on recruiting Moroccan housemaids.

Black magic was likely practiced amongst ancient Arabian peoples, yet it is still prevalent today long after the arrival of Islam. When people fall ill or experience terrible events in their lives, it is almost always blamed on the "evil eye". It is surely the fault of someone who cast a black magic spell on you. While in Saudi Arabia, and amongst Middle Eastern peoples in general, I had to learn not to praise anyone on their beauty or good luck. To compliment a parent on the beauty of their child is an especially bad idea. Even the most modern individual will avoid inviting the jealous eye to destroy something precious.

Witchcraft is taken very seriously by the Saudi religious establishment. The religious police, Mutawa, have an actual anti-witchcraft unit and a sorcery hotline. Those afflicted by a spell or curse are rescued by the religious police who will reverse any detrimental effects by treatment with Quranic incantations. Those accused of witchcraft or sorcery can expect to be executed by beheading.

Fortune-telling and dream interpretation are "haram" (forbidden) in Saudi society.

Unfortunately, the Saudis' (and other Gulf residents) belief in magic makes them easy targets for swindlers. Certain types of scams are popular in UAE and other wealthy Persian Gulf countries, especially what is called "the money-doubling scheme." These rackets are usually run by West Africans who come into the Persian Gulf countries on visit visas. The crooks will temporarily rent a small apartment or set up a room in a cheap hotel. A tout will be placed on the street to put the word out. The hotel front desk staff is paid to look the other way. The crooks promise huge returns for a relatively modest investment. The "mark", or victim, will be told that powerful magic will double or even triple their money. Or the crooks tell them they have a magic liquid that can turn paper currency into double its value.

The mark is asked to return the following day to pick up his profits. Often the hotel room or apartment is by then deserted. But some cons take the scam further. The victims return the following day and are shown their original investment with a nice addition of money produced by the so-called magic. Of course, the marks are convinced the magic really works and become excited about a bigger profit. The crooks promise to perform even stronger magic and triple the investment. So the victims hand over more money and that's when the cons disappear. No matter how often these scams are reported in the newspapers, many still fall prey to the crooks.

In 2009, a hoax swept across Saudi Arabia like a desert sandstorm. A rumor spread about old Singer sewing machines containing a substance called "red mercury" which has never been proven to exist. Those owning the old machines were convinced the mythical substance was worth a fortune. It was said red mercury could cure chronic diseases, uncover hidden treasures of gold and ward off evil spirits. Some believed it could be used to make nuclear bombs. Wealthier people paid up to $50,000 to acquire one of the battered old sewing machines. Tailor shops were broken into and the machines stolen. There were reports of people fighting over the machines in the street.

Then there are the "jinni" (plural of jinn), known as genies in the West, Walt Disney-like beings likely to spring from an old lamp or bottle to grant the lucky person three wishes. Arab and North African legends consider jinni to be supernatural creatures that can do evil or good. Jinni are mentioned often in the Quran. Saudis in particular have a strong belief in them. Some claim to have had personal experiences with jinni and believe their lives have been forever changed: the blind regain sight, the sick are miraculously healed, and the crippled walk again.

On the other side are the jinni that curse the unfortunate. Some believe a jinn can take possession of a human body in much the same way some Christians believe a human can be possessed by a demon.

Honor killings, a horrific custom tantamount to murder, are still common and widespread in today's world.

In parts of the Middle East and Asia, women are seen as property with no rights of their own. They also carry the family's honor. Their chastity, or suspected lack thereof, can mean life or death for a woman. Just a suspicion of inappropriate behavior might be enough to doom her.

There is nothing in the Quran that permits or endorses honor killings. It is a cultural phenomenon that can be traced to pre-Islamic traditions. In this case I speak of Saudi Arabia specifically, where the law prohibits the sexes from mingling. A Saudi woman might be killed by a brother, father or husband in an attempt to "restore the family honor." A woman perhaps observed speaking to a male stranger in public, dressing in what the family considers a provocative manner, or even refusing an arranged marriage can be regarded as disgracing the family honor. Gay women and men are also at risk for honor killings by their families.

In most instances women are not given a chance to defend themselves. Few cases ever make it into the press, especially in the insular world of Saudi Arabia. Some women simply disappear; they "drown" in the family swimming pool or tragically "electrocute" themselves. The few Saudi women's rights groups that exist have made little progress in changing the cultural mindset. Honor killings are regarded as acceptable and even necessary to keep society balanced. In the male Saudi mind all women are adulteresses who cannot be trusted. Thus all Saudi women are required by the government to have a male guardian who watches her behavior and makes important decisions for her.

Honor killings do not occur just among Muslims. The custom can be found in Hindu, Sikh, Jewish and Christian societies. It has been outlawed in conservative but progressive countries such as Jordan, but the practice continues even in Jordan. Unfortunately the grisly custom has also made its way to the West with certain immigrant groups attempting to maintain their traditions. Today Turkey and Pakistan have the highest number of honor killings in the world. In Pakistan female victims of sexual assault are often jailed because rape is seen as adultery on the woman's part. These women are often killed by male relatives, or even forced to marry their attacker to restore the family honor.

The ancient beliefs and practices cannot simply be erased. But along with these deeply held beliefs is the rigid control of the government and the religious establishment. The Saudi people, especially women, are so constrained by all these factors it is no wonder their society is inert. It is true that nowadays more Saudi women are going to school and holding jobs. But until they can gain some independence from male guardians, drive their own vehicles, and have some control over their own lives, Saudi society will not progress beyond what it is now.

Saudi Arabia is the only country in the world which prohibits women from driving. Again, the law has no basis in the Quran. It is simply a cultural tradition unique to Saudi Arabia. A few years ago a group of Saudi women in Riyadh dismissed their chauffeurs and drove in a convoy through central Riyadh. Many of the women were academics from a local university. All were arrested by the religious police, some of whom actually demanded the women be beheaded. The women and their male relatives were accused of renouncing Islam, a crime carrying the death sentence. A commission was assembled to investigate, but no scholar could come up with a religious law that banned women from driving. A religious sheikh proclaimed the women drivers as evil. He issued a *fatwa* declaring that women would not be allowed to drive because it might degrade their dignity. The religious establishment in general seems to believe that allowing women to drive is immoral. Many of the women lost their jobs. No doubt some honor killings resulted from this incident, but no stories were publicized.

Saudi women continue to demand their right to drive. A few brave souls have got into the family car and again driven openly on the streets of Riyadh. Some are even accompanied by their husbands. Sometimes their actions are tolerated by the government, but there have been isolated cases of arrests.

I do not anticipate that Saudi women will be allowed to drive any time soon. If the government were to allow it, a precedent would be set and other doors of independence might open for women.

A Different Kind of Wedding

I came to work one Monday morning to find Gabrielle in a state of excitement. "We're invited to a Saudi wedding on Thursday night!" She told me that our mutual friend Nadia had been issued an invitation by a Saudi friend. The bride's mother told Nadia to bring along her friends if she wished. Nadia was a pleasant middle-aged Egyptian woman who worked as a translator and nursing aide on the female surgical ward in the hospital. She was a thoroughly modern Muslim woman who wore her dark brown hair in a short bouffant. She favored casual trousers and colorful blouses off-duty. She never wore a scarf.

I was delighted and felt fortunate to be able to attend another Saudi wedding. But this one would turn out to be far different from the wedding I'd attended shortly after arriving in Saudi Arabia.

In recent years in Saudi (and other Gulf countries), the price of a bride has become so prohibitive that many grooms cannot afford to marry a Saudi girl. The families of brides are demanding increasingly extravagant dowries for their daughters. Some men go into deep debt in order to arrange a marriage with a Saudi girl. The families and the girls themselves often demand a lavish, expensive wedding on top of the dowry. Saudi men who cannot afford this must go outside the country to find a bride, but only after the Saudi government has approved the marriage. In order that poorer couples, and even handicapped couples, can marry, the government is now sponsoring and paying for mass weddings.

Nadia, Gabrielle, and I booked a little van through our recreation center in order to get to the wedding which would be held at the Sahara Hotel. The Sahara was the only four-star hotel in Tabuk and located at the edge of the city. Vicky, my Alabama friend, kindly loaned me the same black dress I'd worn to the first wedding. Gabrielle and Nadia agreed to come to my flat and then we'd go down and wait for the van together.

On Thursday evening I was still getting myself together when I heard a knock on my door. It was Gabrielle and Nadia all dressed up for the occasion. Gabrielle wore a deep royal blue velvet skirt with a pearl-grey long-sleeved sweater. Her face literally glowed with excitement. "I can hardly wait to see what a Saudi wedding is all about. Do you think my outfit is suitable for the occasion?"

"Your clothing is perfect," said Nadia, looking beautiful in a long Arabic-style embroidered dress in brilliant turquoise. "You will fit in well."

The three of us donned our abayas and found the van waiting for us at the gate to our compound. As we climbed out of the van at the Sahara Hotel we were quickly engulfed and swept along into the banquet room by a river of Saudi women cloaked in black. The room was not unlike an aircraft hangar, a massive space designed with Saudi large-scale gatherings in mind. The floor was finished in intricate parquet wood which stretched at least one hundred feet to the distant walls. The voices of hundreds of women echoed back and forth across the space.

A large stage was situated at the far end of the room. Off to its right was a small door. Aside from the big double doors entering the banquet room, it was the only other door in the enormous room. I never dreamed that later in the evening the hundreds of guests would have to struggle through that tiny door to get to the food. I suspect the reason for the separate room was so male kitchen staff could circulate freely out of sight of the Saudi women.

The big double doors slammed shut behind us and the Saudi women proceeded to throw off their abayas and transform into the exotic birds of paradise I beheld at the first wedding. But Gabrielle had never witnessed this remarkable metamorphosis. She gazed around in awe at the beautifully clothed women. Her mouth gaped open with surprise. "Who would have thought that Saudi women looked like *this* under their abayas? I can't believe these are the same blacked-out figures we see every day in public." I smiled at Gabrielle, "Quite a surprise, isn't it."

The bride's mother appeared and welcomed us warmly. She seated Gabrielle, Nadia, and me together at a vast round table right next to the stage we'd noticed earlier.

Nadia proceeded to give us a bit of history of the bride and groom. "The bride," she explained, "is a Bukhari which means she is descended from central Asian people. Even before the Saudis discovered oil, Muslims from central Asia came to Saudi Arabia for the annual pilgrimage to Mecca. Many of them stayed on in the country. Even though Bukhari families are second or third generation Saudi citizens the Saudi government implements strict rules regarding marriage. Bukhari families are considered inferior in the Saudi hierarchy. The government does not consider them "pure" Saudis. The family of a Bukhari woman may only arrange a marriage for her with a Saudi of similar low rank, perhaps a man from the Balawi or Rashidi tribe."

I later did some research on the Al Rashidi tribe. They remain a formidable enemy of the Al Saud family because they sided with the Ottoman Empire when their leader, Ibn Saud, was trying to unite Arabia under one rule in the early 1900s. The betrayal has never been forgotten. The Balawi tribe hails from Tabuk, but I never found out why they are disfavored by the Al Saud family. Tribal memories are long. Ancient disputes and loyalties are still alive and well in Saudi Arabia.

Nadia went on with her story, "On the other hand, a Bukhari man, a Saudi citizen in every other way, is not permitted to marry a Saudi woman under any circumstance. If he wishes to marry he must go outside of Saudi to find perhaps an Egyptian or Iraqi bride."

I surreptitiously studied the bride's side of the family. Their features were distinctively Asiatic; round faces, and eyes with epicanthic folds, not unlike the Mongols. This seemed likely since the Mongols overran central Asia in the thirteenth century. But though their features were Asian, most of the bride's relatives were fair with hazel eyes and light brown hair. I noticed several of these women had striking green eyes. Most of the ladies were dressed stylishly and appeared to have a modern, urban demeanor about them.

The women of the groom's family were a far different story. They looked as if they had just stepped out of the desert for the evening. Apparently they did not favor tables and chairs for they had spread a few bright blankets and all sat on the floor. To me they looked like what I always thought true Bedouin women might look like. Fierce-looking women who appeared somewhat uncomfortable in the surroundings of a modern four-star hotel. They stood out in their uniqueness and I found them fascinating. All the women were dressed alike in brilliantly-colored satin dresses that hung straight from shoulders to feet. As they arrived in the banquet room I saw that none wore face veils, only a gauzy black scarf over their hair and a black cloak of similar light fabric, through which peeked their bright dresses. Their skin was dark with high cheekbones and proud hawkish noses. The younger women were handsome with luxurious raven hair; two or three had hair reaching the backs of their knees. The older ladies amongst the group were tough-looking, their leathery, heat-and-wind-ravaged faces tattooed with faded blue designs. Their calloused and work-roughened hands were covered with distinctive red henna designs. I did not see any of them mingle with the bride's family. When it was time to eat I saw that the groom's relatives had a large tray they took to the buffet tables and loaded up with rice, lamb, and vegetables. While other guests in the room ate at the big round tables, using forks and knives, the groom's relatives, sitting again on the floor, proceeded to eat with their hands. These Bedouin ladies made a stark contrast to all those sitting at the tables, but only the Western guests took notice.

The music was provided by the usual female Yemeni band, ever present at female gatherings. The bride's mother, a gracious lady resplendent in a long emerald silk gown, approached and encouraged us to get up and dance. I'd been invited to dance at the first wedding I attended, but had passed up the chance. This time I was determined to try it. Nadia grabbed Gabrielle and me by our hands and pushed us toward the dance floor. "*Yalla* (move) let's dance!" she shouted happily. We each tied a scarf around our hips and tried some belly dance moves.

Like many Egyptian women, Nadia danced beautifully, but Gabrielle and I felt rather awkward.

Suddenly we saw the group of Bedouin ladies get up off the floor and move to the dance area. Immediately the Yemeni band changed the music to something sounding primeval and tribal. Their dancing was different. None of the ladies moved about much and they kept their arms straight at their sides. The young women with the knee-length hair swung their gorgeous tresses, entire body shaking and vibrating as they all ululated. I felt I was seeing a performance which may not have changed much for centuries. Something ancient, etched in tradition, and time.

Around 10:30 p.m. we suddenly heard a clamorous knocking on the banquet room doors. "The bride and groom have arrived," smiled Nadia excitedly. The wedding guests rushed to don their abayas and veils. The colorful women of moments ago became a sea of black once more. The banquet room doors flew open and the bride and groom entered the room preceded by little boys and girls scattering rose petals before them. Another small girl carried a white satin pillow on which sat a beautifully-bound copy of the Quran. Her little face was flushed and solemn with the responsibility. The couple appeared very young. The bride was dressed in a long white Western-style wedding dress heavily embroidered with crystals and tiny pearls. She wore a sheer white veil over her hair and face, kept in place by a glittering tiara. The groom wore traditional male Saudi dress, but with the addition of a rich brown robe highlighted with gold embroidery. His features were similar to that of his female relatives with dark skin and proud cheekbones. The couple was followed, according to Nadia, by a multitude of male relatives from both sides of the family. The procession moved forward accompanied by deafening music, both grand and tribal. The music sent chills up my spine. As the couple entered the room the wedding guests started trilling, and the great room vibrated and echoed with the sound.

The bride and groom stepped up on the stage and sat in matching chairs. The music changed again, and the males from both families danced shoulder to shoulder in two lines facing each other, perhaps symbolizing a bonding of the two families. The bride's mother ascended the stage to help with the dowry ceremony. The groom gently lifted his bride's veil and began attaching gold to her. She blushed and smiled shyly at her groom. Our table was close to the stage so I was able to study her face. The bride's heavy theatrical makeup could not hide her intriguing hazel eyes and creamy skin. Tenderly the groom put in her earrings, placed a ring on every finger, seven gold bangles on each arm and three heavy necklaces around her slim neck. The female members of both families then came to the stage and attached their own gifts of gold to the bride. She soon glittered with a wealth of gold, her dowry to keep always.

The wedding party descended from the stage and passed through the small door on the right side of the room. It was time for the bride and groom to cut the cake, a tradition borrowed from Western culture. As the door opened I caught a glimpse of the wedding cake, a many-tiered white confection slathered with brilliant blue icing and blue silk flowers. By the time the couple and members of the wedding party crowded into the room we were unable to see the actual cake-cutting.

The groom and men of both families then left the room to attend their own wedding party in another part of the hotel. The female guests removed their abayas and veils. The bride returned to her chair on the stage and sat looking very solemn.

The bride's mother climbed to the stage and announced that everyone was now welcome to eat. We'd expected a traditional "goat grab", but a buffet meal was on offer. There was a gigantic rush as hundreds of Saudi females made for the small door to the room containing the buffet tables. A log jam of hungry women struggled to squeeze through the single door. It reminded me again of the joke among expats that if the Saudi people ever learned to queue they'd be dangerous!

Nadia, Gabrielle and I hung back; we didn't want to be caught in the frenzy. We watched as little children darted in between the adults' legs to get at the food. Gabrielle commented dryly, "A bit like the running of the Pamplona bulls, isn't it?" We finally ventured into the fray and got tossed about like corks in a choppy sea. I managed to get some salad on my plate and fought my way in the direction of the tray holding roast goat and rice. As I leaned over several people to grab some rice and meat, I felt something cold and wet fall on my sandaled feet. I looked down to see the salad from my plate being raked off onto my sandals by a babe in arms. The beautiful infant gurgled and smiled when I looked over at him. Someone bumped into the wedding cake and it teetered precariously on its moorings. But no matter, for the crowd soon turned on the cake, hacking it into brick-like slabs and carting it off like prized trophies. With food in hand, like a salmon swimming upstream, I fought my way out of the packed room. Gabrielle struggled to escape from another guest's fork caught in her open-weave sweater. The fork was finally yanked out and left a gaping hole in the sweater. Somewhere along the way we lost Nadia. Finally we reached our table and sat down with relief. Gabrielle grumbled, "Why the bloody hell did I wear good clothing to this bear garden (British slang term for a chaotic event)? The wedding's been lovely," she said, "but I almost didn't survive the buffet."

Nadia eventually reappeared at our table, not looking this way or that, and mumbling in Arabic. Her beautifully coiffed hair was now in disarray and a splash of yogurt was smeared across her turquoise dress. But she smiled graciously, "It was a bit difficult to get our food wasn't it?" An understatement! Bruised and elbowed, we all felt like we'd fought a war to get our supper.

While Arab tradition stresses extravagant and extended greetings on arrival with cheek-kissing and polite formality, not so at the end of a function. The meal was apparently the culmination of the evening. The wedding guests ate quickly and then flocked to the exits again draped in black. Male family members waited outside in big Suburbans or a variety of other vehicles. They picked up their women and everybody headed home. The banquet room was deserted in a matter of minutes. The room looked like a cattle stampede had just passed through. I pitied the hotel staff members who had to clean up the mess. Nadia, Gabrielle, and I found the hospital van waiting outside and like Cinderella's we were home just before our midnight curfew.

Arranged marriages are still common in many other countries of the Middle East. All of our current Arab friends, mostly Syrians, are living in arranged marriages. When a man makes a decision to marry, he informs his mother. She will then call on friends and family seeking a suitable young woman. Men can meet prospective brides under close supervision and eventually a mutually agreeable match is made. Even after the couple is formally engaged, an older responsible chaperone supervises the couple as they meet and get to know each other. In modern Arab society, except for Saudi and other fundamentalist societies, marriage is not forced on a woman. She may or may not choose to marry the man who is proposing. Most of our friends are happy in their marriages, no more or less so than Western marriages. The arrangements seem to work out well for the most part.

In Jeddah, the most modern and progressive city in the Kingdom, social freedom between Saudi men and women is slowly developing. According to friends currently living in Jeddah, they sometimes see young unmarried Saudi men and women out together, albeit at private functions only. They are likely from wealthy, powerful families who find it easier to buck the system and get away with it. The old traditions and customs in most of the rest of Saudi Arabia will likely go on the same as they have for centuries.

Shelly with good friend Fawzia in Tabuk, Saudi Arabia

Co- Workers at Northwest Armed Forces Hospital Tabuk, Saudi Arabia

Dr. Chalasani, Shelly, & Dr. Usha

Dr. Mohammed & Dr. Faisal ("The Boys") with Gabrielle

Shelly with Patrick & Jane in Tabuk, Saudi Arabia

Anna & Rafik in Aqaba, Jordan
Rafik played a double for Omar Sharif in the movie _Lawrence of Arabia_

Rough camping at the Red Sea

Shelly at the camel market
Everybody wanted to be in the photo

Al Khazneh or The
Treasury in Petra,
Jordan

Archaeological
Sites

Tomb at Mada'in in Saleh,
Saudi Arabia

Gold and more gold

Bread Bakery

Aqaba, Jordan looking into Eilat, Israel

Hijaz railway station built by Ottoman Turks

Old district of Jeddah, Saudi Arabia

Shelly Anderson

Discovering the Red Sea

I could not live in Saudi Arabia and not see the Red Sea. Many Western staff in the hospital learned to dive and joined one of several expatriate diving clubs around Tabuk. Their stories of the beauties of the Red Sea astonished me. The more I heard the more I wished I could swim.

My first major trip outside of Tabuk was to Duba beach camp, a facility owned by the hospital. The camp was located near Duba, a small city on the northeastern coast of the Red Sea. The hospital recreation center organized a trip every weekend except during the summer. Let me define weekend in Saudi Arabia. Aside from nursing and technical staff who worked shifts, for most employees the work week was 8:00 a.m. to 5:00 p.m. Saturday through Wednesday and 8:00 a.m. to 12:00 noon on Thursdays. The beach bus left Tabuk around 1:00 p.m. on Thursday and returned to Tabuk about 1:00 p.m. on Friday. It seemed a long way to go for just one night.

It was Fawzia who encouraged me to go. "We must go to the Red Sea. We can put our names on the list for next weekend." Only non-Muslims were allowed on the beach trips, but Fawzia was a Muslim and frequently went to Duba. I don't know how she managed it, but she knew a lot of people who apparently eased restrictions for her. I was happy to have her come along, but other Westerners resented her presence. Some had the ridiculous notion she might be spying on them. I doubted it; Fawzia genuinely liked to be around Western people and wanted some fun and freedom just like the rest of us. She left off her head covering at the beach and relaxed. She even wore a traditional one-piece swimsuit albeit with black leggings beneath the suit. Still this was daring indeed even for a liberal Muslim woman.

Those of us taking the trip were expected to bring our own food, toiletries and "Duba mats," a moniker given to thin, colorfully-decorated mattresses used for beach camping. At some point I found out that one of the ancient, wheezing school buses that took us to downtown Tabuk was used as transport to the Red Sea. How on earth could this ancient vehicle transport us 120 miles over desert and mountain passes? "Are they kidding?" I said to Fawzia, "We'll never make it over the mountains in that." She smiled serenely "We have made it every other time. Enshallah (God willing), we will make it this time." A lucky few single women legally traveled to the camp with married couples in their private cars.

On Wednesday evening Fawzia and I went to the market and purchased supplies for our camp-out. Neither of us had a cooler so we chose items like bread, cheese, apples, and nuts. Fawzia assured me that there would be plenty of fresh fish shared by those who went snorkeling. The camp contained a large tank with drinking water, but we still needed several bottles to take with us on the bus. I would soon find out that staying hydrated in the heat and humidity of the coastal climate was difficult indeed.

We rushed home from work on Thursday, changed into cool clothing and lugged our food and belongings to the bus. I was dreading the crowded bus ride. When we climbed on the bus, the smaller Filipino women on the trip were packed three to four to a seat meant for two. Fawzia and I managed to wedge ourselves in the seat right behind the driver. Bags and baskets of food, clothing, snorkeling gear and assorted other sundry were stuffed under seats and in the aisle. As usual the air conditioner was not working. The passengers sweltered miserably waiting for the driver to finish his tea and get on the road. Finally we lurched off on our journey, the decrepit bus groaning and creaking like the geriatric relic it was.

We soon discovered friends and acquaintances also going on the trip that weekend: Paula, an Australian lab tech; Sonja and Anthony, both

Australian ER nurses; Mary Lou, a Canadian lab tech; and Bryn, an Australian English teacher. I especially liked the Australians for their free spirit and amazing water skills. I never met an Australian who wasn't a fantastic swimmer. These people liked and respected Fawzia, and we all felt comfortable with one another. We ended up hanging out together that weekend.

During the four-hour trip to the Red Sea we encountered spectacular landscapes. I felt we had visited the alien landscapes of three distinctly different planets. The first couple of hours we journeyed through dull tan-colored desert sprinkled with malnourished, moisture-starved bushes. All the savage heat of the world lived here. Feverish waves of mirage quivered on the horizon like ghostly dancers. Sun-blasted collections of ancient volcanic slag interrupted bleak expanses of thin, brittle slices of shale. During a brief stop we walked on the flat shale and it shattered and rang to our step like delicate pottery.

The bus crawled along at a steady, plodding pace. My head drooped in the suffocating heat of the bus and I fell asleep. Fawzia, sitting next to me, suddenly jolted my arm. I woke with a start, a little disoriented, to find the bus had pulled into a petrol station. I grumbled to Fawzia, "You didn't have to wake me; we've only stopped to fill the gas tank." But as I sat up from my slumped position, the first thing I noticed was a colossal red cloud sweeping in our direction. On one side of the road I saw bright sunshine and cobalt sky; the other side was obliterated by the boiling red cloud. The stuff of legend, a desert sandstorm! The churning cloud of sand engulfed us and the shrieking wind slammed into the side of our bus with such force the heavy vehicle rocked on its springs. The wind and sand brought with it torrential sheets of chillingly cold rain. The mixture soon coated the bus in mud. Booming thunder slapped our eardrums and brilliant lightning lit the midday darkness. Fawzia grabbed my arm and yanked me into the aisle of the bus. "We must get into the petrol station. If the windows break we will be badly hurt!" she shouted over the roar of the storm. We stumbled off the bus and started toward the petrol station. The wind was icy cold, as if it had just swept off a nearby glacier. As we ran our bared skin was needled by grains of sand that felt like toothy nips from a nasty little terrier.

I'd never experienced anything like this and I was terrified by the sudden violence. We huddled behind counters and displays in the building for fear of the plate glass windows exploding. We waited for the tempest to pass. As suddenly as the storm appeared, it swept over us and was gone. An eerie silence descended. The frightened eyes of our entire group peaked from behind their makeshift blockades to see if it was safe to venture outside. We gingerly stepped out into a new world of rain-fresh air. I was shocked by the condition of our bus on its windward side and amazed at the force of Mother Nature. In a matter of minutes the wind-driven sand had blasted the paint away down to the bare metal. Finally we climbed back on the bus to continue our journey. The former dull tan desert was lit up with a brief display of color after its fresh wash of rain. "Wadis" (wadi is a ravine or arroyo) rushed with muddy water. A brilliant spectrum of rainbow arched across the horizon. I learned later that sandstorms in Saudi Arabia can last a week or longer and occur in both summer and winter.

As we continued on our journey, the landscape evolved into brilliant vistas of pink-red sand, low green shrubbery and bizarre rock formations. Piles of flat corrugated stone resembling Caterpillar equipment tracks were stacked one atop another in straight orderly rows. Enormous boulders dotted the landscape, some smoothly eroded by centuries of wind, others weirdly convoluted, and intricately patterned. In the distance range upon range of sharp, toothy mountains marched on like enormous ruins of a forgotten civilization until they faded into the far—off horizon.

The bus began to climb into a mountain pass, laboring and groaning in mechanical misery. Here the rock was solid, timeless grey granite striated with green and denim-colored bands. Sparse vegetation, feeble bushes, and thorny acacia trees struggled to survive. The bus was barely moving by the time we reached the summit. Fawzia looked over at my worried face. I said, "Are we going to have to get out and push?" She grinned, "Do not worry, the bus always gets us to Duba." The driver stopped at the summit for fifteen minutes or so to allow the ancient engine to cool off. Some of us got off the bus and explored the near surroundings. The air was cool and fresh at this altitude. It would be the last cool air we would feel that weekend. We again boarded the bus, descended the pass and limped into the small city of Duba. The Red Sea stretched before us, sparkling azure and emerald. Charming fishing boats bobbed at their docks. Oil tankers sat patiently in the distance, waiting to fill their holds. Here at sea level the air was cloyingly humid and salty.

On the way to Duba I saw Bedouins, the nomadic desert people, for the first time. Some of these wandering people are considered stateless; they know no borders or citizenships. In the distance I saw black tents erected in groups. A co-worker told me the nomads' tents were made of goat and sheep hair. Flocks of the same black, shaggy goats wandered about nibbling on short, dry clusters of grass, closely watched by children and elderly women. Intermingled with the goats were fat-tailed sheep, an ancient and hardy desert breed. They store large amounts of fat in the tail and rump region. The fat is prized for cooking and soap-making.

I noticed that every camp had a large tanker truck parked nearby. Nowadays the Bedouin take their water with them. Small Toyota pickups called Hilux in the Middle East, the workhorses of these people, were parked haphazardly near the tents. During my time in Saudi, I saw many of these little trucks on my journeys. I was amazed at the uses made by the Bedouins of these tough little vehicles. They hauled everything from water tanks to firewood. But it was the variety of animals tucked into the small truck beds that amused me most. Goats, highly intelligent animals, were packed evenly into orderly, sedate rows where they seemed to stay without being tied or restrained—six per Toyota truck. Sheep, not the smartest animals, were trussed around all four legs and unceremoniously tossed into the truck in disorderly and bleating confusion—four per Toyota truck. Camels, apparently feeling it their due in life to ride, their legs neatly folded, fit nicely without restraint and peered arrogantly over the cab—one per Toyota truck.

The camels amazed me. We came upon a contented camel sitting directly in the middle of the road, chewing its cud, oblivious to traffic. Camels couched on highways are a common sight, but usually later in the evening. I learned that camels sit on the asphalt for the warmth retained from daytime heat. I saw camels everywhere, in shades varying from bright white to charcoal black. Paula, the Australian lab tech, commented, "All the camels are wandering around loose. How do the owners know which camel belongs to whom?" I later visited a camel souq (market) where I learned that each camel had some distinguishing mark recognizable to its owner.

Camels have always been an essential part of Arabian culture. At one time all the desert Bedouin needed to survive was camel milk and dates. The Saudis and Gulf peoples still drink camel milk on a regular basis, though there is high risk of contracting brucellosis because the milk is not pasteurized.

Camels are seen as mean-spirited and disagreeable animals, and often they are. They are highly intelligent creatures, however, and to some almost human in their intuition. A young Saudi man told us all about camels when we visited the camel souq. He said camels will always remember who treated them well or badly. He knew of camels who'd seemingly planned their revenge over a period of time, striking at a cruel owner when he least expected it. Camels have huge square teeth and exceptionally strong legs. They can kill a man with ease. Like most tourists, I would have the pleasure of riding camels several times in both Saudi Arabia and Jordan. I enjoyed their rolling gait, these ships of the desert. They are a very comfortable animal to ride.

From what we saw while passing through Duba, the fishing boats and blue-green sea seemed to be its only interesting feature. Ferries regularly operate from here for Jordan and Egypt. But the streets were dusty and pot-holed. Few pedestrians were about on this smoldering, humid afternoon (anyone with any sense was inside resting under the air conditioning.) Our bus passed through Duba and on down the road to the beach camp some twenty miles distant. About an hour later, our driver suddenly turned off into the desert. Here we were in the midst of nowhere with no evidence of a road. But the driver had made this trip many times, and I supposed he knew where he was going. The bus groaned and creaked over sand dunes for another twenty minutes. Finally, at the crest of a dune, the beach camp appeared in front of us, a village of large, white canvas tents and shabby prefab structures surrounded by a chain-link fence. Our bus rolled to a stop with an almost audible sigh of relief.

The canvas tents were sleeping quarters for four to six people each. The prefab huts nearby contained the common kitchen and bathrooms. If I thought the inside of the bus was stifling, stepping outside nearly made me faint. I was stunned by the force of the heat and the syrupy humidity that settled over me like a heavy wet blanket. It took my breath away. Paula, Sonja, Fawzia and I chose a tent on the periphery of the camp. We were struck by a musty smell when we stepped inside the structure. The floor inside the tent was just sand with several concrete platforms big enough to sleep on. But even with a Duba mat I knew the concrete bed was going to be far too hard to offer any comfort.

Those who could swim and snorkel went off to the reef with their spear guns to catch fish for dinner. Fawzia and I walked to the beach and I dipped my feet into the Red Sea for the first time. The crystal clear water was bath-water-warm and tasted deliciously briny. I could barely comprehend the fact I was actually at the Red Sea. The experience seemed surreal. By now the snorkelers were returning with stories of the stunning beauty of the coral reefs.

I felt frustrated; I wanted to see that beauty with my own eyes. I knew I would be forever sidelined unless I learned to swim and conquer my dread of deep water. Months later I would finally gather up my courage; I not only learned to swim, but also got over my fear of deep water and even learned to snorkel.

The Filipino women, now joined by their husbands and boyfriends who'd driven to the camp in private cars, immediately took over the kitchen and began to cook huge quantities of food for their group. There was the usual racial tension I had come to expect. The Filipinos were resented because there was no chance to use the single kitchen once they appropriated it for their use. They kept the kitchen in their grasp for the entire weekend. I found it unfortunate that racially mixed events or gatherings usually ended up with each nationality sequestered in their own little cliques.

The snorkelers brought back the most amazingly colorful fish I'd ever seen. Sadly their magnificent colors faded quickly in death. Some of the fish looked to weigh at least twenty pounds or more. I asked Sonja, the ER nurse, what sort of fish she'd caught. She described each species, "Well, this big red fellow with the bright blue spots is a sort of "grouper," very common on the coral reefs. And his big blue friend here is a "wrasse," also common in these waters. They can grow to massive size." I was amazed at the wrasse; even in death his scales glowed iridescent turquoise blue, edged in fuchsia pink. This beautiful creature had the misfortune to also taste good.

I knew our group would share the fish so I felt the least I could do was offer to help clean them. Sonja, Paula and I took the fish down to the water and got them ready to cook. Sonja had a razor-sharp filet knife, and she cut the fish to fit in the fry pan. Somebody had even thought to bring a huge old cast iron skillet. Since our group had no access to the kitchen, some of the men built a fire. Bryn filled an old aluminum pot with rice and water and placed it near the fire. The fish was simply floured and fried in butter. Someone else caught some small rock lobsters on the reef and they were put on to boil. The smell of the frying fish was heavenly, the meat white, solid and flaky. Along with the fish we pooled our food resources for the feast and we ate hugely of fresh fish, lobster, rice, fresh vegetables and fruit.

The camp generators were turned off at 10:00 p.m. and most went to their tents to sleep. Fawzia and Sonja went into our tent, wrapped themselves in a blanket on their Duba mats and fell asleep. Paula and I sat chatting near the glowing coals of the fire. When we finally stepped inside our tent to sleep, we immediately stepped back out. The damp night heat had worsened the unpleasant musty smell inside the tent. The old canvas tents were moldy and rotten from their constant exposure to heat and humidity. Paula looked at me and said, "I don't think I can sleep with that rank smell." I agreed with her.

As if the smelly tent wasn't enough, some of the Filipino men brought home-brewed alcohol to the relative freedom of the camp and things got rowdy. We knew we could not sleep in the camp. In search of peace and comfort, Paula and I took our Duba mats and blankets and went to sleep on the beach. We found Anthony already there wrapped in his blanket and gazing at the night sky. He chuckled, "You two couldn't stand it either, eh?" Paula and I lay our Duba mats down on the smooth sand near Anthony. I was surprised at the chilly nip of the night air and wrapped myself tightly in my blanket. A luminous half-moon illuminated the water and sand in soft, silvery light. The three of us chatted for some time. I soon fell asleep soothed by the cool breeze, the sigh of the waves and a radiant display of stars in the night sky. I'd never slept in the open before; it was a delicious experience. I don't think I've ever slept better.

The following day we climbed back on the bus and left the camp around 12:30 p.m. It was a tough and tiring trip, coming and going, for the few hours we actually spent at the beach. But for me it was all worth it to see the Red Sea.

During later excursions to the beach I found other interesting things to do. In the relative cool of early morning I often walked inland to search for desert diamonds, known locally as Saudi diamonds. Saudi diamonds are in fact high-grade quartz, considered a semi-precious stone in the same family as citrine and amethyst. In certain regions of Saudi Arabia the little jewels are scattered on the desert floor in their thousands. I hoped to find a few high-quality stones, but for all their number I knew it would be difficult. They are dull and tan-colored in their rough state, but once cut and polished they can be quite beautiful. The finest Saudi diamond I ever saw belonged to a delightful British woman named Janet who worked in Medical Records. It was a wondrous thing, a huge stone of perfect clarity that flashed with fire. Her husband Ian had the stone set in a 22-karat gold wedding band. Janet was proud of her gorgeous ring and received many compliments on it.

One morning as I was walking in the desert just after sunrise looking for desert diamonds, I was startled by a flicker of movement in my peripheral vision. I turned to see a large tan spider-like creature rise up off the sand on long spiky legs and sprint off at astonishing speed. I knew without a doubt this had to be the infamous camel spider.

Shortly after I arrived in Saudi Arabia Vicky told me about the creature. "Y'all gonna see this thing eventually, especially at the beach. Ugliest damn thing you ever saw!" she exclaimed. I thought she was pulling my leg.

As I looked at this one I felt revulsion and my heart raced at my first sighting of the ugly creature.

An urban legend has grown around the desert camel spider, especially since Iraq war veterans have brought their own stories home. Some of the stories are fabulous: that the creatures are extremely aggressive, they can jump six feet in the air, and they will actually chase down a human. Personally, I don't believe they would pursue a human, or that they are aggressive, but there is no doubt they are terrifying to behold. In the course of my job I process many reports of Iraq veterans with post-traumatic stress disorder. While this disorder is usually due to traumatic incidents in active combat, several veterans have described having nightmares about the giant creatures called camel spiders.

It was years later when I finally researched the beast. Though a member of the Arachnid family, they are not spiders nor are they venomous. Their scientific name is "solpugid." They are common in the desert southwest of the United States, but considerably smaller than their Middle East cousins. Science claims these creatures are harmless to man. But on several beach weekends I talked to people who slept under the stars at night and woke in the morning with frightful wounds on their legs and ankles. I had the opportunity to have a close look at some of the wounds. I cannot be certain if the bites were owed to a camel spider, but the wounds were deep, bloody craters from missing pieces of flesh.

Friends living on a compound in Tabuk caught a camel spider in a large jar, and I was able to study it very closely. The creature's body consisted of two pale tan segments with five appendages on each side. Had the body with the long thin legs been spread out, it would have covered an 8.5"x11" piece of paper. The sight of it made the hair stand up on the back of my neck. No matter the urban legend, I am a believer.

Back in the desert, after collecting dozens of desert diamond specimens, I eventually chose two of similar quality and size, about one carat each. I was told there were shops in Bangkok that specialize in cutting desert diamonds. One acquaintance or another was always traveling to Thailand and most were happy to carry packages of diamonds belonging to several different people. They would drop off the stones at a Bangkok shop and then pick up the finished product before returning to Saudi Arabia. My desert diamonds made the journey and found their way back to me some weeks later. I was impressed by the professional-looking faceting. I took them to a Tabuk goldsmith who made them into stud earrings set in 22 karat gold, which I still treasure.

Travels within the Kingdom

A favorite weekend destination on other little trips within Saudi Arabia was Jeddah. Western expatriates like Jeddah because it is a more liberal city. There was even a uniquely singular hotel that allowed single women to stay, as long as we kept a very low profile.

Jeddah has a population of about two million people and is the largest seaport on the Red Sea. Ancient Saudi tradition says Jeddah is where Eve traveled from to meet Adam. Legend claims Jeddah is the site of Eve's tomb though nothing to that effect is known or marked. I found Jeddah a beautiful city with a terrible summer climate. The winter months are balmy and pleasant, but in summer the temperature can climb to 125 Fahrenheit with 100 percent humidity. A few minutes in the heat and humidity left me soaked with sweat.

But the sites in Jeddah almost make up for the climate. All large Gulf cities have a Corniche, a road that parallels a wide strip of green grass and flower beds which abuts the sea. An intricate metal fence or stone wall lines the water-side and a walking path usually follows the length of the fence. Jeddah's Corniche travels all along the Red Sea coastline for about thirty-five kilometers. Dubai and Abu Dhabi both have a beautiful Corniche lined with sumptuous gardens and brilliant green lawns. Jeddah's Corniche is lined with five-star hotels, fountains, playgrounds and food kiosks. It is famous for its unique statuaries of huge iron bicycles, enormous Arabian lamps and Arabic calligraphy hundreds of feet tall. During the terrible heat of the day the Corniche is deserted, but at night the road comes alive with cars and people. After 10:00 p.m. Saudi families come out for walks and picnics on the lush lawns of the Corniche. Expatriate Arab and Asian families enjoy barbecuing. I have always been amused at Saudi families, who appear to enjoy a picnic nearly anywhere and in almost any weather condition. I have seen them sitting on a concrete boulevard in the midst of a sandstorm. Location and weather does not seem to matter.

I saw Saudi families picnicking on the Corniche made up of generations, from ancient bent elders to babes in arms. No matter the temperature the women in the group were always completely covered in black. I never wore my abaya in Jeddah and never felt the need for head covering. I saw the religious police sometimes, but as long as Western women dressed in conservative street clothes they did not harass us.

Jeddah has beautiful shopping malls with well-known Western brands. The malls also contain high-end beauty salons and luxurious spas. Most salons in the Gulf and much of the Middle East are for women only, private businesses where everyone can relax minus head scarf and abaya.

Most of the cars on the Corniche road are luxury vehicles stuffed with young Saudi males with their cell phones and loud stereos. Not an unusual thing for youths to do in many cities of the world. But the point of the evening parade of young Saudi males is to exchange cell phone numbers with young women. The young ladies are likewise out cruising, but with a chauffeur at the wheel. The young men and women keep the car windows open so they can throw bits of paper back and forth between the cars. I am not sure where the exchange of phone numbers leads, perhaps to passionate telephone conversations, not much else. With the latest communication technology, contact between the sexes is now much easier. This has to be a risky business for the young women involved. The religious police are aware of these exchanges, but it is difficult for them to control. If the young women are caught by the Mutawa in the act of exchanging personal information with a strange male, they are arrested, taken to jail and their families called. Her punishment will depend on how conservative her family is. Recently a young Saudi woman was the victim of an honor killing by her father because he found her having a "romance" with a young man on Facebook.

My last trip within Saudi Arabia before leaving for good involved a party at the German Embassy in Riyadh. Just four months before I left the Kingdom, life presented me with a special surprise. A young woman arrived in Tabuk who would become a life-long friend. Jeanette was a medical transcriptionist from Manitoba, Canada, a petite, curvy girl with a sassy mouth and personality to match. I sensed that Jeanette was an adventurous soul and we clicked right away. We would go on to have many adventures together in places as far flung as Saudi Arabia, London, Dubai, and back in Canada.

Though Tabuk did not have embassies or consulates, cities like Jeddah and Riyadh did. Invitations to embassy functions were much sought after. People would fly from Tabuk to Jeddah or Riyadh, an hour or so by air, to attend the parties. Almost any nationality could attend an Embassy function, but to acquire an invitation we had to know someone who had an "in" with the embassy staff. However, the functions were often snooty and one never saw an Asian at a Western country's embassy party. These parties sometimes required formal dress.

Jeanette heard about a party at the German embassy in Riyadh. It was March, we were bored. Jeanette felt that a party was just the thing for us. I'd never been to an embassy party and assumed it would be like most parties held on just about every Western compound in the Kingdom; heavy drinking, perhaps some dancing and games, and lots of people hooking up. But Jeanette was convincing, "Come on you party pooper, it'll be fun," she said. "You've never been to Riyadh and you've never been to an Embassy party. So come along." I finally agreed, if for nothing else the little trip would alleviate some boredom.

Jeannette contacted her friend, Jill, in Riyadh to see if we could stay with her. Jill was thrilled to host us and agreed immediately. We'd left our decision to the last minute, however, and knew our names would not make it on to the list of embassy party attendees in time. But that was no deterrent for three determined women. We would dress to the nines, confident in our good looks. We agreed that red lipstick, charm and flirtation had always worked in our favor before! Though it was a short flight to Riyadh, Jeanette and I decided to live it up and purchased first-class seats. On the plane we were like two kids, playing with the first-class seats, which folded down into beds, drinking glass after glass of Saudi "champagne" (7-Up and fruit juice), giggling at other passengers and eating whatever was put before us. In this case we were served lamb kebabs and rice, a staple meal on Saudia Airlines. In retrospect I'm sure our fellow passengers found our giddiness annoying; we were so excited to be on a plane heading to a party in Riyadh.

Of course, I did not know that we were headed for an event that Jeanette and I have since referred to as "The German Embassy Incident." I have never let her forget that she very nearly caused an international incident.

Jeanette's British friend Jill had an apartment through her nursing job at Riyadh's King Faisal Hospital. We were lucky to be able to stay with her; it was the only way we could stay in Riyadh since no hotel in that ultra-conservative city would have permitted two single females as guests. Jill arranged for a driver to pick us up at the airport and deliver us to her apartment (most large hospital compounds in Riyadh have legions of drivers to transport single women.) We arrived in front of a large building clad in white marble. The building was one of dozens on a compound near Jill's workplace. Our footsteps echoed as we walked into her cavernous residence which contained four bedrooms, as many bathrooms, and white marble flooring throughout. She had the entire place to herself. This was the first time I'd met Jill and I found her delightful. Taller than either Jeanette or I, she had a generous figure, closely-cropped curly hair and striking brown eyes. She laughed easily and often. The party started the moment we got to Jill's apartment. She'd spent the week preparing "bathtub gin." I was surprised to find that it tasted much like real gin and was quite a good effort as homemade spirits went. That evening we stayed in. Jill ordered delivery of delicious food from a nearby Lebanese restaurant: lamb and chicken kebabs, hummus, eggplant dip, and fresh bread. Jill and Jeanette, ever the dedicated partiers, stayed up much of the night while I went to bed fairly early.

We spent the entire next day preparing ourselves for the Embassy party. Jeanette had put a gorgeous outfit together from purchases in Tabuk. It was a miracle to me, since clothing items on offer there were mostly over-the-top gaudy. She wore a short black dress, made of beautifully draped material, and very high heels in shades of copper and gold. This dress would become known as "the little black dress" in our German Embassy Incident. When Jeanette put that dress on, her curvy figure got a lot of male attention, and we could be sure of some wayward adventure to follow. Since I was leaving Saudi in three months I had some nice outfits made to take home with me. I'd found a scrap of exquisite crimson silk embroidered with gold thread and tiny gilt sequins. I had it made into a fitted vest, under which I wore a sheer black blouse. I'd completed my outfit with a long skirt of lustrous black silk velvet. Jill wore a chic two-piece skirt suit of rose-colored silk. And of course all three of us accessorized with liberal amounts of gold jewelry. It was unfortunate we had to cover everything with an abaya until we reached the embassy. Jill and Jeanette were giggly on a gin high and ready to party. That night I would come to find out just how much Jeanette loved to party and how much trouble she could get into.

Jill called a taxi to deliver us to the German Embassy in downtown Riyadh since all the compound drivers were booked. All the embassies in Riyadh reside in a specific area called the Diplomatic Quarter. The DQ, as it is known to locals, is a vast area where one can find embassies from almost every country in the world. The entire quarter is surrounded by a high wall. It is in fact a self-contained city of its own with malls and restaurants, as well as apartment buildings and luxurious villas to house the hundreds of embassy staff. Many companies rent apartments or villas in the DQ for their employees if they can afford the astronomical rents.

Our taxi passed through a massive iron gate to enter the Diplomatic Quarter itself. It seemed like we drove forever through lush gardens and parks before seeing any buildings. The taxi finally pulled up in front of a flat-roofed, one-storey building covered in nondescript stucco. Apparently this was the place where the party would be held. The building was just one of several that made up the German Embassy compound as a whole. The formal Embassy where the ambassador resides is a large, beautiful building of its own. There is a separate area for Embassy offices and another for formal dinners and dances. As we stepped from the taxi on to the street, we saw dozens of people milling about waiting to go through security screening to gain entrance to the party. The street in front of the building was bumper-to-bumper with taxis and a few luxury cars and limousines.

As we arrived at security the young East Indian guard told us our names were not on the invitee list. We knew this, of course. So Jill began a series of the usual excuses these "gatekeepers" are used to hearing: that Dr. So-and-so was going to call and put our names on the list, but he must have forgotten, can't you let us in anyway, etc. As the litany of excuses continued a drunken German man reeled onto the scene and asked what was going on. The man had obviously started his own party earlier in the day. He was a tall, broad man in his fifties with the red bulbous nose of the dedicated alcoholic. He might once have been a handsome man. His faded blonde hair hung in his rheumy eyes as his gaze took in us three delectable young women. In slurred broken English he introduced himself as Gustav. Jeanette, quick to see an advantage in the situation, explained our plight to Gustav. It took little to convince him. He told the gatekeeper he would sign us in. We breathed a sigh of relief and expressed our everlasting gratitude to Gustav. He responded by giving us a bunch of free drink tickets to be used at the bar in the embassy. And so the night began.

We passed through the gate and entered the stucco building. It was not at all a fancy place, consisting only of two large, plain rooms with a couple of dusty potted palms in the corners. The minute we entered the building, Jill and Jeanette disappeared to find the bar. I grabbed a cola from a nearby ice bucket and surveyed my surroundings. I stuck to sodas all evening and kept an eye on my friends Jeanette and Jill. Jeanette later told me the details of her evening were dim and cloudy. However, she admitted, "What is clear in my mind is the fact everyone at the party got roaring drunk." Jeanette said, "I also have a vague memory of either Jill or I ending up in a Saudi's lap."

I was able to confirm that. I went to the bar to find Jill sitting next to a young Saudi man dressed in a flashy suit made of some sort of shiny navy-blue material. The two were bent over in deep conversation. But Jeanette I found relaxing on the lap of an exotically handsome man in Western dress, her arm draped around his broad shoulders. I laughed and shook my head at her bravura. The man grinned and smiled at the good fortune seated on his lap. Though the man wore tasteful, expensive Western clothing, it was obvious to me he was a Saudi. Men from the Gulf States almost always look not-quite-comfortable in Western dress. They are much more comfortable in their handsome white thobes and gutras.

Jeanette, Jill, and I were surprised to find Saudi men present at the party, an unusual situation. Normally Saudis are not permitted to attend Embassy functions. Westerners are uncomfortable with their presence, and attending these functions is a chance to be free of Saudis for a few hours. But if a Saudi has high connections it may be impossible to refuse them entrance.

I tried to circulate and talk to people, but I'd never been very good at cocktail parties. In fact I felt rather bored. There was no disc jockey in sight, but the bartenders kept music flowing from a console set up behind them. Some people danced, but everyone had become so drunk they could barely stand. I knew that Jeanette, with a few drinks in her, was capable of saying or doing almost anything. I stayed close to her. Jill, I felt, could take care of herself.

The booze continued to flow freely.

Finally the midnight hour was upon us, and the Embassy staff asked everyone to vacate the premises. Jill lived on a compound, but had no curfew to meet. A long line of the inebriated began to stumble out of the party building, dispersing into the murky, languid darkness that falls over Riyadh on hot summer nights. Well, everyone dispersed except for Jill, Jeanette, and me. Jill, somewhat less intoxicated than Jeanette, had gone out earlier to ask the gatekeeper to call us a taxi. Few people in Saudi had cell phones at the time. The technology used by the rest of the world had not quite caught up with the Kingdom.

So the three of us went out and sat down to wait on some benches near the gate. We waited and waited, but no taxi appeared.

The Saudi military generally has a presence when events take place at any embassy. They were indeed present that night, patrolling along the street in front of the embassy compound. But mainly the soldiers kept a watchful eye on all the pretty ladies exiting the party. Jill decided to use her feminine wiles and ask one of the soldiers to call a taxi for us. The soldier appeared to make a call on his radio, but we had no way of knowing what he actually said as he spoke rapid Arabic. The wait continued.

By this time Jeanette was getting restless. If we couldn't get a taxi how on earth were we going to get home? Jeanette decided to take the matter into her own hands when she realized one of the soldiers was leering at us in spite of the fact we wore abayas. Given how long we'd been waiting for a taxi, it was the last straw for Jeanette. She lurched onto her high-heel-clad feet and marched somewhat unsteadily across the sidewalk. She approached the Saudi soldier that Jill had asked to call a taxi for us. He was an unimposing little guy, not more than one hundred pounds, but sporting a mighty rifle. He grinned as Jeanette strode toward him. I looked over at Jill who was by now slightly sober and whispered, "Oh crap, what is she up to?" We watched Jeanette place her hand flat on the soldier's chest and shove him backwards as she shouted, "You never fucking called a taxi, did you?" The young man stumbled and nearly fell. At first he looked merely confused by what had happened, but then his face reddened in anger. Jeanette calmly turned around, walked back to where Jill and I were sitting and continued the wait. I saw the angry young soldier get on his radio and spit out some comments in Arabic. Jill and I looked at Jeanette with horror. Jill whispered fiercely to Jeanette, "What did you do that for? You can't push a soldier! You're gonna get us in deep shit for this!"

Shortly thereafter we saw a number of Saudi police cars and army Jeeps arriving on the scene. A variety of high- and lower-ranking officials spilled out of the vehicles, all of them shouting and carrying on in voluble Arabic. By the time this all happened it was only Jill, Jeanette, and I still waiting. One other loitering straggler, a lone Arab man, approached Jeanette and said, "I do not think you should have done that."

I was flustered and didn't know what to do. I looked at Jill. Her face looked like an angry thundercloud. She approached Jeanette and pointed at a dusty hedge nearby. She ordered Jeanette in no uncertain terms, "Go sit behind that hedge. I'll go talk to the soldiers. I'll do anything I have to do to keep us out of jail." And I gave Jeanette a push towards the hedge. She said not a word, but in her current state appeared mostly unconcerned about the situation she'd started. In the midst of the melee, no one noticed Jeanette move to the hedge and hunker down behind it. Jill strode over to the troops to have a word. I watched her smile and turn on her considerable charm. No go. The soldiers and their superiors were riled up, and there was no calming them. And where was that woman who had caused all this trouble? Jill returned to my side looking frightened. I said to her, "What are we gonna do now?"

The group of military and police officials continued to mill about and shout. Suddenly a big black Mercedes with two German men in the front seats, and diplomatic plates, pulled up beside us. Apparently the East Indian man at the embassy gate had become concerned and quietly contacted someone associated with the German Embassy. The man in the passenger seat got out of the car and approached us. He introduced himself as Ralph. A tall, muscular man with a square jaw, Ralph presented a serious, take-charge attitude. Our saviour was at hand.

Jill explained the situation to Ralph who listened quietly. We had to tell him that the cause of the problem was hiding behind the nearby hedge. He told me quietly, "Get your friend and come back inside the Embassy where you'll be safe. We need to give these guys some time to cool off." I went and pulled Jeanette out from behind the hedge and Ralph escorted us back into the party building. We sat down in the bar, Ralph poured us all a bracing cup of coffee and we chatted amiably.

In hindsight we realized Ralph was a pretty cool guy. We gave the Saudis outside about half an hour or so and then Ralph suggested we all get in his private car so he could personally drive us back to our compound. But we still had to pass through the gate to the main German Embassy where soldiers and police were still milling about. A different soldier stopped us at the gate. Ralph and Jill sat in the front of the vehicle and Jeanette and I in the back. I kept my hand tight on Jeanette's arm and whispered fiercely, "Don't say anything that'll get us in more trouble." The soldier obviously recognized Ralph, and his private vehicle also carried diplomatic plates, so we hoped it would be easy enough for us to pass through the gate. The soldier asked for our residence visa (contained in the small booklet called an "iqama" that expats have to carry at all times.) Jeanette looked at me, having sobered up a bit by now, and whispered, "Honestly, I don't have the iqama with me tonight."

The soldier demanded to know our names. When he came to Jeanette, she said with a straight face, "My name is Julia Watts. I'm sorry sir, but I'm not carrying my iqama with me tonight." The soldier dutifully wrote down our names and then waved us through the gate. All four of us breathed a great sigh of relief. By then Jill was hungry for McDonald's and asked Ralph if we could stop by on our way home. I said to Jill, "How in hell can you think of a hamburger after what we've just been through?" She smiled and shot back, "Well, now we're safe and I'm hungry!" After all the trouble we'd caused Ralph he still took us through the drive-through and then home. As we stumbled into Jill's apartment I said, "Thank God for Ralph." Jill and I looked at Jeanette who by now was looking contrite. "We don't even want to think about what might have happened without the help of Ralph," exclaimed Jill.

The following day we were able to laugh about what happened, but I'll never forget the incident and the awful trouble we nearly found ourselves in. Without Ralph's intervention all three of us would have likely been arrested by the Saudis. The fact that Jill and Jeanette had been drinking would have made it worse for them. In the end we would have all been deported.

About six weeks later Jeanette got a call from Jill who told her about a party at the Canadian Embassy the following weekend. Jill was interested in attending and asked if Jeanette and I would like to come to Riyadh and join her. After the German Embassy Incident I wasn't interested, but Jeanette was eager to go and booked a ticket to Riyadh.

When Jeanette returned to Tabuk she told me about the weekend. Once they were on their way to the Canadian Embassy party, she felt rather reluctant. She thought it might be prudent to stay away from the Diplomatic Quarter for a while. Jill assured Jeanette that surely there would be completely different soldiers at the Canadian Embassy and that she would not be recognized. They got through all the respective check points and arrived in front of the Canadian Embassy without incident. Jill and Jeanette made their way to the bar to start the evening. No sooner did they walk in when they saw a familiar person across the room. None other than Ralph. "I felt so embarrassed, and hoped never to see the guy again," Jeanette told me. "He came over to greet us, shaking his head in disbelief that we'd actually dared to come back to the Diplomatic Quarter after the previous fiasco."

Ralph went on to tell her and Jill about what happened after we left the German Embassy. Apparently things had only gotten worse after we left. The Saudi General of the Diplomatic Quarter demanded a meeting with the German ambassador. The ambassador was put on the spot because he was asked to explain the situation. Ralph said he, too, was interrogated over the incident. The end result was that the German ambassador had to apologize on Jeanette's behalf for having touched the soldier.

Apparently the soldier was ridiculed by his peers for having been pushed by a woman, especially a Western woman. He'd lost considerable face and, no doubt, was exceedingly angry about the incident. Jeanette felt badly about the entire thing, but admitted that she couldn't remember if she'd thanked Ralph appropriately or not. She said that in hindsight she realized we had had a close call, and that it could all have turned out very differently.

Though Jeanette remembered Ralph driving us home that fateful evening, she does not recall shoving the soldier. Perhaps it's best she not remember that she almost created what we called the international incident. And there were no parties at the German Embassy for a long, long time. Jill told us that Jeanette had effectively managed to shut it down.

What a headline it would have made: "WHAT DID A SMALL-TOWN CANADIAN GIRL DO THAT CLOSED THE GERMAN EMBASSY IN RIYADH?"

Carnage on the Roads

Traffic accidents are a fact of life in the Kingdom and the number one cause of death amongst young Saudi males. During the bus trip to and from Duba, we encountered one major motor vehicle accident and several minor ones. Drivers take horrifying chances, passing into oncoming traffic with only inches to spare. Fatal head-on collisions are a frequent sight. Accidents are also common amongst expatriate males who are unfamiliar with Saudi driving conditions and the insane driving habits of the locals. Wherever I traveled in Saudi Arabia the most common sights were smashed-up wrecks littering the sides of roads and highways. Why didn't somebody remove them for scrap? But the wrecks lay where they had met their end, slowly transformed into bare skeletons under the brutal force of the desert sun.

Dr. Mohammed, the young Saudi resident in our department, often asked Gabrielle and me if we'd like to go for a ride in his Porsche Carrera. As much as we would have liked to, we reminded him it was against the law for single women, especially if with a Saudi man. With a little grin he'd say, "No problem, I know all the security people." We laughed as we visualized a ride with Dr. Mohammed. Careening down a desert highway at maximum speed. Weaving in and out of traffic. Stereo blasting Arabic music. One hand adjusting his red-checked gutra in the rearview mirror, the other hand holding a glass of tea, shouting, "NO PROBLEM!"

Aside from the fact it was illegal for Gabrielle or I to ride with Dr. Mohammed, there was the more frightening possibility of involvement in a traffic accident. The young men drive like fiends, blowing carelessly down the streets and highways, weaving in and out of slower traffic. Sometimes they slide by other vehicles on the right shoulder. I am certain they would fly over the top if it were possible. It is common to see drivers suddenly decide to make a left turn from the far right lane. And the horns! In most of the Middle East car horns are an ever-present din on streets at all hours. They are blown for every reason except their true purpose. Though traffic lights exist, little attention is paid to them. From exhausted, bald-tired heaps to sleek, pricey Lamborghinis, all are driven as if jet engines are standard equipment. Such driving is not limited to Saudi men. The hazardous practice seems to be chronic amongst Middle and Far Eastern males in general. Age doesn't appear to be a factor—one can often see Saudi boys barely able to see over the steering wheel chauffeuring cars stuffed with black-draped females and younger children.

A favorite pastime for young Saudi men is attempting to get their SUVs leaning over on two wheels while going round a traffic circle. They circle again and again, each revolution a little faster until the passenger side tips up on two wheels. Once the vehicle is tipped up on its side, the driver has little control over his vehicle and an accident often results.

In the past few years "drifting" (known amongst Saudis as "hagwalah") has become a popular pastime amongst young Saudi males. They push their vehicles to top speed and then steer it into a sideways skid, often flipping the vehicle and rolling it multiple times. It is all the more dangerous because they make use of any straight road including residential neighborhoods and heavily trafficked motorways. Innocent spectators sometimes fall victim to the drift accidents. Often the drivers do not wear seatbelts because safety is seen as being in God's hands. At first some drivers suffered the lash for repeat offenses of drifting, but recently a middle-aged Saudi man was sentenced to beheading for killing two others during a drift accident.

The Saudi religious establishment now considers death by drifting as negligent homicide. Perhaps instead of executing Saudi males for what is essentially a reaction to the awful tedium of their lives, the government could provide some healthy outlets. The youth of Saudi suffer greatly from boredom. Because of total segregation of the sexes, forms of entertainment we take for granted i.e. dating, movie theaters, libraries do not exist in the Kingdom. But nothing can prevent the young men from practicing this dangerous activity. A waste of life on both sides of the equation.

Nonetheless, I soon learned that Islamic culture does not fear death. All is turned over to God. Muslims have a sense of fatalism encompassed in "enshallah" (as Allah wills), the most common statement in the Middle East. Whether you are meant to die (or not) in a motor vehicle accident, or by any means, is entirely in God's hands. There is a passage in the Holy Quran, "Until it is your time, nothing can harm you. When it is your time, nothing can save you." This concept of absolute fatalism is sometimes difficult for a Western mind to grasp.

But one thing nobody ever wanted to do was hit a camel. Of course there was the risk of human death colliding with such a large animal. But the ramifications are dire if you kill a camel. Camels wander everywhere in Saudi, without fences, day and night. Because they lie on warm asphalt roads during cold desert nights there is a huge risk of hitting a recumbent camel at night. Vicky and I knew a Palestinian couple, Nabil and Ibtisam, who both worked in the hospital lab. They went on a desert picnic and returned home after dark via a narrow secondary road. Their aged Toyota SUV slammed into a camel couched on the warm road. The couple was bruised and shaken, but otherwise unhurt. Their SUV was a write-off. Fortunately, because it was lying down when they hit it, the camel did not come through the windshield. Nabil literally drove up and over the creature. He later told us they saw nothing until they were literally on top of the animal. The camel did not survive. And that turned out to be the worst part.

Camels are highly valued animals and worth a great deal of money. In these situations a special investigator is brought to the scene because first priority is to identify the camel's owner. The driver of the vehicle, if not badly injured, is immediately taken to jail. The investigator knows the identifying tribal marks, or particular characteristics of an animal, so that he can contact the owner. Once the owner is notified of the death of his animal, he negotiates with the individual who killed his camel. Nabil and

Ibtisam ended up having to pay 70,000 riyals (more than US $19,000) to the owner, a huge amount of money for them. Nabil was not released from jail until he paid half the fine. Even then Nabil and his family were not allowed to travel outside of Saudi Arabia. They were virtual prisoners in the Kingdom until the entire amount was paid to the camel owner. The couple ended up bankrupting themselves and had to borrow money from family members and friends.

Anthony, an ER nurse who'd seen just about everything, told Gabrielle and me a bizarre story about a Saudi youth. He was blasting down a hilly back road in the dead of night in his sleek Porsche 911. He hit a camel broadside at around 100 mph. The animal apparently exploded on impact and plunged through the windshield before the air bag deployed. Anthony shook his head, "When they brought him into ER I'd never seen such a god-awful mess. I felt sorry for the police and emergency personnel who had to pull the guy out of the chaos of both Porsche and detonated camel." The ophthalmic surgeon took the young man to surgery immediately. Apparently as the air bag deployed, the camel stomach contents were literally driven into the young man's eyes, nose and mouth. His eye orbits were pulverized, his sinuses filled with camel contents. The surgeons picked bits of grass out of his corneas. Amazingly enough the driver wasn't seriously hurt from his chest down and the surgeon managed to save one of his eyes.

Westerners are not immune either to horrific motor vehicle accidents in Saudi. After returning from a weekend at the beach with Jane and Patrick, we learned of a tragedy that had actually occurred during our drive back from the Red Sea. Nigel and Clare, a middle-aged married British couple we knew and liked were with our group on the beach that weekend. On their way home, as they were entering the first mountain pass outside of Duba, their older four-wheel-drive Mitsubishi was side-swiped by a speeding driver in the opposing lane. Apparently as Nigel swerved sharply to avoid the driver he over-corrected and the Mitsubishi's front axle snapped. The vehicle careened over a retaining wall and fell into a deep chasm. Any number of vehicles containing beach-weekend friends were traveling home that day, but those in front and behind Nigel and Clare did not witness the accident.

Apparently the driver who hit them must have kept going.

Their vehicle landed in a ravine so that anyone passing could not have seen it from the road. The poor souls lay there for hours in the heat. Nigel was thrown clear of the vehicle (few observe seatbelt laws in Saudi, including Westerners) and broke his neck. He likely died immediately or soon after impact. Clare was wearing her seatbelt, but sustained horrific injuries during the roll down the ravine. She told us later she was pretty sure she remained conscious, but remembered little of her terrible experience. Her pelvis and both legs were shattered, deep lacerations criss-crossed her torso and numerous smaller bones were fractured. Finally a young Bedouin herdsman with his goats happened upon the vehicle as it lay upside down in the chasm.

In that remote place it was sheer luck they were found at all. By the time the youth notified authorities several more hours passed before help arrived from Duba, the nearest town. Clare said the young herdsman later returned with an elderly woman. She said they did not attempt to touch or move her, but simply sat with her and gave her sips of water. Clare was thankful for the kindness of these desert people, especially as the evening came and darkness fell. She always said their presence helped her not to give up in her desperate circumstances.

At that time EMTs, or even a modern ambulance, did not exist in that remote locale. The Duba police were used to such carnage on the mountain passes, but they were ill-equipped to handle an accident of this magnitude. Clare was extracted from the twisted vehicle and driven in the back of a police car to Duba. The trip quite likely did more injury to her already precarious condition. The hospital in Duba would be considered third-world by Western standards and Clare was merely stabilized there.

The hospital administrators at NWAFH in Tabuk were notified. More hours passed until the NWAFH ambulance arrived in Duba and transferred Clare back to Tabuk. She survived her injuries, her legs and pelvis pinned with multiple rods and plates, her body forever scarred. Her mind more so. Clare remained in ICU for two weeks and then on the surgical ward for a many more weeks undergoing intensive physical therapy. Eventually she managed to get about slowly with a walker, but she said the pain was unrelenting. Her nursing career was over. The expat community came together and organized a huge fundraiser at the British Aerospace compound in Tabuk to help Clare pay for incidentals. When she was well enough she returned to Britain to recuperate as much as she ever would.

The worst accident I ever witnessed occurred on the Duba-Tabuk highway. Gabrielle and I were returning from the Red Sea with our physician co-worker Dr. Walid, his wife Mariam and their two children late on a Friday afternoon. The usual route to the Red Sea from Tabuk is via the Al Ula-Tabuk-Duba Highway, at the time a two-lane primary road. (This was the same road our bus took when I visited Duba beach camp.) The road is of decent quality, but it winds over mountain passes and high ridges.

On our way we passed numerous large cargo trucks slowly negotiating the mountain passes. Most of the drivers are poorly-paid Pakistanis. What stood out in my mind was the fact these truck drivers did not appear to use the gearing-down technique to descend steep grades. Every truck we passed had the brake lights brightly lit. This seemed to me a recipe for disaster. I said to Walid, "All these drivers are using their brakes to get down these hills. There's got to be an awful lot of failures." Gabrielle and Walid agreed. "I would call it a disaster waiting to happen," quipped Walid in his dense French accent.

These are not the well-known 18-wheel trailer trucks of North America. Most of the large cargo trucks driven in Saudi appear ungainly. They are of a high narrow design with a stubby, abbreviated cab, two tires on front and four tires on back. The truck boxes are usually lined with aluminum or wooden railings. They are almost always dangerously over-loaded. Goods are crammed and stacked in a manner far beyond the vehicle's load tolerance. Given the truck's tall, narrow design they become top-heavy and unbalanced when over-burdened. We were some fifty miles from Duba and had just crested a pass. A few miles ahead we saw what appeared to be flames. As we drew closer in the early evening dusk, our horrified minds struggled to take in the single-vehicle accident scene before us. Gabrielle gasped and covered her eyes, "I just can't look." Walid's face took on a grim countenance, "This is very bad. No one can survive this." It was immediately apparent that a large cargo truck had lost its brakes soon after topping the pass. The truck had veered down the steep, long grade and run head-on into a solid wall of granite. The truck impacted with such force the cab was accordioned into a flat slab of metal. I thought the driver might still be encased in the cab which had become his permanent tomb. Pools of burning oil and fiery bits of truck debris added a sense of surrealism to the awful scene. By some miracle the gasoline tank had not exploded. The granite walls, and what was left of the truck cab, were smeared with splatters of blood.

The truck was carrying crates of fruit and lying amongst the scattered produce were two mangled bodies, apparently ejected from the truck before impact. Walid and Mariam, a nurse, got out to see if they could render any medical assistance. Gabrielle and I stayed in the truck and took care of their two children. The nearest emergency vehicles would be some time in reaching the scene. Dozens of cars and trucks were parked haphazardly near the accident scene. A huge crowd of Saudi men and women in thobes and abayas were gathered around the accident site. The crowd laughed and smiled, delighted with the fruit windfall. Gabrielle and I stared with a mix of astonishment and horror as the Saudis stacked the loose fruit into boxes and crammed it into their cars and trucks. No one seemed to take much notice of the mutilated bodies lying amongst the fruit. After all the fruit was free for the taking.

In retrospect I doubt the Saudis meant any disrespect for the dead. With true fatalism they knew nothing could be done for the dead. Their time had come. Walid and Mariam returned to our vehicle. "There is nothing we can do," whispered Walid. Mariam sat without comment, her face a mask of shock. When we reached the top of the pass Walid stopped to pray. We were a quiet group during the remainder of our trip. All the way back to Tabuk we were passed by cars and trucks packed with crates of fruit, a constant reminder of the awful accident scene.

I still see that accident and the aftermath in my dreams.

But an accident scene can be dangerous for the living too. I witnessed many collisions in Saudi Arabia, and later in United Arab

Emirates, where the wreck was surrounded by hundreds of people just minutes after the event occurred. As soon as a wreck is spotted, dozens of cars screech to a halt on both sides of the highway. People run through moving traffic and scramble over high concrete medians, their morbid curiosity goading them to be first at the scene. Collisions with fatalities draw even more spectators. The scene is often so clogged with onlookers the police are prevented from reaching the site. Other wrecks often occur simultaneously among those rubber-necking. In their haste to view the scene, some simply leave their vehicle in the middle of the road to be hit by a passerby.

An ancient practice exists in Saudi and the Gulf region: If you take a life, you must pay the living family for the life taken ("diyyah" meaning blood money.) It is similar to the rule that applies when someone hits and kills a camel. But a camel is often worth much more than a human life. In a situation where a motorist has killed another, unless he is injured badly enough to require hospitalization, he will go directly to jail. No questions asked. I would often see men brought into the hospital in leg chains whether ambulatory or through the emergency room. Whatever his condition the prisoner remained chained to the hospital bed with a guard posted nearby. After recovery, he was taken back to jail and remained there until the blood money was produced by him or his family.

Payment of diyyah applies to all expatriates including Westerners. I saw desperate cases where a Western man was kept in jail for weeks or even months until his distraught family in his home country could come up with the blood money to release him from jail. Sometimes the family of the deceased will pardon the driver, who is then released without paying the fine. Different values are assigned to different people, though according to the Quran, the amount of blood money should not differ based on gender or nationality. In declining order, a Muslim male is considered most valuable. His death could bring his family about $26,000. A Muslim female is generally worth about $13,000, a Christian male about $13,000, and a Christian female about $6500. Those considered inferior by the Saudis, i.e. Hindus, probably won't bring their family more than $1700 for a male and $900 for a female.

A common injury amongst young Saudi men is that caused by their habit of resting the left foot on the dashboard, the leg cocked at the knee, or the leg hanging out the driver's side window. The injury resulting from a leg hanging out the window was less severe since the leg was usually merely severed. But there was worse. One evening I was returning from the grocery store located behind the hospital. As employees we would often take a short cut through the emergency room, then through the hospital and on to our compound. That evening I approached ER carrying two grocery bags. I saw my Australian friend Anthony sitting on the nearby loading dock. He was dressed in his white nursing uniform, holding his head in his hands. I approached him, "What's up Anthony? Taking a break?" He always seemed to be on duty when the worst injuries came into the emergency room. He looked up at me. I saw his face was pale and pinched, his eyes shocked and sad. He spoke slowly, "You know how we always see the young Saudi guys driving with their leg on the dashboard? Well now I know what happens when they're involved in an impact collision. Two guys, they're in ER now. The driver hit a metal light pole at about 90 mph. The passenger flew through the windscreen and he's done for. The driver had his leg on the dash and he's almost literally torn in half. The EMTs brought him in with one leg. I don't know where the other leg is and neither do they." I put my hand on his shoulder and whispered, "I'm so sorry you had to experience this." Anthony broke down in tears. "I've been working in emergency rooms for years and I thought I'd seen it all. Half this guy's insides are outside his body, but he's still alive. How can that be?" I sat with Anthony for some time, a compassionate man grieving for the broken young stranger lying in ER.

We later heard the young Saudi man had died. His agony was over.

Lifestyle of the Western Expatriate

Many Western expats sought the relative freedom and comforts of numerous company compounds around Tabuk. Company compounds are like small islands of freedom in a sea of Saudis. British Aerospace, Halliburton, LSI (a system and software company) and Lockheed Martin are a few. The compounds are populated by many different nationalities: Americans, Canadians, French, Irish, German, for the most part. Some compounds contain families, but most house single men on one-year contracts in the Kingdom.

A compound in Saudi Arabia is defined by a self-contained settlement owned by the company the residents work for. The compounds are surrounded by high walls and self-governed by the owner company and its residents. Single men live in furnished apartments or prefab housing, sometimes shared, sometimes single. Other amenities usually include a kitchen and mess hall for those who don't wish to cook in their residence, as well as a recreation center with swimming pool and perhaps tennis courts. The residents of compounds enjoy privileges and freedoms that many other expats cannot expect. Compounds are rarely ever bothered by the Mutawa (religious police) or the Saudi police.

An invitation can usually guarantee relaxation and genuine alcohol for those who want it. (Embassies bring in top brands of alcohol by diplomatic courier and compounds get their alcohol in amongst equipment and supplies intended for the compound residents.) Single women can overnight freely with a boyfriend or married couple. The

Saudi authorities surely know about the activities on compounds, many illegal according to Saudi laws, but they have no jurisdiction.

Vicky and Anya arranged my first invitation to a compound (LSI). In order to be invited we had to know someone personally living on the compound or garner an invite through a friend or acquaintance who knew someone. Many compounds held evening entertainments such as bingo, board games, dances, or karaoke. The date and time of gatherings were spread by word of mouth. The residents normally charged a small fee to sponsor the functions.

Any non-Muslim could attend these functions, but Muslims were often seen as informants, especially Saudis, and were rarely welcome on any compound. Fawzia did accompany me to a few compounds where her religion was overlooked. She was sometimes welcomed for her beauty and fun-loving spirit, but the majority would not tolerate her presence.

As single women we got to the gatherings any way we could. Married couples would often pick us up, or we would take the hospital bus to a point nearest the compound. Taking the bus was risky because we often had to walk part of the way to our destination. The Mutawa knew where the compounds were. Because they could not enter the compounds, they would sometimes lie in wait for us on the way.

A spirit of cooperation existed amongst people living on compounds. Married couples often volunteered to transport single women to parties even if they were strangers. I met lots of new people in this way. Some women specifically sought out a boyfriend living on a compound. This gave single females a place to go on weekends, an escape from the restrictions of the hospital compound. Other people went to compounds just so they could drink good quality alcohol. I was never too interested in the alcohol, or boyfriends, especially so soon after a bitter divorce, but I spent many pleasant evenings at different compounds. It was a pleasure to sit by a sparkling pool, eat barbecue, talk freely to men, and wear whatever I liked. Life felt almost normal for a few hours.

I met several married couples who would often invite me to stay overnight. Most couples had multiple bedrooms in their homes. Other compounds had unoccupied quarters where single women could spend the night after a party. Fawzia and I met a lovely Canadian couple, Mark and Lisa and their two children, who often invited us to their home. They had us over for Thanksgiving and Christmas with turkey and all the trimmings. The Canadian company Mark worked for shipped everything needed for a holiday meal. As a Muslim, this was Fawzia's first time to share Christmas with a Christian family and eat a traditional meal. She was delighted by the experience.

My favorite compound, and one that welcomed Fawzia, was LSI. The compound was located behind Astra supermarket in downtown Tabuk. On party evenings music in the compound could be heard in the parking lot of the supermarket. I'm sure the Saudis were intensely curious. The Mutawa fumed at the fact they could not enter any compounds to subdue and punish the revelers. We usually took the bus to Astra supermarket and then walked round it to gain entrance to LSI. One time we turned the corner to see two Mutawa standing right beside the entrance to LSI. Since we were a group of six girls, we gritted our teeth and pushed right past them on to the safety of LSI. They were livid, screaming at us and waving their sticks. We totally ignored them which made them all the angrier. They dared not hit us so close to the compound or they would have had a riot on their hands. There was no doubt the residents within the compound would come to our assistance.

A group of us regularly attended a Friday evening barbecue at LSI. Sometimes it was just Fawzia and I, but other times Vicky and Anya came with us. LSI housed a mix of married couples and single men. The barbecue cost only 20 Saudi riyals (about US$5.00) and expats from all over Tabuk attended. The meal was prepared and served by Sri Lankan laborers who worked on the LSI compound. They dreamed up fabulous menus and the food was always delicious. The residents of LSI donated the groceries and all proceeds went to the Sri Lankan men who prepared the food.

I noticed an interesting sub-culture at LSI. I'd not expected to come to Saudi and find real-life rednecks hidden away in a compound, but occasionally they appeared at a Friday barbecue. These guys were unapologetic rednecks who made no secret of the fact they hated the Saudis and anyone who wasn't white and American. The entire group was a cliché; scruffy, beer-bellied, middle-aged men wearing plaid shirts and camouflage hunting caps in the heat of the Saudi summer. They each clutched a quart jar of home-made brew.

One evening Vicky came to the barbecue with Fawzia and me. The rednecks made an appearance that night. Vicky noticed them all sitting at a table together. She raised her eyebrows and grinned, "Well now, feast your eyes on them boys over there, honey," she said in her Alabama drawl, "Those fellas are straight outta the hills. Genuine Bubba Boys right here in Tabuk!"

The Bubba Boys weren't the only oddities in a group I referred to as the fringe element. Every compound had its share of strange characters. But a few of the local compounds were decrepit and ill-maintained; it seemed the more broken down the compound, the more tawdry the residents and their functions. They were men who'd been in Saudi for decades, broken down by heat and home brew. I often wondered how these men functioned at their jobs during the day. The vast majority appeared to be terminal alcoholics. They invited only females to their frequent drinking parties, and only a certain type of woman attended the parties, usually hard drinkers themselves. I never wasted my time going to these compounds; the choice between drunks and a quiet evening in my apartment was obvious.

Trish later met a prime example of the fringe element, a man named Phil. Phil belonged to a unique sub-group. These men were usually older British men and seemed to me like modern holdovers from the British colonial era in India, who at that time would have been called "old India hands." Without exception they'd lived in the Middle East for many years and seemed unable to break free from a life that had become neither British nor Saudi. They drank heavily, lived dissipated lives on the margin of expatriate society, hated the Saudis and no longer knew where they belonged. They drank any kind of alcohol available. If they couldn't get genuine brand-name alcohol through a compound they drank home-brewed sid.

Trish appeared excited when she first told me about meeting Phil. "He's older than me, but he likes me," she gushed. Trish did not say anything about liking Phil. The first time I met him I was shocked to find he was one of the fringe element. A British man, much older than Trish, with the used-up look of the incurable alcoholic. His face was deeply wrinkled and leathery from exposure to the harsh Saudi sun. Phil's vivid blue eyes must have been spectacular in his youth, but were now marred by roadmaps of tiny broken veins. His iron grey hair was shaggy and oily, his teeth broken and yellowed from decades of heavy smoking. Phil had lived in Tabuk for more than thirty years and according to Trish he made a living drilling water wells. He lived in downtown Tabuk and to my great surprise Trish moved in with him. A huge risk for a single woman in the Kingdom.

Phil drove Trish to work and picked her up after work. She was terrified that one day the security checkpoint would ask for a marriage license. Unrelated single men and women were forbidden to ride together in a vehicle, let alone live together. I asked Trish, "Why don't you two arrange a Tabuki marriage, if for nothing else but to protect yourself?" She did not look at me directly, "Well, I did ask Phil. He said no way."

I don't know how Trish managed the stress of her living situation. The few occasions I spent any time with Phil and Trish together I was uncomfortable with the demeaning way he spoke to her. He often told her she was fat; he said it with a rather unpleasant smirk. Trish was anything but fat; she was curvy but a normal weight. Phil was no intellectual heavyweight, but he belittled Trish by telling her she was dumb. Trish chose to make light of it. I once asked her, "Trish, why do you let Phil talk to you that way?" She laughed, "Oh he's only joking!" But I noticed Trish fretted about her supposed "weight problem." Her already low self-esteem dropped a few more degrees. Sometimes Phil simply disappeared in the night, presumably to work on a well, and leave Trish to find her own way to work. Not a simple matter when a single female lived off the hospital bus route. When he left town without notice, Trish had to call one of Phil's male friends to take her to work. She'd stay in her compound apartment until he returned home.

Once Trish invited me to visit her and Phil at his apartment. They came to pick me up from the female compound in Phil's ancient Land Rover. He drove to an old section of Tabuk where we pulled up in front of an ancient building. Here Phil lived in a rambling old flat with myriad rooms. I was aghast at their living conditions. When I entered the flat I felt an air of despondency settle over me. From the entry a long narrow room stretched to a distant kitchen in the back of the flat. Bare light bulbs of low wattage lent a gloomy aura. Coils of sticky fly strips hung dejectedly from the ceiling, thick with corpses of long-dead insects. The floor was covered in an expanse of ancient, scuffed linoleum pocked with holes; it was impossible to tell what color or pattern it might once have been. Years of ground-in layers of dirt and neglect suggested little more than despair had ever lived here. The smell of stale alcohol and cigarette smoke dominated. Phil kept a still in one of the many rooms where he made his own alcohol with whatever resources were available. Trish looked embarrassed, "I try hard to clean up this place, but it's a lost cause." I knew Trish could never clean enough to make the place livable. Phil told me he had a roommate, a young Saudi man who worked with him drilling the water wells. He apparently lived in one of the rooms in the flat, but I never saw him.

Trish went out of her way to make a nice meal that evening. Once we entered the flat Phil disappeared somewhere within the countless rooms. Trish started out by apologizing, "I'm sorry, but he'll be drunk most of the evening, so just try to ignore him." I gave her a quick hug, "Don't worry about Phil. It's nice to be able to spend some time with you." I helped Trish in the kitchen and saw she had contrived a delicious Western-style meal in my honor: meatloaf with mashed potatoes, gravy, and even corn on the cob. We did not see Phil again until we sat down to eat. By then he was reeling drunk. He was usually civil to me, even when drunk. I found the meal delicious and thanked Trish for making some of my favorite comfort foods. Phil proclaimed the meat dry and the gravy tasteless. He said, "We don't eat this sort of slop in England." Trish reddened and shouted at him, "If you don't like it don't eat it!" I felt embarrassed and hurt for Trish's sake. Why did she put up with this awful man?

After supper Phil located some movies and pulled out an ancient video player. We watched a movie or two, which would have been pleasant but for Phil snoring drunkenly on the couch beside Trish and me.

Trish had invited me to stay overnight and showed me to a bedroom in the back of the flat. The room was furnished with a broken lamp and a mattress on the floor. At least I had a blanket. My company that night consisted of the dry husks of long-dead cockroaches and other deceased insects scattered throughout the room. But to my surprise I slept well.

The following morning Trish surprised me with an American-style breakfast with eggs and real bacon. Phil had somehow acquired a closet full of K-rations from U.S. troops during Operation Desert Storm. Most of the packages contained ham and bacon. Phil, looking blurry and hung-over, gave me two precious packages of bacon. I thanked him and told him I appreciated the delicious gesture.

When Trish finally left the Kingdom she entrusted her possessions to Phil. He promised to ship them to her once she was settled in her hometown of Sacramento, California. He also told Trish he would visit her in California, even making mention of the possibility of marriage. When I saw Trish again, several years later, she had neither received her possessions nor a marriage proposal. I thought it fortunate she never married Phil.

Women who hooked up with members of the fringe element seemed to consider themselves fortunate to date a Western man. Bad habits and smarmy conduct were overlooked as long as he was a Western male.

These same women looked down on females who dated men from a different culture. Sadly, it was in this way my friendship with Trish ended. When I immigrated to the United States, I could hardly wait to call and tell her about the wonderful man I'd met while living in United Arab Emirates, the man who became my husband.

Trish was thrilled for me until the question of his nationality came up.

When I told her he was Syrian she was outraged. She shouted at me angrily, "How could you marry an Arab? And a Muslim on top of it all! He'll get a passport out of you and then disappear." I told Trish of our genuine love for each other and that our commitment was real. But she had already passed judgment. She made it clear she didn't want to hear from me again. Seventeen years later my husband and I are still together. I think of it as a loss for Trish who lost a friend because she could not (and would not) look past what she perceived as an insurmountable cultural divide.

I ran into this mind set repeatedly. I knew women who'd been taken advantage of by passport hunters, but I knew from the beginning my husband was different. I later worked at a hospital in the United Arab Emirates. From time to time I would run into a British dietician named Margaret, who worked in the same hospital. She often complained about how difficult it was to meet a nice man, "Every bloody male expat I've met here is a loser. They're either drunks, already married, or psychos!"

One day Margaret asked me if I'd had any luck in meeting decent men. I told her I'd met what I termed a "keeper", my future husband. She reacted with excitement and was filled with questions. How had I met a nice man in the Middle East? Then she asked me where he was from. When I said Syria, her face collapsed. Margaret's smile turned into an ugly sneer and she said, "Oh, so he's a bloody wog then. I really don't understand women like you." She immediately dismissed him and our relationship.

As a single woman in Tabuk I sometimes envied wives who lived on the newer and more luxurious compounds. Initially I viewed them as fortunate to live in their self-contained world of freedom. But in fact many of the wives suffered greatly and their lives were often difficult. It takes a strong woman, single or married, to endure life in the Kingdom. Some wives give up great jobs to accompany their husbands to Saudi Arabia. Some find a local job when they arrive in Saudi Arabia with their husband, especially if they are nurses or other types of medical personnel.

But those without an outside job suddenly find themselves isolated in a closed society with little to do. Most compounds have a driver assigned to chauffeur wives around town because their husbands often work long hours. They go out to shop or buy groceries. But they endure long stretches of idleness and boredom. There is little for the women to do on the compounds except cook, swim, socialize or take care of children if they have any. Some brought their hobbies with them. Marriages shatter when wives finally break under the strain of neglectful husbands, monotony, and the loneliness for family and the familiar things back home.

Some women turn to alcohol and then take the problem home with them. Extramarital affairs occur, especially among husbands who have the freedom to drive and see expats at other compounds. Occasionally I recognized someone's husband at an outside function, not accompanied by their wives. The Western expat community in Tabuk and even in larger Saudi cities is small and insular. It is almost impossible to hide any personal activities.

I saw too many marriages break up for good because a wife could not stand the strain and simply went home. If her husband allowed her to do so.

An odd Danish doctor worked in the OB/GYN department. Given his temper and bullying nature, Gabrielle and I sometimes wondered what his wife might deal with in the home. Dr. Larsen was a bulky dour man of about fifty who never smiled. His taciturn and silent manner hid a temper that could flare in a moment. He often tried to intimidate Gabrielle into doing his routine clerical work before that of others who had already asked, even Dr. Hoey. Gabrielle held her own with him and never set a precedent by accommodating him. He once became so angry he threw the papers he was holding on the floor and stomped out of the office. He slammed the door so hard the entire room shook.

Dr. Larsen and his wife and son had been living in Tabuk for many years. Although we rarely ever saw Birgitte Larsen, we knew she was a striking woman with icy blonde hair and exquisite blue eyes. On the rare occasions we saw Dr. Larsen downtown with his wife, she was dressed in full Saudi regalia with abaya, scarf, and face covered, save for the arresting blue eyes. We always wondered if she chose to dress this way in public or whether her husband forced her to do so. Of course gossip abounded about Birgitte's life with him, that he was insanely jealous of her as well as physically and mentally abusive.

It being Saudi, if Birgitte wanted to leave her husband, she was not free to do so. Even expatriate wives had to produce written permission from their husbands in order to travel outside the country. The Saudi authorities would never allow a married woman, Saudi or otherwise, to travel without their husband's consent. It was likely that many expat wives were trapped in unbearable domestic situations they could not escape.

The Larsens had only one child, a son named Eric. He was born in Saudi Arabia and save for holidays in Denmark, he'd never lived anywhere else. Eric was already sixteen years old and did not attend school. He'd attended public school in Tabuk until the eighth grade. After an expatriate's child has completed eighth grade in Tabuk, their parents must send them off to boarding school, usually in their home country. No higher education is offered to expatriate children in the Kingdom. However, there is no Saudi law that demands an expat parent send their child outside for higher education.

Gabrielle once worked up the courage to ask Dr. Larsen whether Eric was home-schooled by him or Birgitte. "There is no need," he said in his sour, abrupt way, "Eric is getting life experience. It is enough for him." We had no idea what Eric did to occupy himself. We often saw him wandering alone downtown or on the military base. He was a peculiar young man, tall and silent like his father, with the same brooding manner. When we did encounter him in person he would duck into a doorway or otherwise try to avoid speaking to anyone. I was dismayed at the fact this young man was allowed to go without higher schooling.

When I left Tabuk, Eric had just turned eighteen and seemed no closer to going off for further education. I wondered what would happen to this unfortunate young man when his family finally returned to Denmark. What would he do for a living? I visualized his irresponsible father supporting him for the rest of his life.

A Jordanian Adventure

I'd recently made a new friend named Donna who'd just arrived in Tabuk two weeks earlier. She was a vivacious middle-aged blonde with intriguing green eyes and a devil-may-care outlook on life. She appeared in our office one day with a big grin on her round, pretty face. "A bunch of hospital employees are organizing a trip to Aqaba, Jordan next weekend for four days. We're going to Petra too. Ya wanna come along?" she asked in her relaxed Canadian accent. What exciting news! Petra was at the top of my list of sights to see. It's an amazing ancient city located in the south of Jordan. I'd always loved archeology and to visit this magnificent site was a dream come true. I smiled at Donna, "Count me in!"

I turned to Gabrielle "Come on Gab, you need to come along and see Petra too."

"You know I'd love to go," Gabrielle said, "but I'm still not feeling up to a long trip." I was disappointed for I knew she also dreamed of seeing Petra. But, she was still recovering from a bad bout of flu that had laid her low for the past two weeks.

Aqaba is a resort city of about 90,000 people on the northern tip of the Red Sea. Modern Aqaba caters to tourists from all over the world. Jordan is generally considered liberal and progressive by standards of neighboring Middle Eastern countries. It is a secular country, but still more conservative than Westerners are used to. Aqaba is also the site of Lawrence of Arabia's most famous battle. (During World War I

Lawrence and his five hundred allied Bedouin tribesmen drove the occupying Turks from their foothold on the Gulf of Aqaba.) As a matter of interest, the Gulf of Aqaba is part of the Great Rift Valley that begins in East Africa and has been inhabited since about 4000 BCE.

Most of the group planned to travel to Jordan on a small bus provided by the hospital recreation center, but Donna insisted we treat ourselves to a private car. She'd found us a driver by the name of Mohammed, a plump elderly Saudi gentleman with sparkling humorous eyes. He came highly recommended by other hospital staff who utilized his service. He drove an older model Pontiac sedan so clean he must have washed it every day. Mohammed was proud of his beloved car and called it "Blue Lightning." Apparently the delightful old fellow kept a second wife in Aqaba whom he visited often, so he supplemented his income by taking tourists on his trips. The hospital administrators were well aware of Mohammed's sideline business, and strictly speaking single women should not have been in the car with him. But in yet another of the odd contradictions that define life in Saudi, the hospital administration chose to look the other way.

Mohammed picked us up at our compound on a Thursday afternoon for the 130-mile trip to Jordan. Donna and I shared the ride with Anna, an Australian nurse with a quiet, warm manner. At the last moment an Irish nurse named Maeve joined us. None of us knew her well, but she'd heard about us taking a private car to Aqaba and asked Donna if she could share the ride. That was fine with Donna because we could then split the cost four ways. Maeve turned out to be a pleasant woman, but rather odd. She barely spoke, but when she did a flurry of Gaelic, her native tongue, spilled out. Most Irish people I met in Saudi were fluent in Gaelic, a beautiful language, but I didn't understand a word. Maeve apologized and told us she was from a tiny village in County Cork where English was the second language. She said wherever she was her first inclination was always to speak Gaelic.

Mohammed kept us entertained the entire journey with his hilarious jokes in broken English. He was the first Saudi I met who could laugh at himself and the ridiculous antics of his countrymen. Mohammed was also respectful and polite. He treated us like ladies, rushing around the car to open doors for us. Just before dusk we dropped down from the twisty mountain road to a vista of sparkling turquoise water, the Gulf of Aqaba. There before us, at the northeastern tip of the Red Sea, was the confluence point of three different countries: Saudi Arabia, Jordan, and Israel.

As yet we were still several miles from the Saudi-Jordanian border. As Mohammed drove on we could see the city of Aqaba in the near distance, tucked into a cove surrounded by mountains on three sides. We were just in time to savor a spectacular sunset over the distant mountains, dusted with hues of persimmon and rose.

A few minutes later we arrived at the border. Saudi customs consisted of a large square building clad with corrugated steel siding. Long open porticos, supported by aluminum pillars and roofed with the same corrugated steel siding, stretched along either side of the building. Bright fluorescent tubes lit the underside of the porticos. The entire area around the customs building, including a sprawling parking lot, was awash in bright light cast by towering street lights. It was by now almost dark and the recreation center bus had not yet arrived.

Mohammed parked the car under one of the porticos and we all climbed out. It was clear that many of the customs agents knew him as they came forward to greet him with handshakes. We were thankful for Mohammed, who did his best to smooth our crossing into Jordan, but we were still delayed more than an hour on the Saudi side by three insolent Saudi agents. They were gawky young men barely out of their teenage years. Their official green uniforms were ill-fitting, sweat-stained and wrinkled. Our passports were passed endlessly between the three of them as they grinned and smirked at us. They asked Mohammed to unload our luggage from the trunk of his car. Then, with great relish, the agents proceeded to search our suitcases thoroughly. Our clothing soon lay in a heap on the concrete sidewalk. One especially curious youth pulled out various items to examine them more closely. He appeared fascinated by the tampons he found in Anna's bag. She blushed with embarrassment. None of us was about to explain tampons to this repressed and naïve young man. None of them spoke English anyway. Donna, intimidated by nothing, saw Anna's embarrassment and stepped over to the young agent. She grabbed the tampons from his hands and shouted, "Ever heard of the three stooges? You morons are the Saudi version!" They grinned foolishly at Donna, not having understood a word.

The customs boys soon got bored with our suitcases. We picked up our scattered possessions and stuffed them back in our luggage. Mohammed eventually took our passports into the customs building to be stamped with an exit visa. We four women sat down on the curb by his car to wait it out. Nearby we saw a dismantled car. Donna joked and gestured at the car, "We only have to put our stuff back in our suitcases. The poor bugger who owns that car will have to put the entire thing back together when these jokers are done with it."

"The owner is probably rotting in a Saudi jail somewhere," I said, "He'll never see the light of day again."

We were anxious to get into Jordan where we could enjoy three days of relative freedom.

Nearby a scabrous German Shepherd sniffer dog panted on the pavement, perhaps hoping for a car full of drugs to arrive and alleviate his boredom. Finally Mohammed returned from the customs building and handed us our passports. We spoke briefly with him about our return trip and then said goodbye. From there we walked through no-man's land, a quarter-mile concrete walkway between Saudi Arabia and Jordan. The walkway was brightly lit by more of the tall street lights and lined by a high metal fence bristling with razor wire.

Stepping into Jordan was like a cool waterfall washing over our repressed souls. The stress of our hermetically-sealed existence in Saudi fell away like magic. The freedom of Jordan was more felt than seen. A world altogether different from Saudi started at Jordanian customs. As we approached the entrance to the customs building, a smartly-uniformed agent greeted us, "You are all most welcome to our beautiful country." Our entry was handled with efficiency and smiles. Within ten minutes the four of us were outside choosing from a fleet of taxis parked nearby. The four of us climbed into an ancient Peugeot driven by an enthusiastic young man who greeted us in English, "Welcome to Jordan! My name is Ali." We asked Ali to take us to the Aquamarina Hotel where Donna had made reservations for us. Soon we were driving through an industrialized area of Aqaba. The two-lane road was bumper-to-bumper with tanker trucks. Our taxi slowed to a crawl. Ali told us the trucks traveled back and forth from Iraq twenty-four hours a day delivering oil to tanker ships waiting in the Gulf of Aqaba.

At last we pulled up in front of our hotel. We were all excited about staying at a real hotel with bars, restaurants, a swimming pool and even a nightclub. The hotel was located right on the water of the Gulf of Aqaba. Donna and I were soon relaxing with cold gin and tonics as the warm waters of the Gulf lapped at our feet. I sighed with pleasure, "Peace, perfect peace." After almost six months in Saudi Arabia it is hard to describe the joy of such a simple activity. We noticed some Jordanian women garbed in black as they strolled on the beach with their families. But over the weekend we noticed that younger Jordanian ladies tended to dress in colorful outfits with pastel scarves covering their hair.

At last, the remainder of our group arrived in the recreation center bus. They swarmed into the bar, full of stories of their experience at the Saudi-Jordanian border. Because their group was larger the Saudi border agents kept them for over two hours, opened everyone's cases and generally made an entertainment of it. I suspect every Western tourist who used this border crossing was treated to the same nonsense.

Donna and I finished our gin and tonics and then realized we were ravenous. By then Maeve and Anna, both of whom took a short nap in their hotel rooms, made an appearance. We asked them to come along for dinner. The front desk staff recommended a restaurant, a tiny place right on the water of the Gulf of Aqaba. The concierge summoned a taxi for us and once again an old Peugeot showed up at the hotel entrance. The driver, Ziad, was a friendly young man. He told us he'd just returned from working in Saudi. Ziad grinned when he found out we'd just come from there, "Those Saudis, they are crazy people!" Donna shouted from the back seat, "Ziad, can I drive your taxi? You know women can't drive in Saudi!" Maeve and Anna, both shy women, giggled at Donna's audacity. Ziad smiled, stopped the car, and graciously allowed Donna to drive for a few miles. When he took over the wheel again he slowed to turn down a steep hill then rolled to a stop in front of a flat-roofed building. This was our restaurant. Its roof and windows were lit with strings of cheerful holiday lights though it was not Christmas season. I often saw the same seasonal lights displayed in businesses in Tabuk. The colorful lights that Westerners used only during the Christmas season were popular as an everyday decoration here. Anna and Maeve made arrangements with Ziad to come pick us up in two hours while Donna and I headed into the restaurant.

The manager of the restaurant, a distinguished-looking elderly man with salt-and-pepper hair, welcomed us to his establishment. The restaurant served only fish and he led us to a huge tank filled with different varieties. The manager explained the culinary virtues of each fish and asked us to make our choice. The chef would prepare it any way we wished. I ordered my fish deep-fried whole with only salt and pepper to season it.

A waiter stepped forward and led us to a table on the beach, the water near our feet. The evening was cool and we were glad we'd worn sweaters at the suggestion of the hotel staff. I was alarmed when a soldier dressed in a blue camouflage uniform quietly walked past us on the beach holding a gun. I never quite became accustomed to soldiers with guns though I encountered them all over the Middle East. Our waiter told us the soldiers patrolled the beaches twenty-four hours a day. It was then I realized the proximity of Israel in this tension-filled corner of the world.

Our marvelous meal soon arrived, each plate holding a freshly fried fish. The fish was perfectly cooked, the meat delicately white and flaky. Our waiter also brought dishes of hummus, "moutabel" (eggplant dip), sliced fresh vegetables and fragrant discs of Arabic bread still warm from the oven. We asked our waiter if it was possible to have an alcoholic drink. We'd been served alcohol openly in the hotel bar, but here in the restaurant it was handled delicately so as not to offend Muslim families eating nearby. The waiter brought our gin disguised in a little metal teapot with tonic on the side. We gorged ourselves on the delicious food, made all the better by the freedom we felt. After our meal the manager approached. "Would you lovely ladies like to smoke shisha (a water pipe)?

The tobacco flavors we have tonight are apple and cherry." Donna and I chimed in together, "Oh yes please! We'll try the cherry flavor."

I'd smoked a water pipe previously at the Bedouin souq in Tabuk and found I liked it. In my years following stays in Saudi and the United Arab Emirates, and on my return to Canada, I smoked shisha regularly (also known as hubbly-bubbly, nargile or hookah depending on the country.) It is admittedly an unhealthy habit, but there are few activities more relaxing than sitting on the floor with friends, drinking mint tea and smoking hubbly-bubbly. I brought several water pipes back to North America with me. The fruity tobacco and charcoal needed to enjoy the pipes is readily available in Arab import stores in larger cities in Canada and the United States.

That evening Donna and I went to the Aquamarina nightclub and danced late into the night. We avoided drinking any more alcohol because we were off to Petra in the morning. Anna and Maeve did not accompany us to the nightclub because neither was comfortable in a bar scene. I felt as if I were in a nightclub in any Western country. The same loud music, dancing, sweating bodies, and lots of laughter. Donna and I met several new and interesting people that evening, both local and expatriates. We talked at length with a pleasant middle-aged man, Jordanian by birth, but living in Italy. He gave us his business card which described him as an independent film producer by the name of Omer Hadad. He told us his specialty was making documentaries and that he traveled widely. What we found odd was the fact Omer had his little daughter with him whom he introduced as Habiba. She could not have been more than seven or eight years old, a beautiful child with a serious, mature countenance. Nothing was said about a mother or where she might be. Omer must have realized Donna and I were curious about why he brought his daughter with him to a nightclub. He shrugged fatalistically, "It is only Habiba and I. There is no one else to care for her. I cannot leave her in the hotel by herself." Donna had a way with kids and she soon had Habiba chattering and laughing. We didn't know if we should feel sorry or not for the child with her father's itinerant lifestyle.

Donna and I felt embarrassed by the obnoxious antics of another group of Western expats from Saudi. One expat group was loud and foul-mouthed. I encountered many expatriates, not just in the Middle East, who seem to feel bad behavior is okay because they're in a foreign country.

Over the weekend Donna and I walked around downtown Aqaba. Several store owners expressed disgust at the antics of some tourists who visit Aqaba. Many come to Aqaba for the sole purpose of unlimited alcohol consumption. But Western tourists are not the only ones guilty of outrageous behavior. They also mentioned the young Saudi men who come to Aqaba to drink and pursue female tourists. The fact that Jordanian women did not cover completely like Saudi women also made them fair game in the male Saudi mind.

Donna and I reluctantly left the nightclub fairly early that night. But we wanted to be sure we were alert for our trip to Petra the following morning.

Some of our group from Tabuk came to Aqaba to dive. It's one of the finest spots in the world for it. Anna planned to visit Petra the day after Donna and I, but Maeve? Well, we had no idea what Maeve was up to. But Donna and I rose before dawn for our trip to Petra.

The poet John William Burgon wrote about the ancient city of Petra: *"A rose-red city half as old as time."*

Petra is an enchanting city in the south of Jordan, declared a UNESCO world heritage site in 1985. The city was built by the Nabatean culture which began settling the area in the fourth century BCE, but historians believe settlements have existed in the area since about 1200 BCE.

Petra is said to be the site where Moses struck the rock and water spouted forth for the Israelites. In addition to natural springs, the Nabateans were able to harness rainwater with a system of dams and cisterns.

In this way Petra became the center of the commercial and spice trade routes at the time. It became wealthy and powerful by collecting tariffs from the traders and providing them food and shelter. The city began its decline after the Roman Empire occupied it in 106 CE, as by then

Palmyra in Syria had become a more important trading center. Petra was nearly destroyed by an earthquake in 363 CE, and after that the ancient city was lost to Europeans for centuries. But the Bedouin have always lived there. Petra was re-discovered by the explorer Johann Burckhardt in 1812.

To reach Petra our entire group had to split up and share taxis. The way to Petra is a 60-mile drive on a winding, dangerous two-lane road to its nearest town of Wadi Musa (Valley of Moses). I shared a taxi with Donna and Steve, a respiratory therapist from Australia. At the time Wadi Musa essentially consisted of a quiet village and one sleepy old hotel. Today, I understand, there are enormous chain hotels, fast food, and large tour buses disgorging hundreds of tourists. I am thankful I did not have to experience any of this during my visit. I think I would have cried if I'd found fast food restaurants defacing such an ancient, beautiful place.

On the way to Petra we passed near Wadi Rum (The Valley of the Moon), the dramatic setting where Lawrence of Arabia based his operations during the Arab Revolt in 1917. I think Wadi Rum is one of the most breathtakingly beautiful places on earth. It is an ancient, mysterious valley lined by terracotta sandstone and granite rock formations. A vast promenade of rose-gold sand winds between the rock battlements. Mountains and wind-sculpted rock formations line the valley, silent sentinels enrobed in lavender-indigo haze.

T.E. Lawrence described it best in his book, "Seven Pillars of Wisdom": *"Rum the magnificent… vast echoing and Godlike… a processional way greater than imagination… the crimson sunset burned on its stupendous cliffs and slanted ladders of hazy fire down its walled avenue…"*

Petra is a massive site, once home to some 20,000 inhabitants. When I visited the city, the only way in was on foot or on a horse (or camel) hired from locals. I chose to ride a horse, a lovely creature with the delicate concave face of the Arabian steed and a satiny copper-colored hide. She was led the entire way by her owner, a local Bedouin man. The desert Bedouin who live in the area have made a business of guiding tourists, now their main source of income. My guide spoke no English, but we managed. He looked a true desert dweller with a deeply lined face, the skin leathery and tough. While some, like me, opted to be led on horseback, Donna and other members of our group walked.

We started off on a rocky trail, through a shallow valley, that would lead us to the city of Petra. Here the surrounding rocks and cliffs are mainly dull, grey-black basalt. All of a sudden the guide turned right and we passed through a great fissure in the rock. This was the actual entrance to Petra, the "Siq" (literal translation is "shaft"). The cleft had not been visible until we were literally turning into it. Towering golden cliffs immediately rose up on each side of us, some as high as 600 feet. Vertical streaks of dark minerals adorned the cliff faces.

The Siq is one of two entrances to Petra. It is a long narrow canyon, a geologic fault that split centuries ago. No wonder this particular entrance to Petra was so easily defended in ancient times. The walls are smooth and rounded by centuries of water erosion. All along the close canyon walls run channels and large water reservoirs hand-hewn from the rock to capture rainfall. Amazing engineering accomplishments by the Nabateans. The trail through the Siq was rough and uneven, strewn with stones of all sizes. Since my visit the length of this passage has been excavated, dropping it more than six feet, and then flagged with flat stones in a manner to appear ancient. As genuine as the pavement now looks, it is in fact modern.

As we moved forward, the cliffs narrowed overhead so as to nearly touch. In some places there was little room for the horse to pass; I had to dip my head so not to hit it on the stone walls immediately above me. Other than the sharp clatter of the horse's metal shoes striking stones, the Siq was cool and still.

Just when I thought we might forever be in the dark gorge, the trail made a sudden small turn to the left, and we slipped out of the shadows. There in front of us, framed in the narrow cleft in the rock, glowing rose-gold in the early morning sunshine, was Petra's most magnificent tomb, "The Khazneh" (The Treasury). There are thousands upon thousands of photos of The Treasury, but none can do justice to the color and grandeur of the real thing. It felt surreal to me that I was actually here, seeing this wonder. As we emerged from the narrow confines of the Siq we entered a larger, wider canyon. Now the Khazneh, carved from the native sandstone rock face about two thousand years ago, its façade highly decorated with friezes and statues, towered 130 feet above us. The magnificent structure, protected in its little canyon, looked as if its builders and carvers had packed up and left the day before. I sat on my horse and stared, so overwhelmed I forgot to get my camera out for photos.

The Bedouin owner indicated he and his horse would return that evening to take me back. I slid off my horse and looked down. The sand under my feet, and throughout much of Petra, is salmon-pink and seemed to glow, as the Treasury does, in the morning light. First I wanted to see what was inside the structure. I climbed the wide, red-stone steps and entered the dark and quiet Treasury. I was surprised to find only one huge room with two smaller rooms off the back.

Because of its magnificence many archeologists believe The Treasury to be the tomb for the last king of Petra, Aretas III. In recent years a Jordanian archeologist figured that the ground level in front of the structure must have been much lower thousands of years ago. So he excavated beneath the plaza in front of The Treasury and discovered another level. There he found subterranean chambers containing eleven tombs, probably those of the Nabatean monarch and his family.

From my vantage point on the Treasury steps I looked back across the canyon to locate the Siq we'd just exited. I was hard-pressed to find it, the entrance so narrow it all but blended into the rock face.

A few minutes later our official guide joined us at The Treasury. Hamdi was a short, stocky young man, with a round face that contrasted with a long, sharp nose. His English was heavily accented but precise. After introducing himself, Hamdi led our group off on foot. I would have been intimidated had I known how arduous the day's journey would be.

Hamdi led us to a cliff face that towered above us. He pointed up and said to our group of nine, "There is the High Place of Sacrifice. This is difficult climb up and down. Some of you will have problem. Go slow, take care." Donna and I looked up at the hundreds of steps carved out of the stone. They climbed ever higher up the cliff and disappeared somewhere above. Donna gulped and looked at me, "Holy hell, are you kidding me?" Both of us wondered how we were going to make it up there. We had no idea we would be required to climb what turned out to be some seven hundred fifty steps!

Hamdi led the main part of the group up the steps. I said to Donna, "Come on, you can do it. We don't want to miss anything." But Donna had already made up her mind, "Forget it. I'm going to stay on the ground and go the long way." There was another more level path to the center of Petra, but it was much longer and probably not nearly so scenic. Donna and I parted company. "I'll see you on the other side," I called as she trotted off.

As I started my climb, I realized being alone was a blessing. I had the trail to myself. The stillness and quiet belonged to me alone. It was a fortunate day for our group as few other tourists were visiting Petra. I made my way slowly upwards, occasionally stopping to gaze at the winding steps below and turquoise sky above. I had to watch my footing carefully though. The steps were worn and in some places quite slick with fine sand.

About half way up the steps I came upon an ancient Bedouin lady perched on a massive rock. She stood up to greet me, grinning and cackling, and patted me in sympathy. I must have looked weary for she made me sit down and hovered over me like a mother hen. She offered me a bottle of 7-Up and I guzzled the warm, sweet liquid in seconds. I was sure this elderly lady scampered up and down these steps every day, putting my youth to shame. I suspected she looked older than her true age. She was a diminutive old woman, her skin sun-darkened and deeply furrowed. Her forehead and chin were decorated with indigo tribal tattoos. Every time she smiled a mouthful of gold teeth flashed in the bright sunshine. Her hands were knobby and sinewy, hardened from years of toil. She wore a plain full-length dress of faded black cotton. It was decorated with a narrow strip of brilliant embroidery that extended from neck to hem. Spare grey hair peaked from under a loosely-tied black cotton scarf.

I sat with the woman for a few minutes and we communicated as best we could. I gave the ancient crone a handful of Jordanian dinars and continued my upward journey. Before I left she tried to sell me some artifacts, but Hamdi had warned us about clever counterfeits.

Closer to the summit I began to meet stragglers from our group, puffing and red-faced from the climb. Finally I stood at the top. Before me were massive flat stones laid out in a square with channels cut between each of the stones. Hamdi, now at the top with the rest of our group, told us the channels might have been drains for blood. No one is certain of the specific rituals performed here, but it is thought the Nabateans may have sacrificed animals. I gazed around me and could see for miles in every direction. The view was breathtaking. An almost infinite vista of gnarled massifs and rounded rock formations stretched to the horizon, then disappeared in a diaphanous haze. At this altitude the wind was cool and refreshing. I sat down on the stones, warm from the sun, and imagined what it might have been like centuries ago. The spirits of the ancients were all around, in the rock, the wind, the air around me.

Hamdi and most of the group had started down the opposite side of the High Place of Sacrifice. Once again he warned us, "This side more danger, very steep, few steps. Take care." I looked down over the edge of the cliff and sighed. I saw little more than collections of rocks and crags. I started down. It was fortunate I didn't fear heights or the descent would have been terrifying. The vestige of a trail zigzagged down the cliff, so steep it was like descending a ladder. Hamdi was right; there were few actual steps. Just large boulders, ledges of granite, and crumbly shelves of sandstone that slipped and crumbled under my booted feet. In some places I slid down on my backside for fear of falling.

All the way down the sheer cliff I was dazzled by row upon row of vivid bands of color in the rock. One of the most beautiful features of Petra, aside from the amazing facades and tombs, are the astonishing colors of sandstone throughout the city. Brilliant striations of russet, cream, black, and orange flash where the native rosy pink stone is carved and gouged.

Finally I reached the bottom of the valley, my legs shaking from the vertical descent. More Bedouins greeted me with warm sodas and so-called artifacts, but again I refused a purchase. I saw some of our group in the distance, but I did not try to catch up. I believe I enjoyed the hike more because I was not part of the group. I felt like I had Petra all to myself.

Spread out before me was a craggy valley of salmony gold sand strewn with large boulders and scrubby green bushes. All around me, near and far, the towering red cliff faces were lined with hundreds of small tombs carved out of the rock. Most were at a great height above the valley floor, but I thought they might have been closer to the ground in ancient times. Almost all displayed elaborately etched facades. Occasionally I saw a large open room cut out of the colorful rock. These rooms appeared utilitarian in purpose, with pillars and stone benches inside. Each room displayed the exposed bands of colorful sandstone found everywhere in Petra.

As I walked, ceramic potsherds shattered under my feet. The delicate remains of Nabatean vessels carpeted the ground. I picked up some of the pieces to examine them more closely. The workmanship was sophisticated, the ochre-colored shards astonishingly thin with dark red painted designs.

It was now early afternoon and the sun blazed in the cerulean dome of the sky. The red cliffs receded into the distance and I found myself near Petra's geographical center. I stopped to sit on a boulder while others passed by. I felt humbled and moved by this enchanted place. The air was still, tranquil in the afternoon heat. A dusty green fragrance, not unlike sage, suffused the air. Lake-like mirages trembled in the distance, inviting the unwary to seek their treacherous deception. I watched a tiny bronze lizard dart on to a nearby rock. We looked at each other, and I thought he was a lucky fellow to live here in this magical place. He flicked his tail and dashed off in a flash.

The city proper of Petra is spread across a low, wide valley and the Nabateans had to build walls on the north and south to prevent invasion from enemies. After I walked on, I began to see massive, free-standing stone structures with Roman-influenced carvings. Further on a megalithic pillar stood in solitude, surrounded by paving stones that may have been a floor or road. I imagined an ancient temple or grandiose home. The stone floor was hemmed with toppled pillars matching the single one left standing. Perhaps, centuries ago, a roof had been in place.

Nearby was the Temple of the Winged Lions (lions are an oft repeated architectural theme in Petra.) Finally I found myself in what was once the heart of the city. There stood a few walls, once part of a structure called "Qasr al Bint" (Palace of the Daughter), said to have been built for the daughter of a Nabatean king. It must have been a magnificent structure in its time. To one side was a handsome paved street with colonnades along both sides. Over the centuries, many of the huge columns had fallen. This gave me the opportunity to look closely at the inscriptions and exquisite carvings on the stone.

When Christianity reached Petra in the third and fourth centuries, many of the Nabatean tombs were converted into churches. I saw remains of stunningly intricate mosaic floors and Byzantine-style Christian symbols. Petra must have seen generations of gifted builders and artisans.

I found the rest of our group in front of an innocuous-looking structure: a cafeteria nestled under a shelf of rock so as to give the least offense in the ancient setting. And there was Donna sitting on a bench in the shade. "I wasn't sure I'd see you again!" she joked. "What was it like when you got to the top of those stairs?" I laughed, "Well, it wasn't easy getting up there, but the incredible view was worth it. The trail down the other side was a nightmare. Made the seven hundred fifty steps up look like a walk in the park!" Donna shuddered. "I'm so glad I didn't attempt it. I might have made it up those steps, but I would have frozen when I saw the way down. I'd have been terrified." Then I asked her about the route she took. "It sure was a long walk," Donna admitted, "but at least it was all on level ground!"

With that we walked into the cool, dim cafeteria. All the basics were available: water, juice, sodas, small snacks and the ubiquitous squat toilets. To quench our fierce thirst, we guzzled huge quantities of refreshing water and juice.

As Donna and I walked back outside, Hamdi was announcing another hike to the Monastery. He led a much smaller group now because this was the most difficult journey of the day. Hamdi described the trail to the

Monastery, "This is very high place, more than High Place of Sacrifice. Think carefully about it. If you think you cannot get there, do not try." Even some of the fitter members of the group realized their limitations and begged off the trip. Donna and I also declined.

The Monastery group would not return for a couple of hours so the rest of us relaxed. I took the opportunity to look at tombs in the immediate area and picked up beautiful stones as souvenirs for myself.

After about two hours, the group returned exhausted from their climb to the Monastery. They murmured about the beauty of the ancient building, but that the hike had been tremendously challenging. One weary member told us, "At one point we had to climb a rope ladder." I hated to miss anything, but I was so glad I hadn't attempted to see the lofty Monastery. By then it was early evening. The shadows had grown long and the setting sun glanced off the red cliffs in a lustrous display of apricot-rose. But the wind was bitterly cold and we walked briskly to meet our waiting guides and horses. I was deliciously tired and so glad to see my horse that I hugged her.

By the time we reached the Siq to leave Petra there was just light enough to see the Treasury. It stood as it had for centuries, eerie and silent in the dusk. I could almost feel the spirits of the ancients watching as we passed by. It was by now completely dark, but the horses and guides knew their way. One of the guides moved to the front of the group carrying a lantern, a winking firefly of soft yellow light beckoning us home. The locals and their horses live on tourist donations so I gave my guide a generous contribution. A fleet of taxis waited at Wadi Musa. Donna, Steve and I again shared a taxi back to Aqaba. I don't remember the drive back to Aqaba for I slept deeply the entire trip. A splendid, special day I will never forget.

The following morning Donna and I dragged ourselves out of bed, sunburned and exhausted from our day in Petra. But we wanted to go to downtown Aqaba and shop. Fortified by a breakfast of fresh bread, fruit, and tea, we walked downtown. The weather was warm and sunny, though quite humid. We could have taken a taxi, but we didn't want to miss anything along the way. As Donna and I reached the city center, shop owners came to their doorways to greet us and invite us for tea. Though

Aqaba caters to tourists no one pushed their wares on us. In one shop we were greeted by a stunningly handsome middle-aged man named Rafik. He claimed to have been the double for Omar Sharif in the film *Lawrence of Arabia*.

At first we doubted, but he soon produced his movie still-photos. His resemblance to Omar Sharif's character was striking. Rafik was probably in his late fifties with the flashing dark eyes and chiseled features of the legendary Sharif. Rafik proceeded to dress up in his dashing movie costume, then dressed us in similar Arabian costumes. "Let's play dress-up!" giggled Donna. We pulled exquisitely hand-embroidered dresses over our clothing and donned diaphanous veils, glittering with sequins and beads. With the dashing Rafik and our exotic clothing we felt as if we were in a movie. I greatly admired the exquisite embroidery on our dresses, but sadly they were not for sale.

A large antique store stood on the corner of a major intersection. A middle-aged gentleman wearing thick glasses stood in the doorway. He bowed in a courtly fashion "Welcome beautiful ladies. I am Haroun. Please see my shop." He led Donna and me into the long, narrow building lined with glass display cases on one side and various antique items on the other. As is traditional with Arab hospitality, the first order of business is welcoming the guests and making them comfortable. Haroun sat us on little chairs he pulled from behind a display case. He then disappeared into a tiny back room and brewed hot, sugary tea with fresh mint leaves. Haroun served us tea and sat down for some conversation. We drank from miniature tea glasses set on a delicate saucer with a tiny silver spoon on the side. I drank mint tea in many Middle Eastern stores and was always amazed at how the hot brew could be so refreshing in the summer heat.

Haroun had converted the attic of his shop into a sort of personal museum. He showed us artifacts while relating fascinating snippets of local history. His collection contained fragile old Bedouin veils adorned with coins and embroidery, ancient handmade Bedouin silver jewelry, and a variety of antique rifles. Haroun told us these same types of rifles were used by Lawrence of Arabia and his troops when they drove out the Turks and captured the Gulf of Aqaba in 1917.

I fell in love with the heavy, silver Bedouin jewelry. I imagined the tales these precious old items would share if only they could speak. I purchased a piece of history, an old Bedouin veil. The veil was made of thick brown wool and held on the wearer's head with velvet cords. I wanted to try it on, so Haroun adjusted the cords around my head so that only my eyes were exposed. The veil reached my chest and hung heavily with the weight of antique silver coins sewn to the fabric. These were Maria Teresa silver dollars, minted in Austria in the mid to late 1700s. The coins became an important trade item all across the Middle East. Bedouin women also sewed them on to veils and fabric belts as a dowry item.

To cover my hair and complete the ensemble, Haroun draped a large black cotton scarf over my head. The head covering blazed with brilliantly-colored hand embroidery. Then Haroun produced a selection of beautiful long skirts made by local Bedouin women. They were adorned with the same intricate embroidery I admired so much. Haroun told Donna and me that these skirts were worn by Bedouin brides. So I also bought the skirt and the embroidered scarf. I still wear the skirt and am often complimented on its beauty. Haroun gifted me with a silver ring set with a deep green stone. I've never known why he gave me the ring and not Donna. Perhaps it was yet another facet of Arab hospitality. I still wear the ring. Our shopping trip ended with Haroun inviting both Donna and me to his home later that evening. We eagerly accepted his invitation. I considered it an honor to be invited into a private home in the Middle East and always jumped at a chance.

The two of us visited more shops until I felt myself drooping in the heat and humidity. "I'm thirsty and I'm hungry. Let's take a break, Donna!" We chose a small restaurant on the main street and settled at an outdoor table in the shade of an awning. We ate freshly-made tabouli, a finely chopped salad of parsley, tomato, cucumber, and cracked wheat, dressed with lemon juice and olive oil. The cool, crisp salad was served with fresh flat bread from the bakery next door to the café. Donna and I shared a piece of delicate baklava, a divine Mediterranean dessert made with layers of crisp pastry and pistachio nuts bathed in honey and lemon. The setting was so relaxing. As we sipped our mint tea Donna closed her eyes and sighed, "I could sit here all day. I wish we could spend another week in Aqaba."

Feeling refreshed after lunch, we decided to walk back to the hotel. We looked in little shops along the way. Donna wanted a new pair of sports shoes, so we stopped at a sports equipment shop. A young man of perhaps twenty-five years came out from behind the counter and shook our hands. "Welcome to our store. My name is Yasser." Yasser was a beautiful youth, tall and well-built with dark curly hair, brown eyes and a dazzling smile. He wore jeans and a snug green T-shirt. The snug shirt set off his broad shoulders and massive arms. This young man was clearly dedicated to working out. As Donna looked at the selection of sports shoes with Yasser, the shop door opened and another young man stepped in. I had to look twice; although this fellow was dressed differently, he was otherwise a mirror image of his twin brother Yasser! He had the same curly hair, sparkling brown eyes and fit build. He introduced himself as Arafat and Donna giggled, "Your parents are very clever to name you Yasser and Arafat!"

With great charm and salesmanship, the identical young men helped Donna find the shoes she wanted. They even gave her a discount on her purchase. Yasser and his brother grinned mischievously, "Please, you are welcome to come see us anytime." Donna was smitten by both the young men. (She was renowned for her romantic encounters.) "I'm coming back to Aqaba on my next weekend off," she proclaimed with glowing eyes, "and I'm going to sleep with both of them, at the same time if I can." I laughed and wished her luck. In fact a couple of months later Donna returned from a weekend in Aqaba with a big grin on her face. "Yasser and Arafat in stereo!" she crowed. Apparently both had gleefully helped accomplish her goal!

Donna and I had earlier agreed to meet Anna and Maeve at the hotel to compare our shopping finds and discuss our adventures. Anna went to Petra that day, but hadn't yet returned. We met Maeve in the hotel lobby. She chattered excitedly in Gaelic. "Speak English, Maeve!" we exclaimed.

She'd returned from downtown with the oddest thing, a bag of potatoes she purchased at a vegetable market. Maeve told us these were special potatoes, a variety she had never seen outside of Ireland. She was absolutely thrilled to find them. Donna and I chuckled at her strange purchase; they looked like any other potatoes to us. With all the beautifully crafted items in the stores in Aqaba, Maeve's entire day of shopping culminated in a bag of potatoes! But we were all happy with our finds.

That same evening about 8:00 p.m., Haroun, the kindly shopkeeper who'd invited us to his home, arrived at the hotel to pick up Donna and me. He drove an ancient, wheezing Citroen sedan. Haroun and his family lived in a suburb of Aqaba and along the way he pointed out the sights. Finally we pulled up in front of a small villa surrounded by a high cinderblock wall. A metal door painted in brilliant hues of blue creaked open and a short, plump woman in a green headscarf peeked out at us. Haroun introduced the petite women as his wife Fadihah. She smiled at us, kissed us once on each cheek, and welcomed us to her home.

Their house stood at the top of a rise and we could clearly see Eilat, an Israeli city of about 60,000 souls just across the Gulf of Aqaba. (The northern end of the Red Sea is divided into two arms by the Sinai Peninsula; the eastern arm ending in the Gulf of Aqaba and the western arm leading up to the Suez Canal.)

Beyond the metal door we found ourselves in a courtyard lush with flowers, fruit trees, and a riot of shocking pink bougainvillea, climbing up and over the cinderblock walls. In the courtyard under the fruit trees Haroun invited us to sit in comfortable chairs with cushions. It was a beautiful evening, the air warm and soft. The lights of Eilat merged with the lights of Aqaba, twinkling in harmony on the water between us.

Haroun and Fadihah had seven beautiful daughters ranging in age from about five to seventeen years. But the centerpiece of the family was little Ibrahim, the only boy, born four years earlier. Ibrahim knew he was special, the apple of his family's eye. Fadihah kept her headscarf on during our visit, but the daughters left their hair loose and uncovered since their guests were female. The ladies served us Arabic coffee first and then tea with an assortment of delicate pastries sweet with honey. All the daughters spoke some English, so we were able to communicate fairly well. I talked at length with the oldest daughter, Rana, about her upcoming marriage and how it was arranged. She told us her fiancé was a university graduate. She appeared proud of him and seemed happy and optimistic about their future together. The family was obviously traditional, but also open-minded and welcoming. So once again we were treated to the famous hospitality of the Arab peoples.

I awakened early on Friday morning to the calls for prayer from all over Aqaba. No stores were open on Friday morning. This time was reserved for prayer and observance of the Muslim holy day. Anna, Donna and I went to the beach in front of our hotel and relaxed on the chairs provided by the hotel. Anna was still excited about her day in Petra. "Such a magical place," she enthused, "but I was terribly frightened getting down from the High Place of Sacrifice!" I grinned at the memory of my own arduous descent. Donna asked Anna, "Did Maeve show you the potatoes she found yesterday? She sure was excited about them." Anna laughed in her gentle manner, "Well it seems a bit odd, but Maeve is very happy with her find!"

The downtown shops opened around noon so the three of us walked downtown, this time via the public beach promenade. Jordanian families enjoyed the sunny day, picnicking on the beach. Anna was a fan of the movie *Lawrence of Arabia* so she wanted to meet Rafik. He was delighted when we again entered his shop. Anna was enchanted when Rafik dressed her up as he Donna and I the day before. After that we enjoyed a delicious lunch of fresh fruit salad and freshly made yogurt. As the three of us walked back to the hotel we commiserated with each other about returning to Saudi today. Later in the afternoon Mohammed arrived to pick us up in his Blue Lightning and we started back to Tabuk.

We found it psychologically wrenching to pass through the Jordanian border and back into Saudi Arabia. At Saudi customs the same foolish young men again tore our suitcases apart, eager to find any contraband we might have purchased in Jordan. They held us up for two hours while we again sat on the curb and waited them out. The young men looked disappointed when they couldn't find anything to confiscate.

And so we returned to the repression of Saudi Arabia, to fully-covered women and the atmosphere of apathy. What a shock after the warm welcome of Jordan. But I could at least look forward, in two weeks, to flying off for a one-month vacation in Canada.

Bound for Home

Shortly after returning from Jordan, I flew home to Calgary for the month of July. I was anxious to see my family and friends. At the same time, my one-year contract came up for renewal.

I had difficulty deciding whether to spend another year in Saudi or not. My first year in the Kingdom had not been without its difficulties. The stress and strain of everyday life in Saudi had certainly worn me down, and my bout with typhoid took a lot out of me. My parents asked me several times if I planned to go back for a second year. They worried about me the entire time I was in the Kingdom, and so there were many things I did not tell them.

But I thought a month at home in Canada would surely make me feel better. In general I'd enjoyed my adventures in the past year and genuinely liked my department and co-workers. I was proud of myself too for the savings I'd accrued during my first year. The lure of another year of savings finally decided me. Shortly before leaving for home I signed a contract for a second year in Saudi Arabia.

Weeks before leaving on my vacation, I had to figure out how to ship items to Calgary. I bought gifts for my family and close friends, including a large Turkish wool rug for my parents. Shipping should be a fairly straightforward project anywhere else, but like so many simple tasks undertaken in Saudi Arabia it is complicated and frustrating. I hired a company named "Red Sea Express." Their office was not on the regular bus route, so I had to make arrangements for a recreation center car to take me there. The driver picked me up at my compound one evening after work. The shipping company turned out to be a tiny office fronting on a rubbish-strewn street in an older part of Tabuk.

A tiny bell rang above the door as I entered the premises. Two yawning East Indian men emerged from a back room, each clutching a glass of tea. Business appeared slow that day. They first presented me with a mountain of government paperwork. Because of its sheer volume I ended up taking it home to fill out. The Saudi government wanted to know every detail of every item being taken out of Saudi Arabia, the value and whether or not any of the items involved endangered species. I found this laughable considering the shop downtown where spotted cat skins, ivory carvings, and rhinoceros horn daggers were readily available.

Several companies in Tabuk sold metal shipping boxes. The right box was easily found, but getting it back to my flat was a logistical nightmare. My ever-dependable friend Fawzia accompanied me to try to ease the way. She had plenty of experience shipping cargo to her home in Cairo, but even for that short distance it was not a simple task. She took me to a shop in an older district of Tabuk. We entered a long narrow building dimly lit with a few fly-specked light bulbs. The establishment had a corrugated tin roof and a bumpy, hard-packed dirt floor. An obsequious young Indian man rushed over to assist us. Rubbing his hands together he grinned at us, "I am Babu. I am wery (sic) pleased to be knowing you madams." I looked around to see tiers of rickety wooden shelves lining both sides of the building. The shelves were packed neatly with metal boxes of all sizes and colors. I spied a medium-sized box on the top tier, beautifully painted with mosque minarets and flowery arabesques. I turned to Babu and pointed, "I want that one. Can I see it please?" The young man clapped his hands in delight, "Ah yes, madam, is wery (sic) nice box. Is made in Turkey. Wery best box in store."

Babu hurried to the door of his shop and shouted in Hindi at two young Indian men loitering nearby. They rushed into the store with big grins on their faces, their plastic flip-flops slapping against the dirt floor. Babu and his buddies scrambled up to the top tier and among the three of them managed to man-handle the box down off the high shelf. I felt sorry for them; the box was not terribly heavy, but certainly awkward.

When the box finally sat on the floor, Babu produced a large rag and thoroughly dusted the entire box. He spoke broken Arabic so he and Fawzia bartered fiercely on the price. Then it occurred to me. "Fawzia, how will we get this thing back to my flat?" I needn't have worried, my friend would always ease the way. "Don't worry," she smiled, "I will make arrangements."

While I paid Babu for the box and gave him and his delightful helpers a substantial tip, Fawzia went out to the street to hail a taxi. Expatriate females rarely ever took taxis in Tabuk; we'd been warned by our employer of the dangers. Certainly a female would never get in a taxi alone. But on this occasion we had little choice if we were going to get the box back to my flat. Saudi males do drive taxis, one of the few labor professions they will engage in, but on this occasion Fawzia hired an Afghani taxi. An ancient beaten-up Toyota with tires so worn the tread was no longer visible.

As I approached the car, a breeze brought me the foul stench of the sullen Afghan driver. I looked at Fawzia with some concern, "Maybe a Saudi taxi would be a bit safer." She replied, "Don't worry, we are two. And a Saudi taxi driver will never permit us to put your box on his car roof." I knew that was true; Saudis often drove newer cars which they looked after and took pride in. But I'd always felt a little fearful of the big Afghan men and their hazardous old cars. Like most males of his race, he was a tall, fierce-looking man with an angular face and the proud countenance of a people whose country has been invaded repeatedly over the centuries. To ride in this class of taxi in the summer heat is not a pleasant experience. These drivers do not have an easy life in the Middle East and exist on the very edge of expatriate society. Many do not have an actual place to live, usually sleeping and eating in their cars or in decrepit structures abandoned by others.

(As an aside, almost all the taxis in the United Arab Emirates are driven by men from Afghanistan and Waziristan. In UAE these taxis are called "jinglies" because of their driver's love for gaudy metal ornaments dangling from the rearview mirror. Everyone, women too, use the jinglies in UAE, the main mode of transport for those without private vehicles. I later went to work in UAE where as a female I was free to drive. But before I bought myself a car, I was forced to use jinglies to get around. Most females, especially Western women, hated having to take these taxis. Too frequently the rough Afghan driver would stare at us in the rearview mirror and openly masturbate at the same time. In the past few years, large cities in United Arab Emirates have set up taxi companies dedicated to female customers only. The cars are also driven by women, mostly Egyptians.)

Babu and his friends carried the box out to the car. The Afghan slouched silently in his vehicle while the Indian men sweated and shouted at each other in Hindi regarding the best way to get the box in or on top the car. Finally they were able to wrestle my shipping box atop the taxi's already scratched and dented roof. Babu and his friends secured the box with rope wrapped repeatedly through the back and front side windows of the car. The box looked anything but secure, but it was the best that could be done under the circumstances. Fawzia and I were barely settled in the back seat when the Afghan driver tore off with a screech of bald tires. Fawzia shouted something at him in Arabic. He scowled, but slowed down. I held my breath all the way back to the military base, both Fawzia and I holding tightly to the rope running through the car. My next worry was running the security gauntlet. I visualized their dragging the box off the taxi roof and having a bit of fun in delaying us. Fortunately there was a long line of vehicles waiting to enter the base so the guards did not have time to harass us.

I sighed with relief as the taxi pulled up in front of our compound. Fawzia and I got out of the taxi, but the surly Afghan sat without moving. He had no intention of helping us with the box at this end of the trip either. Two Saudi guards loitered near the guard shack smoking cigarettes. They too sat without moving to assist us. Finally Fawzia gestured and shouted several words of angry Arabic at the taxi driver. He climbed out of the car with a murderous look on his leathery brown face. His gnarled and enormously strong hands wrestled with the rope holding my box atop the taxi. Once free, he gave the box a great shove and it clattered to the ground. Without even waiting for payment, the miserable man leaped back in his filthy car and roared off in a cloud of oily smoke.

The two Saudi guards nearby yelped with laughter. I was furious about two small dents in my beautiful box. Fawzia sighed, "I am sorry about the damage. This man he hates women. When I shout at him I thought he wants to kill us." An understatement. Now we had the problem of getting the box up the stairs and into my flat. Fortunately a couple of nurses were just entering our compound after finishing their shift at the hospital. They kindly helped Fawzia and I cart the box upstairs. Fortunately once the box was packed and ready to ship, the personnel from Red Sea Express were allowed to come to my flat and pick up the box, albeit accompanied by a chaperone. Fawzia was a true friend. Considering the murderous Afghan and all, I don't think I could have managed the shipping box episode without her help.

I finally got my passport from the passport office the morning I was leaving for Canada. I breathed a sigh of relief since my flight left late that same evening. I'd booked a driver and car through the recreation center weeks beforehand to be sure I was delivered to the airport in good time. A young Filipino driver, Chito, arrived at the compound that evening to pick me up and delivered me to the airport. I had two hours to wait before my flight to Jeddah and then on to London. Tabuk airport was not a nice place to spend any time. At the time it was an antiquated, squat little building with grimy linoleum floors and beat-up plastic chairs. That was the men's waiting area. The women's section was separate, of course, and awful, but Western females were expected to wait there until our flight was called. The women's area was a tiny, overheated room full of screaming children, shouting women and a bathroom with overflowing toilets. The stench was unimaginable. Whoever was assigned to keep the room clean had obviously given up. Garbage bins overflowed. What the bins didn't contain was ankle-deep on the filthy carpet. The floor was a minefield of dirty diapers, leftover food scraps and crawling babies. While I tried to avoid the stench and mess, it was almost impossible to make myself inconspicuous in the male waiting area. A Mutawa would inevitably appear and herd me into the women's section. I went quietly for this was not a time to argue and risk missing my flight.

I made it home without incident. I spent the month of July at home in Calgary. The weather was rainy and cool that summer. Calgarians complained about the weather, but I soaked up the cool dampness like the dehydrated sponge I was. I arrived just as the Calgary Stampede was getting started. The Calgary Stampede, held for ten days every July, is famous as one of the richest rodeos in the world. Along with the rodeo is a city-wide festival when everyone dresses in western gear and has a good time. I hadn't been to the Stampede in years and enjoyed an entire day there with a group of friends. My parents took me to Banff, and my mother and I went on several shopping expeditions. Banff, a small town in the Canadian Rockies and about 70 miles from Calgary, has always been one of my favorite places. There I spent a relaxing afternoon in the hot springs that Banff is famous for. I caught up on my sleep, visited friends and family and generally enjoyed my break away from "The Magic Kingdom" as some expatriates like to call Saudi Arabia. "The Tragic Kingdom" and "The Evil Empire" are other popular names coined by expats.

All too soon it was time to fly back to Saudi to start my second contract year. At least I felt somewhat refreshed by my holiday.

On my return flight to Saudi Arabia I flew direct from Calgary to London's Heathrow on Air Canada, and then from London to Jeddah on Saudia Airlines. As many times as I traveled through Heathrow I never tired of it. To me Heathrow represents the central hub of the world. I never minded the usual six to eight hours I spent in layover. The airport has great shopping, restaurants, bars and even facilities where it is possible for a traveler to have a shower and relax. And there is no better place to people-watch.

My Saudia flight went smoothly until an hour or so out of Jeddah's King Abdulaziz International Airport. I have since wondered if the terrifying incident about to happen was an omen of my upcoming second year in Saudi Arabia.

The pilot announced bad weather in the area and told the passengers the ride might be bumpy. The flight attendants scurried through the huge aircraft and made sure all the passengers were belted and secure. The so-called bumpy ride was an understatement. The arrival in Jeddah was terrifying. The aircraft was a Boeing 747 with some 400 seats, sold out and full to bursting with passengers. Near Jeddah the plane flew into driving wind and rain. I sat in a window seat and watched the heavy sheets of water sluice over the aircraft windows. Thunder roared and brilliant flashes of lightning seemed so close to the aircraft I wondered if we'd been hit. The roar of the 747 engines in combination with the rain, thunder and lightning was deafening. Some passengers were already shouting in terror. I had flown in all sorts of weather and rarely ever felt nervous about flying, but as we approached Jeddah I felt real terror. As the pilot slowly descended, the fully-loaded, 300-ton aircraft swayed and shook like an inconsequential tinker-toy in the vicious wind. The pilot continued the descent, but I could not imagine how he would land in such weather. I was literally sweating with fear as the thunder boomed and the bolts of lightning lit up the churning black clouds around us. Then suddenly the amber lights of the runway appeared out of the clouds. But something was dreadfully wrong. The runway looked far too close and the plane's nose dipped at a sickeningly steep angle. And the aircraft was still traveling very fast. At the last second, the pilot changed his mind; he must have realized he could not level out enough to land safety. The monstrous engines suddenly accelerated and the G-force slammed us back into our seats. The pilot took the aircraft into a steep climb, the engines shrieking with the effort. The noise of the engine and the storm almost drowned out the screams and shouts of the panicked passengers. The powerful acceleration caused overhead bins to fly open and all manner of belongings were flung about the cabin. I closed my eyes and put my arms over my head and face to avoid getting hit by flying objects. By then I feared my life was going to end on a rain-soaked Jeddah runway. Somehow the pilot gained altitude, the mighty jet shuddering with the strain. When we had finally reached a safe altitude the pilot circled for some time before the control tower mandated another landing attempt. At least Jeddah had a control tower, unlike Tabuk. The landing was rough. The giant aircraft yawed and skewed down the slick runway. I felt my stomach roll and vomit rise into my throat. I wondered how the pilot and his co-pilot felt right now. As the enormous plane braked and rolled to a reasonable taxi speed, every passenger on that flight clapped and cheered. My knees almost buckled as I stood to disembark. I have never been so relieved to step on solid ground. Some of the passengers were badly bruised by flying objects and airport medics rushed to assist the injured. But we all survived. As we reached the airport lounge some of the more devout passengers bowed and kissed the ground.

Of course I still had to get on another airplane to Tabuk. After what I'd just been through I never wanted to get on a plane again as long as I lived. The flight to Tabuk was delayed by two hours while the storm passed. But when the Tabuk flight left Jeddah I was on it, gritting my teeth and clutching the seat arms. Fortunately it was a short flight.

I arrived in Tabuk, where the hospital car and driver were waiting for me, around midnight. This time I was greeted by a young East Indian driver, "Greetings, Madam, my name is Vidy and I drive you home. You have good trip, Madam?" I told him about my terrifying arrival in Jeddah as we walked to his bus parked in front of Tabuk airport. "We should thank the gods then that you are all safely (sic)," Vidy smiled. He delivered me to the gate of the compound and politely bid me good night.

I walked into my cool apartment and slumped down on the couch. Fawzia took care of my flat while I was away and she had obviously been in earlier. She'd left a light on and thoughtfully stocked my little fridge with milk, fresh Arabic bread and my favorite cheddar cheese. She also left a note on the dining table welcoming me back. I felt blessed to have such a friend. I found myself dehydrated and hungry so I enjoyed some of the food Fawzia left me. I was exhausted, but found I couldn't sleep because my body was still on Calgary time, some ten hours difference. Unfortunately, I hadn't left myself much time to recover from jet lag. I had to be at work the following morning. I took a long, hot shower and drifted in and out of sleep for the remainder of the night.

I dragged myself to work the following morning, feeling like I'd been run over by a big truck. I was so jet-lagged I barely remember that day. Gabrielle, Dr. Hoey, and The Sari Gang greeted me with hugs and told me how happy they were to have me back. "The Boys" crowded into the office all smiles and shuffling their feet. They were obviously glad to have me back, but didn't know how to communicate this. Faisal, never a subtle young man, giggled and said to me, "Chilly, you look not so good today!" I shot back at him, "You wouldn't look so good either young Faisal if you'd just traveled all the way from Canada!" Everyone seemed thrilled by the little Canadian souvenirs I'd brought them. All in all I realized I was happy to be back amongst my co-workers. But it still felt stunningly surreal that within just a few hours I could be surrounded by the familiarity of my home country and then suddenly back in the quirks and whimsies of life in the Kingdom. Those who have lived in Saudi Arabia for years say it feels this way every time they travel back and forth from the Kingdom.

During my first week back at work I made a new friend. Trish met me for coffee one morning in the cafeteria. She was accompanied by a petite Irish girl named Catherine from Dublin. She was a secretary by profession and had arrived the week before I returned from vacation. She worked for the director of Materiels Management and her office was located just down the hall from Trish's office. Catherine and I hit it off right away. She was a quiet girl, but with a wicked sense of humor and a delightful Irish brogue. Catherine became a loyal friend, though we didn't see a lot of each other. Shortly after Catherine arrived in Tabuk she fell hard for a much older German man named Tony, though she did not move in with him right away.

I worried about Catherine. She was the epitome of the virginal Irish Catholic girl who'd been educated by nuns and grown up sheltered in the heart of her family. In spite of the fact she was thirty years old, Catherine had never lived on her own. She told me she came to Saudi Arabia because she wanted to buy her own home. She planned to stay two years and save every penny she made for a down payment.

When I first met her Tony I didn't much like him. He was at least twenty years older than Catherine. I tried hard to like him for Catherine's sake, but I found him overbearing and dogmatic. He reminded me somewhat of Trish's boyfriend Phil, though at least Tony wasn't an alcoholic. But he was definitely one of the fringe element, those lone, middle-aged males who'd lived in Saudi Arabia for decades. As with most of his kind he hated the Saudis from whom he made his rather good living. Tony was a structural engineer and lived on a German compound near the hospital. Catherine often invited me to come with her to Tony's place where she would prepare dinner for all three of us. I knew Tony resented my being there. I watched him as his eyes followed Catherine hungrily. She'd made it plain to him from the start there'd be no physical side to their relationship until an engagement ring was placed on her hand.

After a couple of weeks back in Tabuk I settled into my normal routine and eventually got over my jet lag. It was a good thing that I couldn't see into a crystal ball, which just might have told me my second year in Saudi Arabia was going to be tough.

Religious Duties

I had arrived back in Tabuk just as Ramadan began. This would be my first experience of the month of fasting by Muslims.

According to Islamic tradition, Ramadan is the month in which the Prophet Mohammed received the first verses of the Quran from God. Ramadan occurs in the ninth month of the Islamic Hijra calendar and officially begins when the new moon is sighted. Because the calendar is dependent on moon phases, Ramadan occurs about twelve days earlier each year. Muslims fast through the entire month, refraining from food, drink, smoking, and sex from sunrise to sunset. Ramadan is meant to be a time of reflection, to consider those less fortunate, and to make a special effort to be patient and kind in dealing with others. Muslims ask forgiveness for past sins, pray for guidance, and try to make themselves better people through self-discipline and good deeds. In addition to fasting, Muslims are encouraged to read the entire Quran during the month. Those exempt from fasting are children under twelve, pregnant or nursing women, the mentally or physically ill, and those traveling more than forty miles in one day. Ramadan is a month of joy for devout Muslims, sharing special foods and gifts with family, friends, and neighbors, as well as donating food and clothing to the poor. Traditionally the fast is broken each evening by eating dates. Many Saudis open their homes during Ramadan to provide simple foods to strangers in need. At Iftar (breaking the fast) long lines of men, usually poorly-paid laborers and transients, bowls in hand, wait patiently outside Saudi homes for their share of free food. During Ramadan most shops and markets remain open most of the night. There is an air of celebration and Muslims in general seem happy during this time.

In Saudi Arabia Ramadan is an enforced event for Muslims. Any Muslim caught breaking the fast is considered to have committed a crime. Many young Saudis resent being forced to fast. While Muslims who perform Ramadan in the correct way eat lightly when breaking the fast, "The Boys," our young residents in the OB/GYN department, would spend the night partying and eating huge quantities of food. The following morning they'd drag themselves into work sluggish and irritable.

Very little of anything gets done during Ramadan. Saudi Arabia, and much of the Middle East for that matter, comes to a near-standstill. In Saudi the government offices and other official services limp along more inefficiently than normal.

Of course, Ramadan is easier to deal with when it falls in cooler months. But resolve is sorely tested when it falls in the searing summer months. Muslims living in Saudi Arabia and United Arab Emirates work four to five hours per day during Ramadan, then go home to sleep through the afternoon heat. After the sun sets the feasting begins all over again.

Fasting can present grave danger to those taking life-saving medications. Many religiously observant people, especially elderly Muslims, refuse to break their fast by taking their medications. During Ramadan the emergency rooms fill up with diabetics and epileptics, to name a few. Pregnant women are exempt from fasting, but many do so anyway and end up hospitalized with severe dehydration.

Ramadan is a very quiet time for non-Muslim expatriates, who therefore suffer some degree of boredom. By government order the expat compounds must refrain from parties or any other raucous activity that might be overheard by the Saudi general public. Gabrielle and I ate and drank in our office, but we were circumspect and took care to keep the door closed. We respected those fasting in our own department, though they cared little if we ate or drank. They knew we respected them as friends, co-workers and Muslims. But the larger authority dealt harshly with non-Muslim staff observed eating or drinking in view of Muslims.

Some non-Muslims, who seemed to hate Arabs and Muslims in general, actually took the chance of eating and drinking in public to make their point even though they knew they would likely be jailed if caught. The hospital cafeteria remained open for Christian staff, but the windows were covered with curtains so Muslims did not have to see us eating and drinking. There were other perks for Westerners too. The hospital administrators permitted non-essential Christian support staff to work the same abbreviated hours as Muslims. It was easy to adjust to starting work at 8:00 a.m. and leaving by 1:00 p.m. Because the shops downtown remained open much of the night the bus schedule was changed to accommodate late shoppers. The later the hour, the cooler the weather.

Fawzia, Gabrielle, and I often went down in the cool of evening to have supper at the Caravan. Sometimes Catherine came with us, though she, like Anya, refused to eat anywhere outside of her own home or at other compounds. She would sit with us and drink coffee while we ate.

Ramadan ends with the festival of "Eid Al-Fitr" (Festival of the Conclusion of the Fast) one of the most important Islamic celebrations. The other main Islamic celebration is "Eid Al-Adha" (Festival of Sacrifice) which occurs after Hajj, the annual pilgrimage to Mecca. Eid Al-Fitr is a happy time for Muslim families. Children receive new clothing, adults dress in their best, gifts are exchanged and friends and family visit back and forth. Charity ("zakat") is also practiced at Eid Al-Fitr when donations are given to the poor or to a local mosque.

The annual pilgrimage to Mecca, Saudi Arabia, the Hajj, occurs in the twelfth month of the Islamic calendar. The Hajj is the largest pilgrimage of its kind in the world. It must be carried out at least once in the lifetime of every able-bodied Muslim who can afford it. The Hajj is a demonstration of solidarity amongst Muslims and their submission to God. Males, no matter their status, all wear a seamless white garment so each man is equal. Women wear abayas and scarves while attending the Hajj, but their face is supposed to remain uncovered under the eyes of God.

The Hajj is associated with the life of the prophet Mohammed, but the pilgrimage to Mecca is considered by Muslims to stretch back thousands of years to the time of Abraham. As many as two million people converge simultaneously on Mecca for the week of Hajj. Each Hajji performs a series of rituals: Walk counter-clockwise, seven times, around the "Kaaba," the cube-shaped building which represents the Muslim direction of prayer; kiss the black stone embedded in the Eastern corner of the Kaaba (Muslim tradition holds that the shiny black stone fell from Heaven to show Adam and Eve where to build an altar); and dash back and forth between the hills of Al-Safa and Al-Marwah. (The run represents Abraham's commandment from God to leave his wife Hagar and son Ismael in the desert.) According to tradition Hagar left her son to run from one hill to the other seven times searching for water and help for her and Ismael. Returning empty-handed she found that while Ismael had been lying kicking at the sand, he uncovered a spring now known as the Zamzam well. All pilgrims drink from the Zamzam well (believed to be a miracle source of water as a reward to Hagar from God); stand vigil on the plains of Mount Arafat and then in the last act of Hajj throw stones in a ritual stoning of the Devil. Male pilgrims shave their heads, perform a ritual of animal sacrifice (usually a sheep or goat), and celebrate the four-day festival of Eid al Adha. The meat from the thousands of goat, sheep, and cattle sacrifices is flash-frozen and shipped to needy Muslims all over the world. Saudi Arabia has spent billions of dollars improving Hajj facilities, starting with a massive air terminal in Jeddah reserved solely for pilgrims. (It is fortunate the Saudi government has the financial resources to maintain the holy sites.)

One of the best parts of Ramadan for me were the frequent invitations for Iftar meals at co-workers homes. Fawzia prepared delicious Ramadan delicacies and often invited me to share Iftar with her.

My friend Vicky worked with a young Syrian man in the lab. Mahmoud and his family, including his mother, wife, and two children, lived in downtown Tabuk. Vicky was often asked to his home for dinners and celebrations such as baby showers. In Western culture a married man inviting a single female into his family home would be a rare thing. Assumptions would be made about an ulterior motive. But in Arab culture and tradition, hospitality is open to all. There were certainly plenty of men working in the hospital, Arab, Asian, or otherwise, whose intentions were suspect. But Vicky knew the invitations to Mahmoud's home included his entire family. He had taken a liking to Vicky as a person and wanted his family to meet her. Vicky was easy to like with her southern twang, brilliant blue eyes and outgoing personality.

At one of Mahmoud's invitations, when he invited Vicky for an Iftar meal, he told her she was welcome to bring along a friend or two. So Vicky asked me and Anya, our Irish friend, to join her. Vicky had convinced Anya to come along even though she did not usually eat outside her home or at other compounds. The breaking of the fast occurred late in the evening that year, around 9:00 p.m. Vicky, Anya, and I took the hospital bus downtown and proceeded from there on foot. Mahmoud had kindly offered to pick us up at the bus stop, but the religious police were extra vigilant during Ramadan. We did not want to put Mahmoud at risk with the Mutawa. Vicky was sure she remembered how to get to Mahmoud's house, but it was made more difficult after dark. We stumbled down alleyways so dark I could hardly see my hand in front of my face. Anya walked behind me and I heard her curse as she tripped in a pothole. "Vicky darlin', are ya sure you know the way?" Anya inquired in her lilting Irish accent. "Y'all just trust me. We're almost there," Vicky promised.

Individually numbered houses are rare in much of the Middle East. Home delivery of mail is unknown; everyone has a post office box. Usually, only busy, main thoroughfares have names. And in this case the entrance to Mahmoud's house was in an alleyway, another common situation. Directions to most locations depended on landmarks and might be related thus, "Go straight on the main highway, veer left at that sign with the black camel on it, turn right on the dirt road where Mohammed's tailoring shop is, then keep going until you see the clock tower..."

Most homes in the Middle East have a courtyard surrounded by a high wall with entry through a heavy iron door. Vicky stopped suddenly ahead of me and whispered, "I'm pretty sure this is the right house." Vicky lifted the creaky latch on the metal door and we let ourselves into the courtyard. It was as dark as the alleyway. Why hadn't Mahmoud left a light on for us? Vicky went first. I heard her grunt and stumble in the dark, then a quiet, "What the hell...?" Anya and I thought she'd tripped and fallen, and indeed she had, but not over anything we could have expected. Apparently Mahmoud heard us floundering around outside and a light flicked on over the front door. To our amazement, we saw Vicky lying draped awkwardly over a small camel! Anya and I burst out laughing at the strange sight. Vicky struggled to stand, but her abaya was tangled around her legs. The sleepy-eyed young camel looked quite unconcerned and continued to chew contentedly on his hay. The sweet little creature was white in color with gorgeous liquid brown eyes and long lashes. I could not stop myself from touching his soft, curly-haired head. Mahmoud rushed through the front door to help Vicky regain her feet. He apologized profusely, "I am so sorry. I forgot to put the light on for your arrival." Vicky just laughed. "Scared the livin' hell out of me!" she drawled, "thought I'd tripped over a rolled-up rug, until it moved. The little guy's coat feels exactly like a nice wool rug!"

Mahmoud then let us in on a secret and asked us not to repeat it. He told us his brothers were out on a desert road the night before and came across the little camel sitting on the road. They narrowly avoided a messy car-camel accident. In the heat of the moment the brothers decided to shove the camel in the back of their Datsun truck and smuggle it into Mahmoud's courtyard under cover of darkness. The Muslim feast of Eid was due in a few days, the official end of Ramadan. The tender young camel would make a wonderful meal. Had the camel owner or authorities found out about the kidnapping, Mahmoud and his brothers would have been in terrible trouble.

Of course we enjoyed a lovely evening and a delicious dinner with Mahmoud and his family. But after I returned home, I could not move the small camel out of my mind. In a few days he would be slaughtered and enjoyed by Mahmoud and his entire family.

Eventually I did try camel meat in Saudi and found it lean and flavorful. On the other hand I could not have handled dining on Mahmoud's pilfered little camel.

The Wahhabis, a Different Kind of Islam

The Muslim call to prayer has always been a special experience for me, especially the magical evening call. It is what I miss the most about the Middle East. In the shimmer of a tangerine sunset, calls from hundreds of mosques across the city merge to call the people to prayer.

All Muslims follow the five pillars of Islam: fasting during the month of Ramadan, praying five times daily, at least one pilgrimage to Mecca if able, charity for the poor, and belief in God and the Prophet Mohammed. Islam is a way of life, not merely a religion. An observant Muslim's entire life is based on the laws and guidance of the Quran. All aspects of daily life are clearly outlined: What one can eat or drink, what is forbidden or acceptable, how spouses should be treated as well as financial and business matters, sexual matters, family disputes, crime and punishment.

Aside from a small minority of Shiite Muslims in the eastern province, Saudi Arabian people are identified as Sunni Muslims. But they practice an ultra-conservative form of Islam called Wahhabism (also known as Salafis), a movement that claims to adhere to the true understanding of general Islamic principle. An eighteenth century scholar by the name of Mohammed Abd-al-Wahhab believed that Islam could be made pure through violence. He preached against what he considered moral decline and political weakness in the Arabian Peninsula. No other sect compares to the austere Wahhabi interpretation of Islam. The Taliban and other radical extremists have styled themselves after the Wahhabi's strict brand of Islam. The Taliban, though, have taken their version to a vicious and absurd extreme.

When the Prophet Mohammed introduced the new religion of Islam in the seventh century, it was a step forward for women. They owned property and the laws of that time offered them protection. The Prophet's first wife, Khadija, was a powerful woman who inherited her father's business and managed the family fortune. Khadija initially hired The Prophet as an employee and then later proposed marriage to him. How things have changed. It would seem that with the advent of Wahhabism certain elements began a steady backward movement into a sort of Dark Ages that perseveres until today. As the twenty-first century unfolds and the world moves forward, Islamic extremists continue to regress into an ever-more barbaric and feudal way of life.

Unfortunately most of the press about Islam today concentrates on the violence and radicalism of fundamentalists. Those ignorant of the distinctions between different sects of Muslims assume all follow the same violent belief system. In fact the majority of Muslims feel anguish over the hatred directed at them because of a minority of violent radicals.

Saudi Arabia is not tolerant of any other Muslim sects or other religions. Islam is the only officially recognized religion in the Kingdom. Public practice of other religions is illegal. Non-Muslims who wear religious symbols in public risk a skirmish with the religious police. Saudi's Shi'ite Muslims suffer political and economic discrimination by the Saudi government. In fact, Saudis and many other Sunni Muslims do not believe that Shi'ites are "real" Muslims because of their differing beliefs.

Only about ten to twenty percent of the world's Muslims are Shi'ite. There have always been tensions between the Sunni and Shia sects. There are a number of distinct differences between the two, but simply put the chief difference is the belief of who should have succeeded the Prophet Muhammad on his death. Sunnis believe that Abu Bakr, the father of Muhammad's wife Aisha, is the rightful successor to the Prophet. The Shi'ites believe the Prophet Muhammad ordained his cousin and son-in-law Ali as the rightful successor. Thus Islam split into followers of Abu Bakr and followers of Ali. The Shi'ites adhere to a number of rituals that

Sunnis do not practice, and while both factions believe in Mahdi, a spiritual leader who will appear in end times and establish a perfect and just Islamic society, for Shi'ites, the Mahdi is a strong and central focus.

Saudi Arabia takes itself seriously because it is the birthplace of Islam. Saudi kings prefer to be called "The Custodian of the Two Holy Mosques" (Mecca and Medina, the two holiest sites in Islam). Saudi Arabia interprets Quranic law ("sharia") literally, as much in modern times as centuries ago. Punishments like stoning are still practiced today in Saudi, but stoning is also mentioned in the Old Testament of the Bible. The difference is that modern Christians no longer carry out this archaic punishment; the Saudis do. The Quran is the Kingdom's constitution and legal system, and separation of church and state does not exist.

For the most part the oppressively conservative ways of Saudi originate in Wahhabism, but there is also a cultural component. Some laws involving Saudi women are unique to the Kingdom's own social makeup. Over the years the rights of Saudi women have deteriorated abysmally, a cultural phenomenon at odds with the Prophet's original belief in equality for women. This is mainly due to Saudi Arabia's religious leaders (called the "Ulema", Muslim legal scholars) making indiscriminate rules in their continuing efforts to keep Saudi women behind closed doors. I think the recent uproar about women being airbrushed out of Ikea catalogues intended for Saudi customers is the perfect analogy. The more invisible women are the better the Saudi religious establishment likes it.

Women are still not allowed to drive in Saudi Arabia. Saudi women cannot travel internationally or even within the Kingdom without written permission from their husband or a close male relative. Saudi families do not allow their women to leave the home unless accompanied by a male relative. Some Saudi women spend their lives in "purdah", confined to the home and the system of complete sexual segregation. Of note, Waziristan, in the North West Frontier Province of northern Pakistan and Afghanistan, where the Taliban rule, is a far stricter society. There it is said a woman leaves her home only twice in her life: the first time when she marries, the second time when she is carried from her house in her death shroud.

Nowadays a Saudi marriage agreement is usually between the prospective husband and the father of the bride. Much of the time the bride is not allowed any decision-making regarding her own marriage. Saudi men and Muslim men in general, are allowed four wives according to the Quran. This lifestyle is still practiced in Saudi Arabia though it is not so common nowadays. While western society finds the practice reprehensible, in the time of the Prophet Mohammed there was a reason for plural marriages. A great number of men were killed in wars and tribal disputes, thus it was practical to take four wives so that women who had few other options could be protected and provided for.

The Quran stipulates equal treatment for plural wives, but this is difficult since it is human nature that one or two will always be favored over the others. Plural marriage is becoming a thing of the past amongst moderate Muslim men and women. It is no longer affordable for the middle class and is viewed as socially unacceptable among a majority of the younger generation.

"Misyar" is a temporary and usually short-term contract marriage arranged to void the sin of "zina" (sexual relations outside of marriage.) The arrangement has long been an institution in Shi'ite Islam where it is called "muta." It is a controversial arrangement, and because it is not in the Quran, many Sunnis consider it strictly illegal. At the same time it is becoming increasingly popular amongst Saudis. Often called a "traveler's marriage," young male Saudi students attending American universities make use of the practice. When they finish their studies they return to Saudi Arabia and marry a woman chosen by the family. It is used for a variety of reasons, though simply put it is legalized sex. Those against the practice even call it legalized prostitution.

Misyar can meet the needs of divorcees, widows, and widowers who do not wish to engage in another traditional marriage. It can also serve older people who have never been married but would like to try it on a temporary basis. Or a husband might make use of the practice when he does not wish to marry a second time because of the financial burden and responsibilities of having a legal second wife. A contract of no specific time period is made between a man and woman and signed by two legal witnesses. The "wife" is paid an agreed amount by the "husband" and they live separately. Sometimes a wealthy Saudi man may go outside of the Kingdom on vacation and arrange a brief misyar marriage while on vacation. He will usually divorce the woman at the end of the vacation after she receives a mutually agreeable monetary settlement. Some Muslim foreigners working in Saudi and Gulf countries practice misyar rather than live alone and away from their families for long stretches. Most have wives and children in their home country, but this class of worker is usually not allowed to bring his family to his country of employment. The misyar marriage will end in divorce, and once the monetary settlement is made, the husband has no responsibility for his former wife, financially or otherwise. Since children conceived in a misyar marriage are not born into a traditional family situation they suffer considerably. They rarely see their fathers, if at all, and they have few rights compared to those born in traditional marriages. After a divorce in misyar, the father of any children bears no legal responsibility of any kind for those children unless he chooses to.

Every Saudi woman must have a "mahrem," an official male guardian who has the authority and right to make decisions on her behalf. It is not simply a formality, or a system necessarily prescribed by families. A mahrem is sanctioned and enforced by the Saudi government. The mahrem decides whether or not a woman can be educated, travel, work, have a bank account, own a business, and sometimes to receive medical care. Even amongst educated and relatively independent women the mahrem system is in place. Interpretation of the system varies between families, but it affects the lives of all Saudi women. Having a mahrem also applies to foreign women who marry Saudi men.

Without appropriate documentation from a mahrem or the personal appearance of same, a woman could be prohibited from some activities. An example of this was the Saudi female resident, Dr. Khawla, who was part of our OB/GYN department. She wished to travel to Jeddah to a medical conference. In spite of the fact she was a university-educated woman, handling patient responsibilities, she was required to request and receive a letter of permission from her father. Without it she would not even have been able to board a flight to Jeddah. Dr. Khawla attended the medical conference accompanied by one of her many brothers, who likely kept a close eye on her.

Some Saudi women are fortunate to have a mahrem who respects their needs. But a mahrem does not always have his charge's best interests at heart. A Saudi woman is at the mercy of her male guardian.

Some Saudi women own businesses. It is unfortunately common for their male guardian to interfere in the business and even demand large sums of money. The mahrem can easily manipulate the situation to his advantage. It is a simple thing for him to blackmail her; the mahrem's word will always be taken over that of a woman. He has that power. This problem is apparently becoming a major issue, with some women actually losing their businesses. Either her male guardian demands so much money her business goes broke, or she refuses to meet his demands and he shuts down the business.

To my Western eyes the lives of Saudi women seemed distressingly isolated and oppressed. Those not permitted to educate themselves or have a job spend much of their life inside the house. Saudi women who have worked hard to attain a University degree may never be able to get a job. There are no leisure outlets such as libraries or cinemas. Women cannot swim in public or in hotel pools. With few exceptions, women of any nationality cannot stay in a hotel unless accompanied by a male relative. It is illegal for a Saudi woman to live alone. Those who marry usually have many children, but if the husband can afford it he hires Asian maids to care for the household and children.

As a result many Saudi women are so bored they sleep much of the time. Their only other entertainments are shopping or being chauffeured to visit other women. There are rumors of "underground" female basketball teams and exercise clubs. Saudi clerics seem able to find scriptural validation against anything that might perhaps allow women even a small measure of independence.

I met and interacted with a number of Saudi women and I found their strength admirable. On the whole I found them to be resilient, strikingly beautiful, and usually determined to make the best of their cultural restraints. Saudi women own property and businesses, and many are attending universities. They are proud women. They may grumble amongst themselves about the restrictions imposed on them, but they do not want the West to pity them.

The West makes the mistake of assuming Saudi women want the sort of rights Western women have in the context of Western society. That could not be further from the truth. What they want is according to their Islamic beliefs, but before the system was corrupted by rigid tribal customs and radical clerics. Women who were adults before 1979 remember they could drive and go out in public without an abaya or face covering.

The Saudis have attempted to preserve their culture in the face of ever more intrusions from the West courtesy of their oil wealth. Until about 1998, satellite television was forbidden in Saudi Arabia. But satellites eventually found their way into the country and stayed. At first the religious police raided any building sporting a dish, confiscated it, and punished the owner. But satellite dishes became so numerous the Mutawa could not keep up. Up until today both the media and individual citizens are forbidden to criticize the royal family, Islam, or Saudi Arabia. The same rule applies to expatriates. It is also illegal to comment on sexuality or other subjects deemed unsuitable by the religious clerics. Foreign publications are allowed into the country, but advertisements portraying pork products, alcohol, or female flesh are either torn out of the magazine or covered over with black felt pen by government censors.

Censoring is an endless source of amusement and frustration to expats. Trish and I often laughed about it. "Can't you just imagine," I joked, "huge rooms of toiling men, black felt pens clutched in their hands, going through every magazine, book, and music cassette?" We envisaged gigantic boxes of uncensored matter arriving every day, the censors slogging round the clock to keep the Kingdom pure from outside corruption. Trish wondered, "Do you think the government has a big budget for black felt pens? They must go through hundreds of thousands in a year."

Tabuk is a relatively small city so it was rare to find a Western magazine of any type. But sometimes I'd stumble on an imported magazine in the Astra supermarket. The publications were expensive and for that I got a torn-up magazine with black marks covering everything the censors considered unsuitable. If a page or pages contained too large a job for the black felt pen, the offending material was simply torn out of the magazine. On the two occasions I wasted my money on a magazine, I was left in the midst of a story with no ending. One time I was thrilled to find a rare National Geographic magazine, one of my favorite publications. I should have looked inside before purchase, but in my excitement I did not. When I got home with my treasure, I found little remaining of the magazine's contents. An extensive article about an ancient civilization featured hand-drawn dioramas with numerous nude humans. Page after page of nude figures had either been blacked over or the pages simply ripped out. I was astounded by the ignorance of it.

Medical articles containing information about AIDS or sexually transmitted disease were also censored.

The government controls all domestic radio and television stations. Satellite television and Internet are hugely popular amongst young Saudis, but the Internet is closely monitored and strictly censored by the Saudi government. Preventing Saudi citizens from corruption by the West only serves to make the people more curious about what they are missing. It is human nature. What is forbidden becomes ever more desirable.

Even maps do not escape the censors; Saudi Arabia's loathing for Israel is evident on any Middle Eastern map in the Kingdom. The word "Israel" is blacked out with felt pen and Palestine written in.

Archaic Justice

When I arrived in Saudi Arabia almost the first thing I heard about was the dreaded Mutawa (religious police). These government-authorized men enforce various interpretations of "sharia" (Islamic) law, a concept developed within the Wahhabi sect. They have the power to arrest individuals whom they perceive as having broken a moral code: unrelated males and females caught socializing, homosexual behavior, prostitution, enforcement of Islamic dress codes, enforcement of dietary laws (consumption or sale of pork products or alcohol), and making sure all businesses close during prayer time.

But mostly they are known as rigid and cruel, little more than government-supported street thugs. Ask anyone who has lived in Saudi Arabia and most will surely have a hair-raising story to tell you about the Mutawa. A great many younger Saudis are losing patience with the religious police, increasingly resentful over their intrusion into the personal lives of Saudi citizens.

(The Mutawa, however, are not alone in the Middle East. In the ultra-Orthodox Jewish [Heredi sect] community in Jerusalem, "modesty patrols" wander the streets making sure Orthodox women are dressed and behaving in a manner according to custom.)

What I found most terrifying about the Mutawa is their unpredictability, their often arbitrary decision-making, according to their own personal concept of morality. Very little has any basis in the Quran.

During my early days in Tabuk it was rare to see a Mutawa downtown. Non-Muslim female expats felt relatively safe going to the souq wearing only an abaya with no head covering. But suddenly everything changed. Like long-dormant plants regenerating after a heavy rain, swarms of Mutawa appeared within a matter of days. We began to see madness downtown. The religious thugs began their enforcement by segregating, by sex, all hospital buses to the souq and grocery stores. Women were abruptly forbidden to enter certain businesses such as the music store. The Mutawa feared we would mistakenly (perhaps even intentionally) touch a male customer while perusing music titles. For women the entire transaction of buying music had to be conducted with a clerk through a tiny window in the storefront.

That was only the beginning. Normally non-Muslim male and female shoppers wait out prayer time business closures by walking around or sitting on benches along the street. But then the Mutawa arrived. All women were ordered to stay within a walled enclosure in the center of the souq during prayer time. The area contained picnic tables and benches, so it was comfortable enough. Since women of all nationalities were gathered in the enclosure, I sometimes had the good fortune to interact with Saudi women. Most were curious about Western women. If we appeared friendly they would sometimes approach us wanting to try out their scant English skills. If Fawzia was along to translate we could have a real conversation. Some just wanted to touch our hair. At that time Western women wore their hair free of covering, which seemed to fascinate the Saudi women. I was approached numerous times by women of all ages who just wanted to touch my auburn hair. I did not mind.

But for the Muslim men it was another story. I felt sorry for them. The Mutawa, accompanied by the local police, would start at one end of the main street of the souq and literally herd the men into the nearest mosque. The Mutawa would beat stragglers with their long, stout sticks. Any man who attempted an escape was literally chased down and herded back to the main crowd. Moreover, Mutawa drove small Toyota trucks up and down the main street shouting, "Salah, salah, salah" (prayer/worship), via a loudspeaker. I was appalled by this forced practice of religion. Of course non-Muslim men were caught up in the drive to the mosque. They protested about the fact they were not Muslims, but their appeals were usually ignored by the Mutawa. Non-Muslims are not allowed to enter Saudi mosques, so these men milled about outside until the prayer finished. Muslim and non-Muslim men began to avoid downtown in the evenings.

Mutawa prowled the streets on foot and in black Chevrolet Suburbans with blacked-out windows. Arabic writing decorated the side doors. Fawzia and I were waiting at the bus stop one evening when one of the Suburbans squealed to a stop nearby. I asked Fawzia what the writing said. Without hesitation she translated, "The Commission for the Promotion of Virtue and Prevention of Vice." The doors of the Suburban burst open and a mob of skinny, bearded Mutawa, gripping long sticks, exploded from within. They looked loaded for bear. They immediately surrounded a young Asian man who was standing on the street near us. He was slim and well-dressed, not seeming to be causing any mischief. I watched in horror as the Mutawa set about beating the young man with their stout sticks. I felt sickened by the thudding blows landing on the poor soul. He fell to the ground and curled up tightly, trying to avoid the blows. Finally the Mutawa hauled the young man to his feet, pushed him toward the vehicle and literally threw him into the back seat of the Suburban. All the while he shouted, "What have I done? What have I done?" The Mutawa yelled back something about looking at women. I tried to watch obliquely without drawing attention to us after Fawzia warned me in a loud whisper, "Look away, pretend not to see this!"

The Mutawa jumped into the truck with their victim, slammed the doors, and careened off into the night. Chills ran up my spine as I wondered what they might do to the young man. We'd all heard stories of deaths and disappearance of some in Mutawa custody. In 2007 two people died within two weeks while in the custody of the Saudi religious police. There was the half-serious, half-joking story about the "one-way helicopter ride," an efficient manner to dispose of dissidents and other types perceived as troublesome. Simply take the victim on a helicopter ride deep into the desert and chuck him out the door from a great height.

I came to believe this likely happened. (Our young OB/GYN resident, Dr. Mohammad, certainly believed it. Gabrielle and I once asked him if he knew of a specific case. He skillfully avoided the question and left our office. We never asked him that question again.)

Waves of Mutawa activity wax and wane in Saudi. At times they are everywhere, but other times they are rarely observed. They are seen as an instrument of the Al Saud ruling family, a useful device to control the masses. I would go on to have my own terrifying experience with the Mutawa. In spite of it I knew, of course, the evil members of the Mutawa comprised only a tiny fraction of Saudis.

Probably the most sobering interpretation of Islamic law in Saudi is the manner of execution by public beheading. Again, this is an archaic punishment carried out today as it was centuries ago. The practice now occurs only in Saudi Arabia and only rarely in Iran. Though still part of the legal system in Yemen and Qatar, no actual beheadings have ever been reported in those countries. No one knows the true number of beheadings in Saudi every year.

Most large towns and cities in Saudi have what Western expats call "chop-chop square." This can be a public square or even a car park cleared of traffic. Executions are traditionally held after Friday prayers. The executioner is a respected and highly paid employee of the government, a job handed down through generations of the same families. The executions draw huge crowds. Some attend for the entertainment value; by all reports it is not unusual to see Saudi children running and playing among the crowd. But what shocks our Western mind most is that beheading is a common occurrence in Saudi and simply accepted as justice done.

For justice is swift in Saudi Arabia, especially for murderers and drug traffickers. A criminal code does not exist. Civil law does not exist. There is no separation of church and state. Punishment is dispensed according to Wahhabi interpretation of Sharia, the law of the Quran, taken literally even now in the twenty-first century. Some crimes punishable by death are drug trafficking, murder, rape, homosexuality, witchcraft, and apostasy from Islam. Occasionally an arbitrary decision is declared by an Islamic judge's interpretation of Sharia. There is no minimum or maximum sentence for serious crimes, no such thing as a plea bargain. The person who commits these crimes knows the sentence is death. On entering Saudi Arabia the message on every customs card is very clear, written in large red letters, "Penalty for drug smuggling and trafficking is death." For thieves, a sharp knife is used to amputate the right hand, but only after at least three offenses of theft.

I often thought I might attend a Friday beheading, but I could not bring myself to view such a horrifying event. Some Western expats did attend the Friday executions and returned with blood-chilling stories.

My Australian friend Anthony, the Emergency room nurse, decided to see for himself what Saudi justice was all about. As if he didn't see enough in the ER. At work on Saturday he came to tell Gabrielle and me what he saw. His face was pale, "Bloody hell, that was the most awful thing I've ever seen." Gabrielle saw the look on Anthony's face and said, "You better sit down Anthony. You don't look quite right."

Anthony sat in our comfy chair behind the office door and began, "There was a huge crowd in attendance. Mutawa circulated through the crowd and pulled us Western observers to the front. They wanted us to see the decapitation at close range. I watched as the police laid a large piece of plastic on the ground. It occurred to me that its purpose was to catch the arterial spray."

Anthony stopped talking for a moment, trying to gather himself and tell us the worst part of his story.

"The criminal was brought to the square, blindfolded, with hands bound behind his back. He was made to kneel facing east toward Mecca. His hair and shirt collar was pushed aside to expose the back of his neck. A policeman announced the prisoner's name and his crime to the crowd. Some British bloke standing beside me said the poor sod was given a sedative. They don't want a prisoner screaming and crying for mercy. Show himself to be a coward, like."

Anthony spoke in little gasps. "The executioner came out of a nearby mosque. He was a big bastard, muscular, skin black as coal. He walked slowly to his victim. No expression on his face. He held the sword in one hand; bloody thing looked about four feet long. Stood on the prisoner's left, tapped the sword against his neck. The guy's head jerked up. The big guy swung that sword, still one-handed, in a huge arc, and down onto the victim's neck. Must be a strong bastard 'cause the head came off with one swing."

Anthony's voice dropped to a whisper, "I looked away then, but I still saw the blood spray about six feet. I started walking away, couldn't look back. But I heard the poor sod's head drop to the pavement with a thunk.

"I wish I'd not gone to see that."

Not all murderers will die. Some will receive clemency from the victim's family at the last moment, sparing his life. The executioner may visit the victim's family to plead for forgiveness for the criminal. Sometimes the family agrees to do so. Or the family might demand "blood money" (monetary compensation) from the prisoner. A rich man may be able to arrange this, but not a humble laborer who literally has only the clothes on his back.

Execution of women is usually carried out with a gun or by stoning, but beheading is occasionally used. Even in the midst of her beheading a woman must remain covered. A small slit is made in her abaya over the back of her neck. (One hopes the executioner has good aim.)

While in Tabuk I was told a story by several physicians who'd worked in the Kingdom for years. I am not certain if the story is true or not, but given the absurdity that is Saudi Arabia I cannot totally discount the story. There were apparently instances when a criminal from the upper class had been caught committing enough thefts to warrant removal of his right hand. But because of the criminal's importance, either through wealth, tribal affiliation, or important connections in the Saudi hierarchy, only part of the extremity was removed in the operating room. Then the part was immediately re-attached. A symbolic gesture, but relatively meaningless.

After hearing Anthony's awful story, I'm glad I never witnessed an execution. I knew the image would haunt me forever.

Preserving My Sanity

I'd settled into my second year in Saudi, but there were times I wondered if I'd made a mistake staying for another year. It was great fun when adventures came along, like trips to Jordan and Petra, but otherwise everyday life in Saudi could be tough. Boredom is ever present. More and more I felt psychologically exhausted and depressed. I wanted to give up and return to Canada. But it felt like such a big step back, and I really wanted to finish my second year. Then there was the corruption, madness, and power games amongst the hospital administration, which affected everyone right down to the housekeeping staff.

We began to see more military activity with fighter jets zooming around at all hours. One morning Jane came to our office to see me on some matter when the roar of a jet stopped us in mid conversation. As the noise subsided she quipped, "A nice little war would be a pleasant diversion, relieve our boredom."

Finally I found my own solution to boredom. For a long time I'd been putting off learning to swim because I was just plain scared. I'd been terrified of deep water all my life. For one reason or another I was at the recreation center almost every day, and every day I would gaze at the swimming pool wishing I could swim. I envied the brave souls who went off to the beach to dive and snorkel. They came back full of stories; amazing creatures on the reef, colors so fantastic they couldn't even begin to describe them. The more I heard about others' adventures in the Red Sea, the more frustrated I felt.

Then I heard about an employee of the recreation center offering swimming lessons for women. So I decided the time had come for me to learn. I couldn't put it off any longer. I didn't feel too enthusiastic about the lessons at first, and I was also self-conscious about the fact I was no beauty in a swimsuit. At the first lesson a half-dozen women showed up. The male instructor, a tall Swede named Bendt, came to the edge of the pool and announced with a shrug, "The hospital administrators say that even for swimming lessons I cannot get in the pool with females!" Bendt smirked humorously. "They fear that I will have to touch you, and I told them it would be impossible to teach you if I cannot get in the pool or touch you!" Everyone groaned. The long reach of Saudi sexual segregation even extended to a swimming pool frequented only by Westerners! Even here single men and women were assigned separate swimming times, although single women could use the pool on family day (married couples with children), but single males could not.

I already knew how to float and dog-paddle so I had somewhat of an advantage. But within a couple of weeks I was the only one showing up for lessons, and Bendt was not willing to go on with just one student. I felt completely abandoned, but something kept me practicing. I went to the pool every evening after work. I gradually developed my own odd version of a breast stroke and swam laps from one side of the pool to the other. But I was still too frightened to venture into the deep end.

A few weeks passed and still I continued to go to the pool every day. When I returned from yet another beach weekend with Jane and Patrick, I came away even more determined to conquer my fear of deep water. If I didn't, I knew I would never see the reef, the colors, and the wonderful creatures. Jane knew of my frustration and finally one day she said, "I'll meet you at the pool after work. I have a plan. You swim next to the side of the pool while I swim beside you. If you panic you have only to put your hand on the side and stay there."

After work Jane and I met in the pool. I started out swimming at the side of the pool with Jane right beside me. I was amazed when I made it into twelve feet of water with very little trepidation. I hung at the side of the pool in the deep water, hardly believing what I had just achieved. I was further astonished to find that treading water came naturally to me.

What an incredible feeling of fulfillment! In those few moments I'd finally freed myself from a lifetime of fear. Jane grinned and shouted, "I knew you could do it! Come practice every day and Patrick and I will take you snorkeling."

Once I was comfortable in deep water nothing could keep me away from the pool. I swam every evening after work and on the weekend. I worked my way up to fifty laps every day. Gabrielle, already an accomplished swimmer, decided to join me after work. Jane, Gabrielle, and I often did laps together, chatting as we swam. The inches fell from my arms, shoulders and middle. I found I loved the water more than I could ever have imagined. Swimming became the major factor in helping me to cope with life in Saudi Arabia. No matter the kind of day I had I knew I could get in the pool after work and find freedom and stress relief.

True to their word, Jane and Patrick invited me to the beach with them for snorkeling. As a single woman I was allowed to travel with married couples. The distance from Tabuk to Duba is not great, but it takes longer than need be because of frequent police and military checkpoints on the way. Tedious. At least every 25 miles we were stopped by two or three scrawny young Saudi males in uniform, each holding the omnipresent automatic weapon. These lonely desert checkpoints must be hardship postings indeed. The police and soldiers usually walked around our vehicle and peered in the windows to see what we were carrying. But mostly they stared at Jane and me, or any other Western female who might be inside. I felt nervous the first few times I encountered a checkpoint, but I soon realized that they are common in most of the Middle East.

While we waited at each checkpoint, Jane filled the time with her wicked brand of humor. She didn't like Saudis much, and she often made fun of them. One time she pointed out a particularly dull-looking youth and whispered to me, "Look at that poor sod. Bet his gene pool hasn't been stirred in a while!" It was unfortunately true. The police and military personnel we saw on these isolated stretches of road often looked like leftovers, those who hadn't made it into the mainstream of recruits. Jane would quip wickedly, "This lot looks like their sister was their mother." Inbreeding is a real problem given the popularity of marriage between first cousins.

My excitement grew as we neared the Red Sea. Now I could swim! Now I could slip off the edge of that reef and see the beauty I'd been missing. Most divers and snorkelers wear full-body suits, footwear, and gloves to prevent coral injuries and contact with jelly fish. Footwear is a necessity because of stone fish, one of the most dangerous creatures in Arabian waters. It possesses one of the world's deadliest venoms. The creatures prefer shallow water and are notoriously difficult to identify because of their effective camouflage. Along that part of the Red Sea swimmers have to walk through shallow water over old coral banks to get to the reef edge and deep water, increasing the chances of stepping on a stone fish. Unfortunate victims say the pain of the stone fish venom is excruciating. Immediate first aid is required with transport to a center that has anti-venom.

But nothing could have intimidated me at that point. The recreation center boasted a well-stocked dive equipment shop where I'd purchased a high quality snorkel, mask and diving gloves. For my feet I had only a pair of tattered sports shoes, but they proved adequate. I tried out my snorkel and mask in the shallow water on the reef. Even in the shallow water I was amazed at the richness of life. This old coral was thickly populated with small versions of the giant clams that are indigenous to the Red Sea. Gloriously-colored fish in brilliant hues of yellow, blue, and tangerine swam close to peer at me.

With single-minded intent I finally decided I was ready to go over the reef. I was tentative about going into the sea, but my interest in what I'd see was stronger than my fear. All my effort to learn to swim and conquer my fear peaked at this very moment.

I sat down on the reef shelf and peered over the edge into thirty feet of crystalline blue-green water. Jane was waiting for me in the water by the reef edge, dressed in her black and pink wetsuit. "You ready?" she asked. I grinned and slipped into the warm, azure water. Jane took my hand and we floated together for a moment. I looked down into the deep water through my mask and felt momentarily disoriented. Everything appeared blurry. Then my vision cleared, and an explosion of color and motion assaulted my senses: forests of coral in brilliant fuchsia and purple, huge lazy grouper fish in stunning shades of turquoise and red, neon-yellow angel fish, and schools of tiny silver dart-like fish zipped about in perfect unison. The entire undersea world was backlit by the cobalt and aquamarine colors produced by depth. The sea floor dropped away beneath me, the water so clear I could see a group of scuba divers thirty feet below. I saw Patrick wave at me from amongst the group.

Jane gradually let go of my hand. I felt no fear. I hung there in awe, astonished by the beauty around me. A flotilla of small jelly fish drifted near, transparent and delicate, the rippling streamers on their underside edged in shocking pink. My mind kept marveling that such incredible colors could exist. After a half hour of bobbing comfortably on the gentle waves, I climbed back on top of the coral ledge to reflect on what I'd seen.

I consider my first glide over the reef as one of the most beautiful moments of my life, all the more so because I had to work so hard to achieve it. It was a personal victory over one of my greatest fears. That night I went to my tent exhausted. I was lulled to sleep by the sound of breaking waves and the scent of the salty night air.

Earlier that evening happy groups of divers and snorkelers dotted the beach, cooking the fish and lobsters they'd caught that day. Jane and Patrick invited me to dine with them on slices of big red grouper they had fried in a pan of melted butter. As we chatted, they congratulated me repeatedly. "You did this on your own," enthused Jane. "You should be so bloody proud of yourself!"

"Honestly," I said to Jane, "I don't know that I could have done it without your help and encouragement." I was so deeply grateful to her.

When darkness fell, the party crowd brought out their booze, and things got loud and unruly. Another group, including Patrick, Jane and me, pitched our tents further up the beach; we'd already heard about the late night parties. I understood their need to let loose on the freedom of the beach, but I felt no desire to join them. The Saudi beach patrol drove by several times a night in their Toyota Hilux trucks. After the partiers went to sleep, we'd hear the patrol truck laboring along the sandy beach from some distance, back and forth throughout the night. The soldiers were dressed in dark green uniforms with matching caps. One man drove while two others stood in the box of the vehicle slumped over the 50-calibre machine gun mounted on every truck. I wondered if they ever got the chance to use the big gun. The beach patrol must have known there was alcohol in the camp, but to give them credit they rarely hassled the beach crowd. As long as we were far away from Saudi citizens, our Western habits weren't a big threat. The patrol came by more frequently during daylight hours. Sometimes as many as four or five different patrol trucks passed by in an hour. It was, of course, a soldier's best chance to ogle women in revealing beach attire!

After learning to swim and snorkel, I went on as many beach trips as I could manage. I often went with Dr. Walid, Dr. Hosni, their wives Mariam and Hala, and their children. Both doctors worked in our department and almost always asked Gabrielle and me to join them on their beach trips. Dr. Walid and Dr. Hosni were Syrian by birth, but Belgian citizens. Walid's wife, Mariam, was a tall native Belgian with a quiet and pleasant demeanor. Dr. Hosni met his wife, Hala, in Belgian, but she was also of Syrian birth. Hala was a petite woman with dark brown eyes and a feisty spirit. Both couples had two small children, whom Gabrielle often babysat. As a group we always had great fun together. Gabrielle and Mariam both knew how to swim and snorkel, but they were wary of the Red Sea. Hala was a modest woman who did not swim. The ladies preferred to stay on the beach with the children, but I never missed a chance to snorkel.

Walid's vehicle, an elderly Toyota SUV, was subject to breakdowns. Most expat males bought used vehicles while living in Saudi because it was difficult for foreigners to get a car loan. No one ever knew how long they might stay in the country so, for most, the purchase of a new vehicle was not worth the trouble. Not to mention the high likelihood of your new vehicle being trashed in a motor vehicle accident.

On one trip to the Red Sea with Walid and Miriam, we were barely out of Tabuk before we heard the thump, thump of a flat tire. Mariam and the children, and Gabrielle and I, sat by the side of the road while Walid set about changing the tire.

It was still early morning, the air searingly hot, and the desert empty. I gazed over the distant vista, finding joy in the breathtaking beauty. Waves of heat frolicked on the horizon while cloud shadows drifted silently over the golden desert sand and far mountains.

Soon our peace was shattered. Bedouins began to arrive. Where had they come from? Only minutes ago the terrain was bereft of any living thing. Small Toyota trucks careened to a stop by our crippled SUV and soon a traffic jam blocked the entire highway. Males ranging from toddlers to bent old men gathered round our vehicle. We knew the men had a genuine desire to help, but the situation soon turned into a comedy. Everyone gestured and shouted in voluble Arabic, advising Walid of the best technique to change the tire. Walid simply smiled and entertained their advice in good humor.

Then from the distant mirage of heat we watched a herd of shaggy black goats approach us. They were accompanied by their minder, an elderly woman wearing a long dress covered in dust. The creatures escaped her supervision and were soon mixed amongst the collection of Toyota trucks. Their bleating protests added to the cacophony of shouting men. The old woman, astonishingly agile for her age, skillfully re-grouped her charges and herded them away.

The Bedouin men cast many glances at us women. We laughed about our situation, knowing the Bedouin men thought Walid a wealthy and lucky man to have three wives and two children! Within a few minutes the tire was changed. The collection of Bedouin men picked up their children, jumped in their trucks, and disappeared into the desert in a cloud of dust.

I never had a dull moment at the Red Sea. The first time I went snorkeling with Walid the sea was fairly rough with cresting waves pulling us about. He'd bought a new spear gun and was eager to try it out. A brisk wind blew that day, but once in the water we forgot about the choppy sea. We first inspected some fish traps that Walid set the weekend before. We found the traps contained small grouper and other edible fish. We planned to eat the fish so decided to return later and collect them fresh. We ate everything we caught. Any fish left over was taken home in an icebox.

That weekend I brought a disposable underwater camera hoping to get some shots of the reefs. It was difficult to get decent photos because the sea was rough. Every time I'd get set up to take a picture another wave would crash over me. But my photos turned out better than I expected.

We never knew in what condition we would find the Red Sea. Sometimes the water was calm and crystal clear, like swimming in liquid glass. At those times I could see the bottom far below me, the emerald depths alive with colorful fish and massive stands of coral.

After leaving the fish traps behind, Walid and I glided over to look at a towering coral formation. Suddenly an enormous moray eel slid out from a hole inside the coral. It grimaced pugnaciously, its gaping mouth lined with razor teeth. The eel, dark brown in color with darker brown spots, was long and sinuous, pure muscle. While underwater images are distorted in size and shape, I knew this eel was at least five feet long because we could see his tail sticking out the opposite side of the coral formation. Moray eels are territorial creatures, but apparently they rarely bite unless aggravated. I felt a little frightened when this one continued to dart his head in and out of his hole in the coral. This huge fellow was obviously threatened by our presence near his home. Moray eels have two sets of jaws and teeth. Long, sharp teeth line the mouth and secure the prey. A second set of jaws (called pharyngeal jaws) further down the throat also has teeth. These jaws come up into the mouth and grasp the prey to pull it down into the esophagus. Because moray teeth are backward-facing they cannot release their prey once caught. If it bites a human hand in mistaking it for prey, a large and strong moray can drown a human. A moray's teeth will not release even in death. The jaws must be pried off a human victim. While I didn't actually think of all that at the time I just knew I wanted to be away from there right away. Walid pointed at the eel with his spear gun, but I signaled him not to kill this impressive creature. We swam away to safety.

On one occasion I was frightened quite badly in the sea, though the experience never kept me away from the water. It happened on another weekend when I went on a beach trip with Walid, Hosni and their wives and families. The Red Sea appeared fairly calm that weekend and I was anxious to get in the water. Hosni was just off a busy week of on-call duty and wanted to have a nap. So Walid and I put on our equipment and went into the sea. As usual we checked the fish traps. The water was beautifully clear and there was plenty to see.

A person should never snorkel or dive in open water without a partner, but suddenly I found myself alone in the sea. I surfaced briefly to look for Walid's snorkel, but I found the water had suddenly become choppy. I could see little over the waves. But I felt no fear or even apprehension at the time. Instead of doing the sensible thing and going to shore immediately, I decided to take one more, small excursion in the immediate area. I'd already discovered I could easily lose track of time, and sometimes place, while snorkeling. Any snorkeler or diver will tell you your world narrows to the sound of your own breathing and the extraordinary sights around you.

I am not sure how much time passed, perhaps an hour or less. When I surfaced to swim to shore, I was horrified by my situation. I found I had drifted a good half mile or more beyond our beach camp. I realized I'd been carried by currents so subtle I was not aware of it, but, nevertheless, strong enough to pull me laterally. I treaded water and took a moment to orient myself. From my perspective in the water the entire shoreline looked pretty much the same. Over the shifting waves I could see I wasn't too far from shore. So I moved close to the coral shelf and swam beside it back around a point of land. I was soon able to see our beach camp in the distance. It was then, as I swam, that I felt the current pulling me sideways. I felt thankful a more aggressive current hadn't dragged me out to sea or so far down the shoreline I would be lost. I was so relieved when I stepped on shore. I'd learned a valuable lesson that day.

To my great surprise I found Walid already back in camp. I was furious at him and my own poor judgment. I shouted at him for leaving me alone in the sea. Both Hosni and Mariam also castigated him for abandoning me. But Dr. Walid did not seem concerned about the situation.

On more than one occasion Walid showed a lack of common sense. Once Gabrielle and I traveled to the beach with Walid, Mariam and the children; (Hosni and Hala did not accompany us on that trip.) Outside of Duba there are few definite roads into beach sites, but it is usually possible to find rough tracks left by others. It was worth looking for a well-worn track because it usually indicated a relatively accessible route. But Walid loved to turn off the road at his whim, tracks or not. We drove for at least an hour with no clear route in front of us. I think Walid was driving in circles as we were no nearer the Red Sea shore than when we turned off the road. I heard Gabrielle mumble from the back seat, "Are we lost, do ya think?" Walid spluttered with indignation. Of course we weren't lost; he knew exactly where we were. We three women smirked at each other and fell silent.

Eventually we found ourselves in a shallow canyon surrounded by smooth sandstone walls. A lovely little canyon, it was filled with green acacia trees and huge golden sand dunes sculpted by wind pooling in the canyon. Walid stopped to take stock of the situation. On the opposite side of the canyon a natural opening cleaved the wall. Perhaps it was a way out. Walid decided to plow through the high dunes to get to it. Had I been driving I would never have attempted that route. He pointed the four-wheel-drive at the first huge dune, meaning to either go over it or through it.

I knew for certain we would be stuck because the dune was too high and wide to drive through. Walid gunned the engine and made a run at it. In the middle of the dune our vehicle came to a sudden halt, high-centered and stuck fast. The sand came midway up the doors. I heard Gabrielle mutter again, "Bloody hell, we'll be here forever." No one knew we were here and we had no idea where we were. None of us could open our doors for sand so Walid and I rolled down the side windows and climbed out of the vehicle. Mariam, Gabrielle, and the children stayed inside. I hiked to the top of the highest dune hoping to see a meaningful landmark. I thought we had to be close to the Red Sea, but to my horror I could see nothing but more sand in every direction.

I returned to the truck and by then Walid had the shovels out. There was little choice but to start shoveling and hope for the best. We did not expect Gabrielle and Mariam to get out and help. I knew I was the strongest of the women and could shovel more effectively. Moving heavy sand in high temperatures and energy-sucking humidity is not an ideal way to spend time. Mariam and Gabrielle occasionally handed out either water or cola to keep us hydrated. After an hour of digging, Walid thought he'd try to drive out of the dune, but in spite of rocking the truck back and forth we remained stuck. We continued to dig.

Eventually Walid drained half the air from the tires; a hard tire tends to pile up sand in front of it, but a softer tire will usually crawl over sand. Walid and I climbed back into the truck. With a giant heave and screaming engine we finally rolled out of our predicament. Walid was quiet and clearly chastened by the experience. He carefully found his way out of the canyon, avoiding larger dunes as much as possible. We'd wasted the entire morning and much of the afternoon digging ourselves out. By now the sun was dipping towards the west, and we were able to get our bearings. We soon arrived at the Red Sea and set up camp.

I'd camped before in North America, but never so roughly as we did at the Red Sea. There were no posted beaches in the region we frequented. Other than the hospital beach camp, none was developed. Most beaches could not be accessed without a four-wheel drive vehicle. We each brought a tent, blankets, food and boxes of bottled water, everything we thought we'd need. If an important item was forgotten we did without it for the weekend. The nearest town was Duba, fifteen to twenty miles distant after the highway was reached. There were no toilet facilities and no trees or shrubs to protect modesty; the back of an inland sand dune sufficed. It didn't matter.

I fell in love with camping at the Red Sea and never missed a chance to go to the beach, where I was never bored!

Mada'in Saleh – Petra's Elder Sister

I'd been interested in archeology most of my adult life and visited many famous sites in North America and some in the United Kingdom. So when the hospital recreation center announced a tour to a place called Mada'in Saleh (cities of Saleh), an ancient site about three hundred and forty miles south of Tabuk, I jumped at the opportunity. In 2008 UNESCO proclaimed Mada'in Saleh a World Heritage Site. This archeological treasure lies near the holy city of Medina on the west coast of the Kingdom.

The Nabateans built Mada'in Saleh, the same civilization that built Petra, its sister city in Jordan. Over 2000 years ago these magnificent cities were the superstars of the camel caravan route carrying incense (frankincense and myrrh) and spices to Mediterranean ports. The Nabateans became enormously wealthy by collecting tolls from the caravans. Inscriptions found in the region of Mada'in Saleh indicate an even older Arab civilization dating as far back as the sixth to fourth centuries BCE. Some historians believe the Queen of Sheba may have come from this region, the center of the ancient biblical land of Midian.

To have seen Mada'in Saleh is far and away the highlight of my two years in Saudi Arabia. Petra in Jordan is a splendid place, but Mada'in Saleh in Saudi Arabia has a special magic of its own. It is in a spectacularly beautiful setting, and the most magnificent archeological site I have ever seen. For me, the special allure of Mada'in Saleh is that I had the honor to see it at all. It is difficult to access, and few outside the

Kingdom ever have the privilege of seeing it. Its remote location, the requirement for government permission and the restrictions on getting into Saudi means it is often empty of tourists. Expatriates already living in the Kingdom represent the bulk of visitors to Mada'in Saleh.

Few Saudis ever visit Mada'in Saleh. In fact many avoid it. In the third century BCE, the Thamud tribe settled in the area. They were idol-worshippers, and their society suffered under despotic rulers. A pre-Islamic prophet named Saleh came to the area and called on them to convert to monotheism. The Thamudis made fun of him and demanded he perform a miracle to prove the existence of one God. They asked Saleh to produce a pregnant camel and so he did. Saleh warned the Thamudis to care for the animal and not harm it, but the Thamudis killed the sacred camel. When after three days they did not repent Saleh called upon God to destroy them and so he did. Centuries later, some highly superstitious Saudis still consider Mada'in Saleh a cursed place.

Saudis have little interest in anything from their ancient past. Given the country's oil wealth and the modern conveniences, many Saudis seem almost ashamed of it. Ancient structures are often razed and replaced with modern steel and glass buildings. Others are "restored" to the point where the structure no longer resembles the original. It is said that when Mecca and Medina were modernized to accommodate more religious pilgrims, several ancient structures of significant Islamic heritage were bulldozed. The space was paved over for parking lots and accommodations.

Of course, I was excited by the trip, and I decided to invite Trish to come along. I'd noticed she was again living in her flat on the floor below me after a stint of living downtown with her boyfriend Phil. Curious, I asked her why she was back living on the compound.

"Phil got a contract to drill a water well somewhere east of Tabuk," Trish explained. "He's way out there in the desert and doesn't know when he'll be back. No point me staying downtown. Too hard to get to work."

"So you'll be around awhile," I said, "Why don't you come along to Mada'in Saleh? We haven't seen much of each other, so it'd be a chance for us to spend some time together."

Trish smiled, "That would be nice. Sure I'll go."

About fifteen people signed up for the trip and we rode in a minibus provided by the recreation center. Oddly enough, Western males and females were permitted to travel together on these types of trips. Our group consisted of Western expats, Filipinos, and two blonde German nurses, who kept to themselves. The German women spent most of the trip complaining about the heat and dust. They also made racially charged comments about Arabs and Filipinos in earshot of the Filipinos traveling with us. I wondered why such people even bothered to go on these trips. Trish came, but probably shouldn't have, because her stomach was acting up. On the other hand one of my favorite Australians was part of our group, an athletic, humorous young woman named Christina.

We left in the coolness before dawn. Three hours later we stopped for breakfast in a tiny oasis town called Tayma. This area has great archeological significance for its place in biblical Midian, but nowadays it's barely a wide spot in the road. The group ate in a roadside restaurant staffed by several Turkish men. We were served fresh-baked flat bread, boiled eggs, a white cheese, black olives, fresh tomatoes, garlicky "foul" (beans) and gallons of hot mint tea. I

Aside from the foul beans, it was the first time I'd had an Arabic-style breakfast. I found it refreshingly different and delicious. Trish was feeling terrible by the time we reached Tayma. In fact, the bus driver had to stop twice on the road so Trish could get off and vomit. I was worried about how she would do on the rest of the trip.

We were required to take a security escort on the trip, as ordered by the Prince of Tabuk. Abdul Rahman Saeed was a devilishly handsome young Saudi man with sparkling brown eyes and, following a hot trend amongst young Saudi males at the time, shoulder-length black hair. Abdul fancied himself, but he was a humorous, pleasant sort who interacted well with our group. In spite of his lack of English skills it was obvious he was used to being around Western people. Our group leader, Nicolas, an employee of the recreation center, told us Abdul was provided for our protection against hostile Bedouin. He was more likely along to make sure we didn't wander off the prescribed route. Abdul Rahman led our bus in his brand new Nissan Pathfinder. He normally worked as a security guard for the Prince of Tabuk. He wore a shoulder holster containing a scratched, rusty-looking handgun. At one point our entourage stopped because Abdul wished to display his marksmanship skills. We soon discovered Abdul could not hit the flat side of a barn at five paces! Christina giggled, "So much for protection. What if us girls are kidnapped by Bedouin? We'd have been carried off into the desert while Abdul figured out how to un-holster his trusty sidearm!"

A rather sobering fact is that this remote region of Saudi Arabia still sees its share of centuries-old tribal feuds. Occasionally a feud will flare up and Mada'in Saleh will close to tourists until the unrest settles down. Even if in-country expats are able to obtain a permit, it may not always be safe to travel in the area. There continue to be persistent reports of attacks on Western travelers in the area. As recently as 2007 three French expatriates from Riyadh (who were also, incidentally, Muslims) were shot and killed on the roadside near Mada'in Saleh. The killers have never been identified. Mada'in Saleh has been closed several times since.

Like all road trips I took in Saudi Arabia, I was fascinated by the different landscapes. On the journey from Tabuk to Mada'in Saleh, the first fifty miles or so consisted of a two-lane asphalt-covered road with bone-jarring potholes and loose gravel. The surrounding terrain was bleakly desolate, almost featureless, a monotone canvas of small grey-brown stones and sand. No vegetation at all. The landscape gradually changed into tawny-colored sand with an occasional thorny acacia tree.

I love acacia trees. They are starkly handsome with their dark greenery spread wide to create a flat top. The trunks are gnarled and contorted, exquisite bonsai of the desert. Their thorns are terrible things, long and sharp as a straight razor. They can pierce and slash tender human flesh with ease. Once while attending a desert picnic, I stumbled upon a dried acacia thorn lying on the ground. I was wearing open-topped shoes and the thorn was at such an angle it buried itself in a major vein on the top of my foot. The wound bled profusely for some time.

But camels dine on the thorny branches apparently without harm. Where there are camels, the acacia trees are trimmed neatly across their base according to how high camel heads can reach.

I saw a lot of Bedouin camps in the distance as we traveled the asphalt highway. Frequently the bus driver slowed or stopped to allow camels to cross the road. The haughty beasts took their time. Some stopped mid-road, seemingly just to smirk at the bus. We neared a town named Quariba, where small piles of rose-colored rocks began to appear more frequently. As the miles passed the rocks evolved into great monoliths, and later sheer cliffs of striated, rose-gold sandstone.

Midway through the trip we made a rest stop at a petrol station. A metal enclosure, about the size of a typical outhouse, was set up behind the station with a filthy squat toilet inside. No running water. The stench was so terrible the Filipina women covered their mouth and nose with a handkerchief. Trish, pale and obviously ill, stumbled off the bus and came over to lean on me. She took one look at the toilet facilities and exclaimed, "What a hellhole. As if I didn't feel awful enough!" But we had no other choice, so the ladies in our group lined up and waited patiently for a turn in the hellhole.

Christina and I noticed an encampment of Bedouin tents standing near the outhouse. Two young women, without veils, scurried from their tents and approached our group of women. Both wore shimmery satin blouses, one in vivid neon pink and the other dazzling lime green; two desert roses in this rather mean setting. Chunky old silver Bedouin bracelets clanked together on their slim wrists and massive old silver necklaces collared their slender necks. Their long, voluminous skirts were made of plain black cotton. Both had beautifully-embroidered headscarves thrown loosely over their hair. Though young, their faces were already brown and leathery from the desert sun. They smiled broadly and beckoned us to come drink tea with them. One took my arm and pulled gently, "Ahlan wa sahlan! Chai!" (Welcome, tea!) pointing to her tent. The two bigoted German women in our group sneered rudely at the invitation, expressing disgust at sharing anything with these desert women. Christina and I would have joined the Bedouin women for tea in a second, but with great regret we had to say no, the bus was waiting. Their excited young faces fell with disappointment.

One of the things I liked most about Christina was her openness and genuine enjoyment in interacting with other cultures. She said to me with some sadness, "I'm sure sorry we had to miss that opportunity. It would have been great fun." I agreed. What an experience it would have been. And once again, the fantastic Arabian hospitality: Two young women of the desert, with little of their own in all likelihood, offering the comfort of their family home to perfect strangers from a completely different culture. In desert tradition even an enemy can be welcomed into the family tent for three days.

Back on the road, we drove for another hour or so. Finally the bus descended from the desert plateau into a basin surrounded by reddish-brown sandstone cliffs. The valley was filled with groves of date palms, their delicate fronds creating a vast blue-green carpet across the entire valley. Everywhere the humid air was alive with the sound of countless irrigation pumps, laboring to keep the date palms hydrated. We entered the ancient oasis village of Al Ula, a settlement that dates to the seventh and sixth centuries BCE. After the Romans conquered Petra in about 100 CE, the Nabateans moved their capital to Mada'in Saleh, located about thirteen miles north of Al Ula. Al Ula has since been the major settlement in the region.

We pulled up in front of a quaint local hotel that had surely seen better days. A two-storey structure covered in flaking paint that had once been white. The building was surrounded by a fence of rusted metal stakes, long-dead vines clinging to it. As our group entered the lobby, a grinning East Indian clerk first separated males from females. He led us women to the first floor where several rooms held three or four single beds each. A single squat toilet and shower head were located in a room in the hallway. The males were roomed on the floor above us. The hotel itself was relatively clean, though I noted the sheets on my single bed had not seen detergent in some time. I wasn't bothered. I'd brought along a couple of my own towels and simply laid one of them over my pillow.

The bed was quite comfortable. I shared a room with Christina, Trish and two giggly Filipinas named Ascencion and Lourdes.

A curious thing attracted my attention. On every bedside table I noticed a sticker with a bright green arrow on it. Through the years I saw the arrows in every Middle Eastern hotel room I ever stayed in. Much later I found out the small green arrow pointed in the direction of Mecca for the convenience of Muslim guests wishing to pray.

The restaurant in the hotel served pretty much the same food as the restaurant in Tayma. There was no menu; food items were simply brought by the East Indian wait staff and set on a big table in the center of the dining room. Roast chicken, fresh flatbread, olives, boiled eggs, fresh tomatoes and cucumbers, and hot mint tea. The same food appeared at every meal. Our entire group, males and females, ate together in the hotel restaurant and it became our gathering place over the next two days.

Local Saudi men came and went from the restaurant with less of the usual staring brought on by a group of Westerners. The Indian waiters were gracious and chattered with all of us in broken English. They were a delightful bunch and couldn't do enough for us. It seemed the locals and the hotel staff was used to the occasional foreigners coming to see their wondrous neighbor, Mada'in Saleh.

The dashing Abdul Rahman Saeed joined us in the restaurant that evening. It was clear Abdul enjoyed his time with us. He asked if I, the strong-looking lady with the pretty red hair, was married. Surely I must have borne many children. He seemed puzzled by the fact I was not married and had no children. Abdul said he had one wife, but wished to have four, the limit allowed in Islam. I wasn't sure if Abdul was making a marriage proposal or if he was simply curious about me. I hadn't the heart to tell Abdul my hair color came straight out of a bottle!

The following morning we rose before dawn to go to Mada'in Saleh. By now Trish was so ill she could not come with us that first day. Christina and I made sure she was comfortable and had a good supply of water, juice and crackers before we left.

Before the bus departed for Mada'in Saleh the hotel kitchen provided our group with boxes of bottled water. The same smiling waiters stacked the water in the back seats of our bus. The kitchen also sent along bread, cheese and fresh fruit to share among our group. We would need all of the water. By the time the sun rose the temperature was already in the high nineties. Before we left Al Ula the following day I gave each member of the wait staff a much-deserved gift of money for their great service. I noticed some other members of our group did the same.

On the short drive to Mada'in Saleh the narrow road zigzagged between vertical walls of golden sandstone. As we left Al Ula I saw decrepit old mud brick buildings slowly being reclaimed by nature. This was a much older part of Al Ula where nobody lived anymore.

We arrived at the gate to Mada'in Saleh. Several security guards in tan uniforms slouched against a small shed, constructed of dented aluminum siding. All carried the usual automatic weapons. We watched as Abdul climbed out of his Nissan and proceeded to sit down with the security guards. Tea was brought from inside the shed and the group set about drinking it together as our group sweltered in the hot bus. Apart from the traditional greetings and sharing of tea, apparently Abdul had to sort out some red tape as well. Our group leader Nicolas told us this trip had involved three months of paperwork and "baksheesh" (bribes) on the part of the recreation center director.

As we waited, I looked at my surroundings. The immediate landscape was amazing, vast stretches of golden sand with scatterings of convoluted beige rock formations. In the far distance smooth and rounded mountains ringed the entire area. An occasional flat-topped acacia tree adorned the expanse of sand. There was little other vegetation.

Finally Abdul rose and climbed back into his Nissan. One of the Mada'in Saleh security guards swung open the entrance gate, climbed into a dusty Jeep and led the way. Our little bus passed through the gate and struggled along a rudimentary track with deep sand on both sides. It would be a simple matter for the bus to get stuck.

I was breathless with excitement to see this marvelous place. The bus followed Abdul and the security guard. The bus pulled to a stop. Our group got out and stood gazing at the wonders all around us.

Rising out of the landscape of sand were monolithic boulders of golden sandstone standing in solitary splendor. Carved into each was an intricately carved façade with an entrance in the middle. The lintels were crenelated and embellished with carved urns and figures of birds. Each of the monoliths contained one gigantic tomb, likely reserved for the wealthy and powerful. I saw similar, but less elaborate, tomb facades in the distance cut into the base of sandstone outcroppings, lined up one after another like sentries. Most of these tombs were built between 100 BCE and 76 CE and appeared extraordinarily preserved in the dry climate. Some of the carvings on the facades display distinctly Roman embellishments, a moment in time when Rome occupied the region. Mada'in Saleh was already ancient when the Romans were here. When we arrived at the site, I'd noticed a newer-looking chain link fence topped with razor wire surrounding the immediate area. The reason for this became clear. Some of the tomb fronts were scarred with bullet holes and graffiti.

At one time the living residents of Mada'in Saleh resided nearby in what were probably mud huts, little of which remains today. According to recent archeological investigations, the hub of the actual city still lies beneath the sands: ruins of homes, temples, streets, markets and military housing. The Nabateans drilled wells and dug rainwater tanks in the area, still used by the local Bedouins today. Other recent discoveries have been made in nearby stands of towering rock formations: ancient inscriptions, dedications to gods, drawings and sacred niches and chambers.

Most of our group drifted off. I rejoiced in my solitude. I wanted to explore on my own, to contemplate this majestic place alone. The afternoon was breathlessly hot with an occasional whisper of a breeze. The silence roared in the still desert heat. The air was flawlessly clear, the kind of crisp clarity found only in remote places as yet unadulterated by pollution. I climbed into a tomb and sat quietly. The tomb was cool and dim, but details were illuminated by one brilliant shaft of sunshine that crept in silently. Long narrow niches lined the walls where the dead had once rested.

As the massive weight of the centuries enfolded and settled around me, I felt tears in my eyes. I could scarcely believe I was here, that I could come to this remarkable country, to this remote place, and live this experience. I thought I was the most fortunate person on earth. If only these rooms and the spirits within could talk. What fantastic mysteries might they share with me? I thought of these ancient structures enduring in their desert solitude, steadfast in the hush of time immemorial. I was momentarily awed by the thought that Mada'in Saleh had been here centuries before me and would be here, I hoped, centuries after me. I felt humbled and small in life's grand scheme.

Eventually I met up with Christina, sitting on a rock by herself. I approached and sat down to share the rock with her. Her face held a look of wonder. I suspect mine looked the same. "Isn't this the most magnificent place?" I said to Christina. She sighed, "Pure magic. The landscape, the tombs, the colors, it's astonishing. I've never seen a more beautiful archeological site."

Our group spent the entire day at Mada'in Saleh. We returned to Al Ula in the radiance of a cinnamon sunset. I never saw a sunset in Saudi that wasn't spectacular. I was sunburned and filthy with dust and sand, but overjoyed with the excitement of my day. We arrived back at the hotel and got cleaned up for supper. Some of our group gathered in the hotel restaurant. We chattered amongst ourselves, sharing stories of our day in Mada'in Saleh. Then Trish showed up and said she felt better. "Oh Trish, you have to try to come with us tomorrow," I told her. "It's the most beautiful place."

The waiters again served the same food at supper: roast chicken, fresh bread, olives, boiled eggs and mint tea. A bit tiresome after a couple of days, but still I enjoyed the food because it was well-prepared, and there was always plenty of it. Anyway we were all ravenous after our day in the heat and dust.

Later that evening some of us decided to go to the small souq in downtown Al Ula. The entire market took up only one street. We did not wear our abayas that evening, but we did dress conservatively with long sleeves and modest necklines. The local Saudis, both men and women, were welcoming and curious. Some stopped us to practice their few words of English. I again got the feeling that the local people had seen their share of foreigners visiting their pretty town.

Trish and I found ourselves in a tiny cubbyhole of a gold shop. I tried on a bracelet made of 22-karat gold coins, an extravagant thing, heavy and warm on my wrist. Trish was enthusiastic, "It's gorgeous, you gotta buy it!" Bemused, I shot back, "Oh sure, it's easy for you to spend *my* money!" But in the end I succumbed to the precious bracelet. To this day I can remember what I paid for it: 800 Saudi riyals or about USD $200. Would that we could still buy gold for that price!

Our room was very quiet that night. Christina and I passed out the minute our heads hit the pillows. Even the Filipina girls, Ascencion and Lourdes, didn't do much giggling that evening. The effect of that day's sun, heat, and strenuous exercise made us all sleep like babies. But we were up the following morning and on the bus just after daybreak, eager for another day at Mada'in Saleh. This time Trish felt well enough to come along.

On the second day Abdul and the same security guard led our group to the old Hijazi railway stations located near Mada'in Saleh. These were the main stations built by the Ottoman Turks at the turn of the twentieth century. At one time the tracks linked Medina (the holy city south of Al Ula) to Damascus and on to Jerusalem. During the Arab Revolt of 1916-18 Lawrence of Arabia and his Bedouin tribesmen blew up parts of the track, the main supply line for the Turkish troops. I'd always been fascinated by T.E. Lawrence and imagined his ghostly presence about to appear at any moment to give us a guided tour.

The stations were in the process of renovation by the Saudi government. Modern red tile roofs jarred against the old stone walls of the stations. Workmen carelessly slapped fresh cement over cracks in the old stonework, history literally disappearing under the Saudi government's concept of restoration. A recently "restored" Ottoman castle stood nearby; it looked as if it had been built the week before. What a shame. But the history of this place was fascinating. Our group spent a couple of hours looking around the rail yard and clambering over an old locomotive permanently on display in one of the stations. Soon we climbed back on the bus and traveled back through a different section of Mada'in Saleh. Here we stopped to look at a natural spring and more tombs built in cliffs.

And then it was all over. We started our trip back to Tabuk quite late, around 3:00 p.m. We again stopped in the tiny town of Tayma to have supper, but this time at a larger restaurant. About this time we noticed that our trusty guide Abdul had disappeared. I suppose he thought we were close enough to Tabuk to find our way. Our entire group was seated at a long table, males and females together. We were objects of curiosity and everyone in the restaurant stared at us. We were able to order off a menu this time, but most food items were some sort of chicken dish.

Trish, who was by now feeling strong and hungry, exclaimed over the menu, "Chicken, chicken and more chicken! Can't somebody make a burger for me? I'd kill for a burger." One of our young Arab waiters tried hard to get Trish what she wanted. He brought a plate from the kitchen and set it proudly in front of her. On it teetered a huge pile of iceberg lettuce leaves with a blob of mayonnaise and two sliced tomatoes sitting on the top. Atop the mayonnaise and tomatoes sat a round patty of charred minced meat that looked pretty much like a hamburger should look. Minus the bun. Trish looked at the waiter, "What the heck is this?" The young man answered, "Is burger madam." Trish asked, "Where's the bun?" I don't think the waiter knew exactly what a bun was, but he appeared to smile in understanding and scurried off to the kitchen. He returned with another plate containing a long piece of crusty French bread cut in half. I think Trish was determined to be difficult. She said, "That's not a bun." The waiter replied, somewhat exasperated, "Is best we can do, madam."

Trish sighed and stuffed the lettuce, tomato, mayonnaise and burger in the French bread. I peered across the table at her and commented, "That looks quite good, Trish." She was disgusted, "It ain't Dairy Queen, but what did I really expect to get in a teeny, tiny town at the ends of the earth."

The rest of our group started in on our plates of chicken and rice. The waiter came by and whispered in our group leader's ear. Apparently there were Mutawa lurking about outside the restaurant, having been alerted to Westerners in the area. Like many restaurants in Saudi Arabia, I'd noticed the room could be divided up, and each table made private with a curtain. The waiter pulled a long curtain around our entire group to enclose us all at the one long table where we sat. A few minutes later we heard the front door of the restaurant slam and then men scuffling and shouting at each other. It was apparent the Mutawa had come to check on the situation. But soon things were quiet again. The Mutawa had left, the restaurant manager apparently having convinced the religious police that, behind a curtain, he had our corrupting Western influence under control.

The Kingdom, especially the northwest Hijaz desert, has an opulent history. The region is situated on an ancient frankincense route that once stretched from Yemen north to the Mediterranean. Civilizations along the way date back to 1000 BCE and have left many rich archeological sites. Currently, what is termed "tourism" in Saudi refers mostly to religious pilgrims who come from all over the world to visit Mecca. And, of course, expatriates living in Saudi Arabia make up the biggest percentage of domestic tourists.

The Saudi government has indicated an interest in attracting international tourists, especially those drawn to the ancient history of this primeval land. A select few American and British tour companies sometimes offer costly, but limited tours, of Saudi Arabia. But most of the sites which could draw thousands of tourists are off-limits or inaccessible for some reason.

Archeology and ancient finds are sensitive subjects in Saudi Arabia. The religious establishment is hostile to archeology, fearful of discovering anything vaguely related to ancient religion (pre-Islamic), or any connection to early Judaism or Christianity. For the most part, even finds of major significance in Saudi Arabia are quickly enclosed in a chain-link fence and topped with razor wire. Each has signs declaring, "Archeological area, unlawful to trespass, subject to penalty." I saw many such sites during my travels in the Kingdom, vague but visible outlines of ruins covered with sand and fenced off to all.

Veneration of objects is forbidden in Islam, but it is only the Saudis and other ultra-conservatives who include historic artifacts in that belief.

Witness the Taliban and their destruction of the ancient Buddhas in Afghanistan. They considered them graven images, incompatible with their version of Islam.

And so, potentially amazing discoveries, sure to attract international tourists to a country eager to promote itself as a tourist destination, lie silent under the sands of Saudi Arabia.

The Saudi Ministry of Tourism has actually begun training a special branch of Mutawa to deal with tourists, so-called "tourism ambassadors." Consider a place like Mada'in Saleh, a site often visited by expatriates whose groups include both single men and women. The location is so remote that non-Muslim females never wear an abaya or headscarf. Considering the religious police and their propensity for fanaticism and violence, I seriously doubt they would tolerate these situations. The plan seems likely to end in disaster. Mutawa tourism ambassadors, indeed. The very idea is ludicrous.

In fact, I returned from my delightful trip to Mada'in Saleh directly into a life-threatening situation with the Mutawa.

An Attack by the Religious Police

I wore my abaya in public just as soon as I arrived in Tabuk, but at that time Western women didn't wear head scarves because we were not strictly mandated to do so. We never had any problems downtown, other than the typical encounters with staring men groping their crotches.

During my second year in Tabuk, however, a wave of ultra-fundamentalism swept over Saudi Arabia. With this came the Mutawa, the feared Saudi religious police. More and more of them began to show up on the streets of Tabuk. Dozens of scruffy-looking men in ankle-length white robes roamed the streets with straight wooden sticks clutched in their hands. The sticks they wielded were stout and at least five feet long. Their militant eyes scanned the crowds for what they considered violations of their own warped religious beliefs.

Initially the Mutawa made themselves busy at prayer call by herding Muslim males to the mosque, whether they wanted to pray or not. But we Western women left our heads uncovered and were never harassed.

On a chilly December evening shortly before Christmas I was downtown alone. I was standing on the street, about to enter the photo-developing shop, when I heard furtive shuffling footsteps behind me. Turning, I saw a Mutawa dressed in the characteristic white robe, his callused feet cracked and filthy with street dust, striding toward me. His long bony face sprouted an unkempt beard and his flat shark-like eyes blazed with religious fervor. He was, of course, carrying the stout stick used by all Mutawa. I felt disgust and wondered why these vicious characters just couldn't let people go about their business.

The Mutawa stopped close enough to shout at me, "Cover your head!" I saw the cold hatred in his eyes, and it chilled me to the core.

At first, I confess I did not think he was serious. Furthermore, I was not carrying a scarf with me. In the past few weeks I heard the Mutawa had approached a few Western women and told them to cover their head. None of us, of course, took the Mutawa seriously. But this individual seemed more aggressive than usual, more intent on forcing compliance. I tried not to let it show on my face when I felt genuine fear trickle into my belly.

He again shouted, "Cover your head!" I roared back, "Leave me alone!" I was surprised at his command of English. A lot of these men seemed educated, but it is said they are little more than ex-convicts whose only job qualification is to memorize the Quran in order to reduce their sentences.

Walking away from the Mutawa usually worked, and I moved down the street as quickly as I could; I was frightened. Still I had no inkling that the fiend would pursue me. But tonight would be different. Tonight, it seemed, the religious police intended to enforce the head covering.

Though still nervous, I continued shopping and soon held a heavy bag of purchases. About an hour later I was in a fabric store examining a bolt of silk when something went THWACK on the bolt beside me. I will never forget the sound of that Mutawa stick striking the fabric. I turned to see the same angry Mutawa. His stick was raised as if to strike me. His fanatical eyes shone with purpose. Ah, now he had me cornered, the better to deal with this disobedient female. I stood there facing him. Hatred flashed in his eyes.

I glanced at the nearby shopkeeper, but he quickly dropped to the floor behind his counter. I knew I could not count on his help because the merchants were terrified of the Mutawa.

Now I was truly terrified, and I knew I had to head straight for our bus stop a couple of blocks away. There would be hospital employees there; people I hoped would help me. I pushed past the enraged Mutawa and left the shop. His proximity made my skin crawl. He followed me, screaming, "Cover your head! Cover your head! Cover your head!" Had I a scarf in my bag I would have put it on at once, but I had nothing.

Once I reached the street I saw my exit was cut off. Attracted by the commotion, a crowd had amassed in seconds. Hundreds seemed to pop up out of the pavement, creating an impenetrable arc of sweating bodies around the store entrance. In those seconds I realized the crowd was entirely made up of Saudi and Asian men. Perhaps I hoped to see a sympathetic female face, but not one woman was amongst the crowd. I was now in the midst of a ghastly situation.

The pursuing Mutawa had somehow got ahead of me and stood at the front of the crowd. Nearby I saw another Mutawa appear, a corpulent slug of a man with the same mean eyes as my pursuer. He was accompanied by two local policemen. The officers stood casually with their hands behind their backs, both wearing a completely neutral expression.

Suddenly, the first Mutawa stepped toward me. His stout stick slammed down on my forehead and stars of light flashed in my head. The stick slammed into me again. And again. I raised my arms to protect further blows to my head. Waves of fetid body odor surged off the enraged man and I choked with nausea. I made the mistake of looking into his eyes, murderous eyes mad with fanaticism. Blows landed on my shoulders and chest. He hit me so hard across my stomach the wind was knocked out of me. At that moment I was afraid if I lost consciousness he would beat me to death. The adrenalin kicked in and I was in full "fight or flight" mode.

Enraged, I turned on my attacker and swung my loaded shopping bag into his ugly face. The Mutawa was momentarily unbalanced by the blow but barely hesitated. My action had only made him angrier and once again he began to thrash me viciously about the head. The second short, fat one suddenly started toward me with his stick raised. Both of them were stunned by the fact I had tried to defend myself. Oh God, I thought, were both of them going to finish me off? The two policemen, their faces vacant, watched silently with hands clasped behind their backs. "You cowardly dogs," I thought, "standing by while two crazy men beat a lone woman."

The watching crowd fell eerily silent. I saw sympathy on some faces, sick fascination on others. I began to panic because I was hemmed in on all sides by the hushed and growing crowd of spectators. Time stood still for me. I felt dazed, out of options. I felt something wet trickle down my face; I thought I might be bleeding from one of the blows to my head. Dizzy with pain and terror, I remember thinking, "I'm going to die on this dirty Saudi street. My poor parents."

Suddenly, out of the crowd leapt a tall, burly young man, whom I thought I recognized. He grabbed my elbow in his strong hands, punched his way through the silent crowd and said to me, "Run; run as fast as you can!"

Gripping my arm, he ran with me, his strength and speed carrying me along. I wasn't a teenager, and I wasn't particularly fit, but I had never run faster. My savior dragged and half-carried me all the way to the bus stop.

When we reached safety, I looked up to identify my brawny rescuer. I was shocked to see Abraham, the handsome Pakistani cook who worked in our hospital recreation center. His face was flushed with fear and effort, sweat pouring off his forehead. I was amazed at his courage, literally risking his life for me.

"Thank you, "I gasped, "Thank you!" I said it repeatedly, not knowing how to express my immense gratitude.

"I have to go," Abraham panted, "those evil ones will be looking for me!"

He disappeared quickly. Abraham was both Christian and Asian and we both knew if the Mutawa caught him they would arrest him. In jail, without a doubt, he would be beaten, even tortured. After Abraham disappeared around a corner, I saw that a number of female hospital employees were waiting for the bus. These women quickly gathered around me.

A young English nurse stepped forward. I recognized her from the hospital but didn't know her name. Her clear blue eyes registered alarm as she quickly assessed my condition, "What the hell happened to you? Why is there blood all over your face?"

I reached up to my throbbing head and my hand came away covered with blood. One of the blows to my head had lacerated my scalp above my left eye. Someone in the crowd handed me a Kleenex which I pressed to the wound. I gasped out my story and the group of women looked horrified.

The nurse was quickly examining my head and face. "Those bloody bastards. What have they done to you?"

I must have looked a mess, my face smeared with street dust, sweat, tears, and blood. I was still shaking with anger and fear. Meanwhile, the leftover adrenaline was dissolving into a terrible fatigue. I was terrified those same Mutawa would appear at any moment and my ordeal would continue. I prayed the bus would arrive.

My intention was to go straight home, but the young nurse encouraged me to go to the emergency room. "I think you need sutures, it's a deep cut." The other women, angry and stirred up, advised me, "You have to report this attack."

The bus finally arrived, and I was again the center of attention. Those getting off the bus saw the scene of tension and a crowd gathered around me. I heard people, male and female, muttering angrily about the attack. The bus ride back to the hospital seemed to take forever. The atmosphere in the vehicle was hot and angry. I felt awful, my stomach roiled with nausea and my exhaustion overwhelming; I wanted to lie down right there and go to sleep. But my ordeal was not over.

The young nurse accompanied me to the emergency room. She was my guardian angel, though in the midst of it all I never learned her name. I was led into an examining room where I lay down with a groan. My entire body ached with pain and weariness. My lacerated, bleeding scalp throbbed with every heart beat. As usual the emergency room was full of auto accident victims and screaming children. I wanted to go home and sleep, but I knew I had to make an official record of the attack. It took some time before a physician came to examine me. I was attended by a young Saudi resident who ordered a CT scan and quickly placed six stitches in my scalp. He asked me what had happened. I told him and I thought I saw a brief moment of shame flicker across his face, but after the story he made no comment. Perhaps I imagined it.

The attending nurse and physician had me undress for further examination. I looked down and saw extensive purple bruising over my chest, arms and stomach which resembled churning black storm clouds. I remember thinking that I was going to die on that Saudi street. But here I was, intact and feeling lucky I had survived. My thoughts were full of Abraham, my savior, and a mantra ran through my mind, "Thank you, thank you, thank you."

The physician ordered an injection of Pethidine (Middle Eastern equivalent of Demerol) because he said I'd be in a lot of pain later. I just wanted to go home, but by then the Saudi military police had shown up to interview me. Two inbred-looking characters in green uniforms slouched into the exam room and took my statement. Neither had much command of English, and I wondered what sort of report they came up with. They had no authority over any incidents outside of the military compound and, through an interpreter, they told me I would be required to make a report at the civil police station in downtown Tabuk. Would this torment never end?

I was fearful to ride downtown with these two. Just because they were military police did not mean they had my best interests in mind. But by then the Pethidine had taken effect. Between my fatigue and the opiate coursing through my system, I just didn't care. So I climbed into the back seat of the ancient military Jeep, and the two MPs delivered me downtown to the central police station.

The Jeep stopped in front of a high concrete wall with thick strands of razor wire along the top. It was late, perhaps midnight, the night sky black and moonless. I climbed out of the Jeep and shivered in the chilly night air. The military police accompanied me through a creaking, beat-up metal door into the police compound. I saw before me a vast courtyard paved with sand and ringed by a collection of crumbling cinderblock structures, their purpose unclear. The same concrete walls, at least 12 feet high, ringed the entire place. The decrepit structures around the courtyard held black holes of windows devoid of covering which stared back at me like soulless eyes. Just standing in this place made my skin crawl. This was the sort of gruesome place I would have pictured had I ever been asked to describe a third-world jail. A grisly picture of the Auschwitz gate flashed through my mind, "Abandon hope, all ye who enter here." What I saw next confirmed my thoughts.

In the center of the courtyard I saw a wretched-looking young Asian man on his knees, chained to a scraggly tree. He wore only a pair of filthy, tattered shorts and I knew he must be numb with cold. My escorts grinned and one made a gesture of swinging a sword, "He chop-chop bukhra, enshallah." Oh God, this poor soul was to be executed tomorrow. I watched with horror as one of the soldiers walked over to the kneeling man and kicked him squarely in the ribs. The young man gasped and fell on his side. I knew that condemned prisoners were often chained in public the day prior to their execution for the purpose of "public shaming." Anyone was welcome to come and kick, hit, spit on or generally harass a prisoner.

Even in my drugged state, the hair stood up on the back of my neck at the horrifying reality of this experience.

I was taken into the police station proper and led down a long corridor. The floors and walls were filthy with decades of dirt and neglect. The air smelled of stale sweat, cigarette smoke, and the ubiquitous scent of Arabic coffee. We entered a small, cluttered office and I was directed to sit in a vast, dilapidated leather arm chair. My military escort left and indicated they would wait in the Jeep for me. I was now by myself for the first time. The old chair I sat in was saggy but comfortable. Despite my own pain, my mind kept going back to the condemned man outside and I wanted to cry.

The office was overly warm and quiet. I felt my eyes droop and my head dropped to my chest. I struggled to stay awake, fearful of nodding off in my drugged and fatigued state. I was bolted to wakefulness by the creak of the arm chair next to me. I opened my eyes to see a fully-covered Saudi female slumped in the chair, I assumed to keep me company in the presence of men. The lady said not a word, but I murmured to the featureless black veil over her face, "Shukran" (thank you), Madam."

Suddenly I heard a commotion in the hallway outside the office, men shouting in Arabic and the scurry of feet. A short, plump Saudi policeman of indeterminate age popped into the room with a wide smile on his face. I wondered what he found to smile about in this grisly place.

In fairly good English the plump man said to me, "I am Sergeant Ahmed Al-Fahani and it is my duty to talk to you tonight." The sergeant was dressed in an unkempt khaki police uniform with huge patches of sweat decorating the underarms of his jacket. He had an unctuous manner about him, and I saw that the smile he wore did not reach his eyes. This man gave me the creeps. He asked me to tell him about the incident that night. I described in detail what had happened, and though he made sympathetic noises I knew he simply did not care. The only advice he could give me was to report the incident to the Canadian Embassy in Riyadh. I knew this trip had been a waste of time. He stood up behind his cluttered desk, still smiling, and indicated the interview was over.

One of the military policemen came back to the office to escort me to the Jeep. As soon as I saw him I wondered if he had kicked the prisoner again on his way in here. As I stood to leave, Sergeant Al-Fahani came from behind his desk and slipped a small, sweat-stained piece of paper into my hand. "If you need anything, call me," he whispered. The emphasis on "anything" made me feel like laughing hysterically.

I was led back down the filthy hallway and heads poked out of offices all along the way. Grinning Saudi policemen, all in the same untidy green uniforms, had a good look at me as I passed. Once again we walked by the wretched prisoner, and I felt sick at his coming fate. I thought about him all the way back to the military compound, and though I'd never know, I imagined his thoughts of terror for the morrow. By now I knew about the horrifying method of execution in Saudi, the flash of the sword, a head rolling. I was haunted by the images for weeks to come.

When finally I reached my apartment it was almost 3:00 a.m. As I stripped off my sweat- and fear-soaked clothing, the sergeant's piece of paper fell out of a pocket. When I unfolded the paper to find his name and phone number, I burst out laughing. I knew there was only one thing the sergeant wanted from me, and true to Saudi male form, he had taken his opportunity. While I was telling my story to him, my head throbbing and muscles aching, he was only thinking about how he could pick me up. I stepped into the shower, luxuriating in the cleansing water as it washed away the dirt and fear of my experience.

Later that week I saw Abraham in the recreation center and gave him a hug. Tears rolled down my face. I said, "I don't know how to thank you. You literally saved my life."

I knew his wage was meager and I tried to offer him a reward. But he stood straight and refused my offer. I thought I might have insulted him. "I did what I knew was right," Abraham said humbly, "and no thanks is necessary."

The following day, a hospital-wide meeting was called regarding head covering for non-Muslim women. I was asked to tell my story again to the crowd. Other staff members looked angry, but the hospital administrators, all Saudis, wore the same neutral expression. I knew the incident was nothing more than an annoying inconvenience to them. Women were told that head covering was now mandatory anywhere outside our compound, especially downtown. I was quite happy to do so, but many Western women were angry at being forced to cover their head. I was shocked when one disturbed individual came to me and said, "This is your fault." I turned on her, "You go downtown and get beat up, then come tell me what you think."

After the attack I was terrified to go downtown alone or even to the grocery store on the compound. I was a prisoner in my own apartment. During the first week after the attack Fawzia went to get my groceries. But she was a wise lady and knew this could not go on. She sat down and talked with me one day. "You cannot lock yourself up," she said. "It is a terrible thing that happened to you, but you must make yourself brave again and continue with your life." Fawzia offered to go downtown with me the first time after the attack. Gabrielle also went with us that night to support me. As we neared downtown on the bus I wondered if I could even get off the bus. I sweated with fear and anxiety though it was a cool evening. It took weeks for me to feel more comfortable. There were

Mutawa everywhere now, and though I always wore my abaya and head-covering I never again traveled downtown alone.

The Mutawa problem grew steadily worse across the entire Kingdom. Their extremism is the stuff of legend, nightmarish legend. Probably the single worst case of their fanaticism occurred in 2002 when a fire broke out in a girls' school in Mecca, the center of Islam. Apparently no fire alarms or fire extinguishers were available inside the building. The girls were screaming to get out of the flames and smoke, but were beaten back by the Mutawa because none of them was wearing an abaya or head covering in the rush to escape. The fire-fighters were prevented from helping the girls by the Mutawa because it was considered a sin to touch or see them uncovered. Fifteen girls died, and many more were injured. The incident incited a huge outcry by Saudi citizens. It is impossible to grasp how fanatical these religious police can be to disregard human life to this extent.

After my terrifying experience, head coverings became unquestionably mandatory for all females.

Farewell to Saudi

My world began to crumble after the Mutawa incident. Gabrielle announced that she was not going to finish her contract and would leave Tabuk for good. "I have to go. My health is suffering from the stress of this place, and Jonathan needs me while he's attending University." Gabrielle was speaking of her young adult son, who lived in London. The night she left I was devastated. It was the end of an era. The special little world we had created in our office would never be the same. I very quickly gained a new office mate, Sheila, a secretary from Dublin. She was a pleasant girl to work with, but very young and lacking imagination. She saw no humor in "The Boys" or anything else Gabrielle and I found so amusing in our department. Sheila's only goals were learning to dive, joining the Diving Club at our recreation center, and finding a boyfriend. She soon achieved all her goals, and her entire life revolved around weekend dive trips to the Red Sea and the expat party circuit. The first boyfriend soon fell by the wayside and after that Sheila seemed to have a new man every other week.

Two weeks later my Irish friend Catherine, also announced she was leaving Tabuk for good. Tony, her longtime boyfriend, told her he'd accepted a job in United Arab Emirates. Catherine intended to follow him. About eighteen months later I started a new job in a hospital in the United Arab Emirates, and found Catherine working at the same hospital. Tony and Catherine had finally become engaged, but eventually Tony ended the relationship. Catherine soon returned to Dublin for good.

After Catherine left Tabuk, I still had my faithful friend Fawzia. But my spirit was broken. I could no longer summon up the excitement and adventurous spirit that had kept me going for the past year and a half in Saudi. Exhausted emotionally and physically, I came to a decision to leave Saudi for good on completion of my second contract. I was experiencing serious depression and found it difficult to cope with even the smallest everyday incidents. I had no more energy to give to Saudi Arabia. In retrospect I realized that the Mutawa attack had been the final straw, the defining incident that would push me to leave the Kingdom for good.

By January I was coasting through the last six months of my second contract, relieved that I had made a decision not to re-contract for a third year. Fawzia and my new friend Jeanette, who arrived in Tabuk shortly before I left for good, made my last few months in Tabuk bearable, and we actually had a lot of fun. Jeanette quickly got to know people on other compounds and we attended a lot of expat functions: bingos, Trivial Pursuit nights, theme dinners, dances, and get-togethers. I hadn't done a lot of this kind of socializing up until then, and it helped pass the time. But my decision to leave Saudi Arabia never faltered.

It was difficult for me to say goodbye to Fawzia. She'd been such a loyal and loving friend throughout my two years in Saudi Arabia. She gave me a special parting gift of a Quranic verse written on a beautiful copper plate. We managed to keep in contact for a couple of years, but as so often happens in the expat life we eventually lost contact. Along with a couple of other friends, including Donna, who also drifted into the great unknown, my greatest regret is losing track of my friend Fawzia.

Afterword

In June I left Saudi Arabia. Jeanette was traveling to Canada at the same time. (She had to quit her job in Tabuk and go home to take care of her sick mother.)

A few days prior to our departure we needed to obtain our travelers checks. Now here is a ploy that can be extremely useful in Saudi Arabia, and, to be honest, I often exploited it. So it seemed fitting that just before leaving Saudi Arabia Jeanette and I used the tactic for the last time. We took an early bus to downtown Tabuk, to National Commercial Bank, hoping to avoid the sort of melee we always expected in these situations. We thought we were being clever.

But as we approached the bank we could see the place was packed with milling Saudi men and hundreds of Filipinos. (We guessed a lot of Filipinos were also planning to go on holidays.) So I said to Jeanette, "Look we're gonna be here forever, so I think we've got to use the "secret weapon" in a situation like this." Jeanette agreed, "Oh absolutely, this is the time and place for it." A fervent feminist would shudder at our plan! But as a female in Saudi sometimes we did what was necessary to smooth the way.

Jeanette and I darted into a small alley and furtively lined our lips with brilliant red lipstick. We also pulled our headscarves just a little looser so as to display Jeanette's blonde hair and my auburn tresses. We made a grand entrance through the bank's front doors and every male head in the place turned. No definite queues existed; there is no such thing in Saudi

Arabia. In a bank or any other public establishment in Saudi, males of all stripes will demand to be served first. But any woman, Saudi or otherwise, is fully within her rights to push to the front of a crowd of men. Failing to do so, a woman is unlikely to ever get served in a crowded situation. I have seen Saudi women aggressively push through a crowd of men like black-clad dervishes, shoving and slapping them away like pesky flies. The crowd of men will scowl and mutter, but they will let women pass. As is the right of women, Jeanette and I shoved our way to the front of the crowd. The Saudi male employees behind the counter grinned at us. We grinned back with our luscious red lips and gorgeous hair. Many of the Filipino males glared at us, and I didn't blame them.

A handsome young Saudi man in a neatly-pressed, dazzling white thobe rushed over to us from a side office. He exclaimed in awkward English, "I am Mohammed Al Dossari, please to come to my office to have the service." As Jeanette and I were seated in his office, we smiled shrewdly at each other. The "secret weapon" never failed. Mohammed snapped his fingers smartly at a loitering tea boy. A fixture in just about every establishment in the Kingdom, the young Indian fellow dashed off to perform his task. Soon after the tea boy placed little glasses of hot mint tea in front of Jeanette and me. We told Mohammed Al Dossari we needed travelers checks in U.S. dollars. He rushed back out to the counter to summon an underling, giving him orders in rapid Arabic. Then Mohammed hurried back into his office, anxious to grab all the time he could with us. He said excitedly, "The checks will be before you so soon. Please to relax and enjoy me!"

Mohammed was so sweet and eager to make a good impression on us that Jeanette and I were hard-pressed not to break out in laughter. Very soon the underling placed the travelers checks in front of us to sign. As we signed each one Mohammed asked about Canada, "I very much like to see this Canada. But they say it is very cold. Is this true?" Jeanette smiled, "It is so cold in the winter we have to plug our cars in to keep them warm." Mohammed looked extremely doubtful at this news; he was sure we were pulling his leg. But he grinned politely and made no comment. We finished signing our checks and rose to leave. Mohammed eagerly reached over the desk to shake our hands. I was always surprised when the occasional Saudi male offered to shake our foreign, female hands. Jeanette and I thanked Mohammed profusely for the great service. He bowed his head slightly as he grasped our hands, "Surely it is so wonderful to meet beautiful Canadian ladies. Please to have nice trip!" Mohammed led us out of his office and through the crowd of males. They parted like the Red Sea. He waved from the front door as Jeanette and I walked away down the street. After half a block we fell about laughing until we saw a couple of Mutawa in the distance. We hastily took a shortcut.

On reaching Canada I had to deal with something quite unexpected, a sort of reverse culture shock. The reality of Western life—bills to pay, rent, insurance, upkeep of a vehicle, too little vacation time—hit me hard. Even with the dangers inherent while living in Saudi Arabia, when a Westerner leaves the expatriate life he/she leaves behind generous wages, free housing and utilities, free medical care, seven to eight weeks of vacation, and enough money to travel and buy items we would never consider at home. The expatriate life can be exceedingly addicting. Lack of any sort of responsibility is something you get used to pretty quickly.

I spent the fall and winter in Calgary, and was quickly reminded of how much I loathe winter. I signed up with a temp agency and took several unsatisfying short-term jobs. I wondered what I was going to do next.

In January I made a decision to apply to Tawam Hospital in the United Arab Emirates. I did not bother going through a recruiter because at the time it was not necessary for certain jobs in UAE. In the space of three weeks I was contacted by Human Resources at Tawam Hospital in the city of Al Ain, had a phone interview, and was hired. My new position would be combination medical transcriptionist and medical secretary in the OB/GYN department. I left for UAE in March and settled into my new job. I liked United Arab Emirates since it was much more liberal than Saudi. I bought a used car—yes women can drive there—and wore conservative but normal street clothing. By then Jeanette was again working in Saudi and often came over to UAE to visit me. What a delightful feeling of freedom we had. Jeanette and I drove all over UAE, shopping, going to the beaches and dancing the nights away at fantastic nightclubs in Dubai.

I should mention here that there are significant differences between Saudi Arabia and the United Arab Emirates where I lived for five years. All women are free to drive and a good percentage of Emirati women hold jobs. Some women even work in the UAE police force and civil service. The local people are less conservative, though by no means liberal either. Most Emiratis are Sunni Muslims and do not follow the beliefs or traditions of the strict Saudi Wahhabis. The capital, Abu Dhabi, is more conservative than Dubai. Tourists from all over the world visit Dubai to see the wonders of Palm Island and the tallest building in the world, Burj Khalifa. Most of the major hotels have bars that serve alcohol. UAE allows some churches, generally Roman Catholic, to operate discreetly in the country.

That is not to say United Arab Emirates is without danger. It is still a relatively conservative Muslim country. The secret police (CID - Criminal Investigation Division) are everywhere. Their agents are clothed in the typical Emirati male national dress so you won't know who they are. Plenty of Westerners languish in Emirati jails over offenses related to alcohol, drugs, making insulting comments about Islam or the UAE government, running afoul of UAE decency laws or photographing what is prohibited, to name a few. Freedom of speech or action is also limited for Emirati citizens, some of whom have been jailed for calling for government reform. Some are held without charges.

I was having a good time in UAE. I liked my job, I could drive anywhere I liked in my car, my wage was generous and I had plenty of vacation time

But my life was about to change in a most unexpected and wonderful way.

About a year after arriving in UAE I met some Lebanese friends for coffee in the hospital cafeteria. With them was a quiet, handsome blue-eyed Syrian man named Ghanem who made my heart melt at first sight. He had the kindest eyes I'd ever seen, and my first thought on meeting him was, "This one is different." At that time we chatted, but made no plans to meet again. I hoped we would somehow meet again because I fell in love with him that day.

Two months later my friend Jeanette again came to visit me from Saudi. We were standing in my favorite bakery waiting for our order of fresh bread. And then I saw Ghanem standing nearby. He saw us and approached immediately. His blue eyes sparkled as he re-introduced himself and smiled shyly. He handed us the pile of fresh, hot bread he was holding, "Take this and enjoy it. I can order more." He worked up the courage that evening to give me his business card. Jeanette and I went to Dubai for the weekend, but my mind was on Ghanem the entire time. I could hardly wait to get home and call him. We had our first date the next week.

A few months later, to my family's surprise, a new immigration law made my father eligible for a United States citizenship because his mother was born in Michigan. My Dad quickly acquired the citizenship and I went home to Canada to apply for my green card through him. One year later I had my green card. I'd long wanted to live in New Mexico so I made plans to return to the United States and wait five years to naturalize. At the time Ghanem and I hadn't made plans for a future together though we knew there could never be anyone else for either of us. Leaving Ghanem behind was the most difficult thing I've ever done, and I cried all the way home. My parents met me in Albuquerque. Within the week I had a job in Las Cruces, New Mexico. Ghanem and I ran up a huge phone bill during this time because we missed each other terribly. We were miserable without each other and for some time I thought I might return to UAE to be with him. However, he obtained a U.S. visit visa and traveled to see me.

Ghanem and I married in Las Cruces, New Mexico on May 2, 1997. We are the love of each other's life.

Life can change in a heartbeat. I fled to Saudi Arabia to try to escape my life, and ended up having the adventure of a lifetime. And meeting the love of my life.

About the Author

Shelly Anderson

Shelly Anderson was born and raised in a rural community in Canada. She moved to Calgary, Canada where she lived until moving to the Kingdom of Saudi Arabia.

It was her successful profession as a medical transcriptionist that led her to accept a job as a transcriptionist in a hospital in Saudi Arabia. During her two years there she wrote reams of letters to friends, family, and former co-workers in Canada, most of whom kept the letters for their entertainment value. Those letters eventually made their way back to Shelly with encouragement from many to write a book about her adventures in the Kingdom.

The Siamese cat the author is holding is Sammi. Shelly left Saudi Arabia and later took a job in United Arab Emirates. She met her future husband there and they adopted Sammi in Abu Dhabi. They brought Sammi with them to the United States where he filled their house with fun for twelve years. He passed away in March 2012 ever missed and remembered with love.

Shelly is a dual citizen Canadian/USA who now resides in El Paso, Texas with her beloved husband Ghanem and two Siamese kittens, Basboos and Barney.

This is Shelly's first book.

shelly@shellyandersonbooks.com

Shelly Anderson